Preying on the State

PREYING ON THE STATE

The Transformation
of Bulgaria after 1989

Venelin I. Ganev

Cornell University Press   *Ithaca and London*

Copyright © 2007 by Cornell University

All rights reserved. Except for brief quotations in a review, this book, or parts thereof, must not be reproduced in any form without permission in writing from the publisher. For information, address Cornell University Press, Sage House, 512 East State Street, Ithaca, New York 14850.

First published 2007 by Cornell University Press
First printing, Cornell Paperbacks, 2013

Library of Congress Cataloging-in-Publication Data
Ganev, Venelin I.
   Preying on the state : the transformation of Bulgaria after 1989 / Venelin I. Ganev
     p. cm.
   Includes bibliographical references and index.
   ISBN 978-0-8014-4564-4 (cloth : alk. paper)
   ISBN 978-0-8014-7902-1 (paper : alk. paper)
   1. Post-communism—Bulgaria. 2. Bulgaria—Politics and government—1990–   I. Title.
DR93.44.G365 2007
949.903'2—dc22
                              2006101256

Cornell University Press strives to use environmentally responsible suppliers and materials to the fullest extent possible in the publishing of its books. Such materials include vegetable-based, low-VOC inks and acid-free papers that are recycled, totally chlorine-free, or partly composed of nonwood fibers. For further information, visit our website at www.cornellpress.cornell.edu.

Cloth printing   10 9 8 7 6 5 4 3 2 1
Paperback printing 10 9 8 7 6 5 4 3 2 1

To my mother, Maria Georgieva Ganeva,
And to the memory of my father,
Iordan Venelinov Ganev, 1926–2004

Contents

Acknowledgments   *ix*

1 The Dysfunctionality of Post-Communist State Structures   *1*

2 The Separation of Party and State as a Logistical Problem   *33*

3 Conversions of Power   *62*

4 Winners as State Breakers in Post-Communism   *95*

5 Weak-State Constitutionalism   *123*

6 The Shrewdness of the Tamed   *151*

7 Post-Communism as an Episode of State Transformation   *175*

Bibliography   *199*

Index   *215*

Acknowledgments

This project began at the Department of Political Science at the University of Chicago in 1997. The writing was not easy, and might not have been completed without the support of the teachers and colleagues who helped me persevere in the icy waters of academia and repeatedly expressed their belief that what appeared to many to be a decidedly unorthodox case and line of inquiry were worth exploring. Inspiring conversations with David D. Laitin and Lloyd Rudolph helped me carry on. I could also rely on a cohesive peer-support group: Julie Alig, Mark Blitz, Elise Giulianno, Gretchen Helmke, Dante Scala, Lynn Tesser, Pete Wolfe, and Jakub Zielinski. I thank them all—it is too bad, indeed, that this group scattered to the four winds.

I conducted important research at the now defunct Center for the Study of Constitutionalism in Eastern Europe at the University of Chicago Law School. I thank my colleagues there—Ania Budzjak, Nida Gelazis, and particularly Dwight Semler—for their assistance and advice.

I am particularly grateful to my best friends on campus, John Kenny and Fonna Forman-Barzilai, who always found the right words to encourage a writer prone to despair. I will always treasure the memory of our conversations, confessions, and debates.

My biggest intellectual debt is to Stephen Holmes. It was Steve who gently but persistently pushed me to consider seriously the problem of post-Communist stateness; it was Steve who provided guidance and provocation every time I needed it. Having him as a teacher and as a friend has been a blessing for which I am truly grateful.

I left Chicago and the project in 2000 but returned to it during my year as a Hoover National Fellow at Stanford University (2003–04). The stimulating atmosphere at Hoover made it possible for me to substantially revise and expand the text. I thank Robert Conquest, Ken Jowitt, Michael McFaul, and John Dunlop for their advice, and Jeremi Suri, Scott Kieff, Joy Taylor Kelly, Tracy Tiele, and the other fellows for their camaraderie.

Throughout the years I have benefited from the generosity of several scholars who spent their precious time discussing my ideas, reading draft chapters, and helping in various ways to improve the quality of my argument: Anna Grzymala-Busse, Georgi Derluguian, Yoshiko Herrera, Martin Krygier, Jim McAdams, Bernard Manin, Wojciech Sadurski, Herman Schwartz, Charles Tilly, and Jan Zielonka. I am much obliged to two remarkable Bulgarian scholars who have repeatedly read draft chapters and discussed the entire project: Antoaneta Dimitrova and Ralitza Peeva. Without their friendly encouragement I would still be lost in the labyrinths of insoluble dilemmas.

The book was completed at Miami University of Ohio, and I acknowledge the support of many colleagues and friends there: Warren Mason, Ryan Berilleaux, and Susan Kay for their mentorship; Gulnaz Sharafutdinova, Doug Shumavon, Steve De Lue, and Sheila Croucher for always being ready to seriously consider yet another one of my bizarre ideas; and Walt Wandersush for gracefully enduring numerous visits by a panicked and confused next-door neighbor. I am especially indebted to Karen Dawisha and Adeed Dawisha, whose constant interventions helped me keep up with self-imposed schedules and whose intellectual guidance proved to be invaluable along the way.

Various drafts of this book's chapters were presented at the Kellogg Institute for International Studies, University of Notre Dame (April 2000), Yale University (April 2001), the European University Institute in Florence (February 2002), Harvard University (March 2004), and Stanford University (April 2004); I am grateful to all participants in these forums for their comments and suggestions. Earlier versions of chapters 4 and 7 appeared in *Communist and Post-Communist Studies*, chapter 2 in *East European Politics and Societies*, and chapter 6 in *Europe–Asia Studies*.

At Cornell University Press, this project was embraced by Roger M. Haydon. His belief in the worthiness of what I had to say and his editorial suggestions ultimately made its realization possible.

I am grateful to my Bulgarian friends whose feedback, counsel, and original points of view were truly precious: Roumen Avramov, Asen Baltov, Sava Beninski, Asen Djingov, Emil Georgiev, Ionko Grozev, Julia Gurkovska, Deyan Kiuranov, Rumyana Kolarova, Malin Komsiiski,

Ivan Krastev, Stephan Kyutchukov, Alexander Mihailov, Ilian Mihov, Stefan Popov, Rossen Potzkov, Kristian Takov, Velizar Shirov, and Marius Velichkov.

Embarking on such an arduous project would not have been possible without the unremitting support of my family. My late aunt Nevena Zheljazkova was always a source of hope and inspiration. My uncle Milcho Spasov, a remarkable intellectual companion and a loving friend, was, miraculously, always able to reenergize my feeble intellectual batteries. My brother, Georgy Ganev, and my sister-in-law, Anna Ganeva, always found a kind and firm word of encouragement when I needed it. My best friend, my wife Mila, somehow managed to inspire me even when I was stuck in a barren desert of self-doubt and on the verge of giving up. Daily walks and talks with Iori, my older son, made the loneliness of intellectual pursuits bearable. And my younger son, Marty, never failed in playing the role of a little magician who could make life beautiful again.

My deepest gratitude goes to those whose unconditional love I could feel every moment along the way: my mother, Maria Ganeva, and my late father, Iordan Ganev, who did not live long enough to see the project completed, but until his last day never doubted that "I tova shte stane," that "it will happen." It is to them that this book is dedicated.

Preying on the State

1 The Dysfunctionality of Post-Communist State Structures

> The very existence of these laws, however, is at most a matter of presumption.
>
> Franz Kafka, "The Problem of Our Laws"

After more than a decade of scholarly research and reflection on political developments in post-Communist Eastern Europe, a consensus has coalesced around the viewpoint that the transformative processes unleashed in 1989 precipitated a rapid and radical weakening of state structures. While debates about how to conceptualize and measure the decline of state power continue unabated, academic observers, policy analysts, and political actors readily agree that throughout the 1990s the infrastructure of governance was stricken by a grave malaise. It was primarily the failures of promarket reforms in early post-Communism that led World Bank officials to the conclusion that "an effective state is vital to the provision of the goods and services—and rules and institutions—that allow markets to flourish and people to lead healthier, happier lives."[1] It was the attempt to integrate East European nations in the European Union that compelled Brussels bureaucrats to insist that a special chapter on "administrative capacity to apply the *acquis*" be included in each country report on the progress toward accession—and until the end of the last century, these reports invariably acknowledged that "the capacity to implement and enforce the *acquis* is weak."[2] Astute

---

1. See *World Development Report 1997* (Washington, D.C.: World Bank, with Oxford University Press, 1998), 1.
2. This particular quote is from the Bulgaria country report for 1998, available at http://europa.eu.int/comm/enlargement/report_11_98/pdf/en/bulgaria_en.pdf.

champions of democracy singled out the syndromes of "the largely non-functional state" as a formidable obstacle to democratic consolidation in the former Soviet world.³ And advocates of liberal constitutionalism insisted that the general directionality of change after 1989 "makes excruciatingly plain that liberal values are threatened just as thoroughly by state incapacity as by despotic power."⁴ That the state was "weaker" than before and "weaker" than it should have been was among the few empirical and normative claims about post-Soviet reality that did not provoke serious dissent throughout the 1990s.

This book is an inquiry into the causes and concrete manifestations of the general trend toward increased dysfunctionality of state structures in early post-Communism. My approach privileges the analysis of structural factors and modes of self-interested elite agency over the examination of the ideological considerations and reformist visions that allegedly guided policymakers. My key argument is that the causes of state malfunctioning go much deeper than the policy preferences of "free marketeers" who deliberately dismantled the state. These causes should be traced to what we might label the historical specificity of post-Communism as an episode of state transformation—a phrase that encompasses the unique institutional legacy of state socialism, the unusual structure of incentives facing powerful elites, and the peculiar dynamics unleashed when fundamental social relations related to the collecting, managing, and distribution of resources were radically altered. The reconfiguration of state structures in post-Communism is not a development that might be attributed to ideas about what constitutes a good polity: rather, it is the outcome of a set of institutional and social processes that crucially—and negatively—affected the organizational basis of effective governance. It is to the systematic exploration of these processes—their multiple dimensions, their institutional implications, their political significance—that this book is devoted.

But the Polish report, issued the same year—at a time when Poland was the undisputed "leader" among the all candidates for full membership—reached essentially the same conclusion:

> Poland has experienced difficulties in implementing planned public administration reforms which are needed to lay the foundations for further improvement of administrative capacity.... Efforts need to be made to enhance the capacity of Polish administrators to implement and enforce legislation in key internal market areas.... There is a need to consolidate the functioning of administrative structures in a sustainable way.

See the Polish report for 1998 at http://europa.eu.int/comm/enlargement/report_11_98/pdf/en/poland_en.pdf.

3. Thomas Carothers, "The End of the Transition Paradigm," *Journal of Democracy* 13, no. 1 (January 2002): 1–17.

4. Stephen Holmes, "What Russia Teaches Us Now," *American Prospect* 8, no. 33 (July 1, 1997), 33.

The State-Centered Perspective on State-Transformation in Post-Communism

To understand the decay of post-Communist state structures, I believe we have to employ a state-centered view of the fluctuation of stateness in early post-Communism. Centering an inquiry into the metamorphoses of state structures on the post-Communist state itself provides the sharp analytical lens we need to examine the empirical processes, the salient features of the historical and institutional setting, and the structure-transforming events and forms of elite behavior related to the dysfunctionality of administrative apparatuses and bureaucratic organizations in post-Communism. This analytical recalibration holds the promise of generating comparative and theoretical insights that may sharpen current understandings of the problems preventing efficient democratic governance in non-Western countries.

The notion of a "state-centered understanding of the state" does not rest on a heuristically stale tautology. As Gianfranco Poggi has cogently explained, this interpretative perspective conveys the conceptually important message that in the modern era "the set of institutions specifically concerned with accumulating and exercising political power" constitutes a distinct domain that may endogenously generate the conflicts and interactions that "affect autonomously, and sometimes decisively, the state's own arrangements and policies."[5] The central premise of the state-centered analysis, therefore, is that neither the "inputs" into the state domain (ideologies and reform proposals submitted by temporarily empowered electoral winners) nor the interplay of broader political forces and larger social constituencies may satisfactorily account for the sudden fluctuations of stateness. Behind such fluctuations lies a dynamic autonomously generated within the state domain itself. The realization that the transformative energy affecting state structures is not reducible to more general patterns of political, economic, and social change necessitates exploration of the historical and institutional peculiarities of post-Communist state structures and, more generally, of post-Communism as an episode of state transformation.

A "state-centered approach to the state" is *not* coterminous with a state-centered approach to post-Communist society or post-Communism *tout court*. I am emphatically *not* arguing that in the former second world the state remains the central driving force behind all important developments and that institutional, social, and economic developments are epiphenomenal to an overarching process of reconfiguration of state

---

5. Gianfranco Poggi, *The State* (Stanford: Stanford University Press, 1990), 98–99.

structures. This book should not be construed as an implicit endorsement of theoretical approaches that posit the primacy of "the state" in an ongoing debate with advocates of the notion that pride of place should be accorded to "society."[6] My claim is more limited: a state-centered approach is worth pursuing only in the light of a particular objective—understanding the causes and manifestations of the dysfunctionality of post-Communist infrastructures of governance. To be sure, this phenomenon has far-reaching social and economic ramifications.[7] But it is not, and should not be, considered a master matrix that will yield insights about everything worth knowing about post-Communism, nor an affirmation of the ontological priority of the state over society in a preexisting hierarchy of forms of social being.

Second, the state-centered approach is not intended to suggest that the state is a unitary actor. In fact, the opposite is true. This approach is uniquely useful for those willing to dissect post-Communist stateness. The maintenance of modern states, Charles Tilly pointed out several decades ago, involves "the combining, consolidation, neutralizing, manipulating of a tough, complicated and well-set web of political relations."[8] To adopt a state-centered perspective on the state means to reopen key issues pertaining to this web of multiple, conflicting, and dynamically evolving political relations. State "weakness," then, will be explainable as resulting from the "consolidating" of certain interactive patterns within the state domain and the "neutralizing" of others. The dysfunctionality of bureaucratic apparatuses will be linked to the "manipulating" of institutionalized hierarchies of state agents. The diminished capacity of administrative structures can be understood as a "recombining" of the preexisting components of a state-centered system of control over flows of resources. It is precisely under the gaze of analysts willing to conjure up basic questions about modern stateness that the apparently unitary character of the post-Communist state can be analytically decomposed.

The general notion that institutional changes affecting the infrastructure of governance should be analyzed from a state-centered perspective is intimately linked to an analytical reevaluation of the legacies of

---

6. For a good review of this debate, see Robert Hanneman and J. Rogers Hollingsworth, "Refocusing the Debate on the Role of the State in Capitalist Societies," in *State Theory and State History*, ed. Rolf Torstendahl (London: Sage, 1992), 38–61.

7. On how state weakness affects interethnic relations and minority policies, for example, see Venelin I. Ganev, "The Politics of Ethnic Reconciliation in Bulgaria," in *National Reconciliation in Eastern Europe*, ed. Henry F. Carey (Boulder: Columbia University Press—East European Monographs, 2003), 319–42.

8. Charles Tilly, "Reflections on the History of European State Making," in *The Formation of National States in Western Europe*, ed. Tilly (Princeton: Princeton University Press, 1975), 25.

state socialism. East European societies were among the most thoroughly etatized in the world. In the words of Valerie Bunce, among modern political regimes "none has approximated ... the sheer size, density and sectoral as well as geographical coverage of the [socialist] party state."[9] Among the empirical "givens" with which every inquiry into the remodeling of state structures should begin, then, is the sprawling grid of organizational entities that Communist state-builders left behind. To be sure, the boundaries that separated this grid from the society in which it was embedded were often blurred. Nonetheless, the state arena constructed by the fallen regimes, marked though it was by the amorphousness of enormity, was distinct enough to warrant notions such as "insiders" and "outsiders." The state-centered approach entails a focus on the former agents—on the ways in which their role and location in the web of political relations evolved—rather than on the latter protagonists.

Concomitantly, this approach clearly suggests that it is *not* warranted to rely mechanically on preconceived notions about existing state structures under Communism in analyses of *post-Communism*. What Kafka said about the laws by which the political arena is allegedly governed—that the very existence of such laws is at most a matter of presumption—should unhesitatingly be applied to post-Communism as well. Simply because the Communist state constructed heavy administrative structures entrusted with economic planning does not mean that these structures could be easily retooled for monitoring post-Communist privatization. Simply because the Communist state maintained a vast and well-equipped police force does not mean that this police force could be instantly redirected to enforce property rights and the rules of market competition. Simply because the Communist state effectively controlled the national wealth does not mean that its resources could be swiftly redeployed for the purposes of post-Communist development. In short, it would be foolhardy to conceive of the institutional legacy of state socialism in terms of functioning tools of governance.

Moreover, the state-centered reevaluation of what the fallen Communist regimes left behind should encompass not only the *institutional* peculiarities of the state domain—what the state "is"—but also its *functional* characteristics, the historically specific modes of husbanding resources and formulating authoritative definitions of political reality. What *became* of the post-Communist state—why it lost its logistical capacity and organizational coherence—is an issue that cannot be analyzed in isolation from what the state was *doing* under the particular circumstances of the 1990s.

---

9. Valerie Bunce, *Subversive Institutions* (Cambridge: Cambridge University Press, 1999), 23–24.

The blending of institutional and functional perspectives in a state-centered reassessment of the legacies of state socialism better clarifies that we should think of such legacies as consisting of sensitive positions in proximity to flows of resources; strategic sites where various assets were stashed; cadre loyalties that permeated the esprit de corps of the civil service; and elite networks privy to scarce knowledge about what is to be found where in the public domain. It should also compel us to recognize that—to put in a formulaic fashion one of the main ideas of this book—the deinstitutionalization of the state is related to its defunctionalization, a conjunction of dynamics that acontextual analyses, blind to the conundrums of post-Communism as an episode of state transformation, will surely miss. The a priori assumption that the positions, sites, loyalties, and networks that constituted socialist stateness provide the institutional basis of novel, democratic modes of governance should be rejected. From a state-centered perspective, scenarios in which the institutional wherewithal bequeathed by the old regimes is *not* instantly and effectively redeployed in pursuit of reform policies are also plausible and worth exploring.

The state-centered perspective entails neither a state-centered interpretation of post-Communism in general nor the notion that dynamically changing post-Communist environments are shaped by a uniquely potent unitary actor, the state. What it does entail is approaching post-Communism as a historically specific episode of state transformation. To Vadim Volkov we owe the insight that sometimes what transpires in the social world is a set of specific historical and institutional circumstances where in "the absence of a general organizing will ... we can postulate neither the existence of the state nor its absence."[10] This peculiar dialectic of state presences and absences is crucial for understanding the reconfiguration of state structures in early post-Communism. The term *dialectic*, of course, is not intended to get across a philosophical idea regarding complex and yet repeatable patterns shaped by acontextual forces. Rather, it is intended to express skepticism about such neat dichotomies as "state-led" vs. "market-driven," "state-controlled" vs. "privately run," and "state-regulated" vs. "unregulated"—as well as appreciation for the simultaneous "thereness" of institutional components, dynamics, and logics of action that might be considered mutually exclusive—or at least reliably compartmentalized—under conditions of established "stateness." An episode of state transformation constitutes an empirical reality resistant to analyses that take institutional frameworks for granted and explore how such frameworks process political

---

10. Vadim Volkov, *Violent Entrepreneurs* (Ithaca: Cornell University Press, 2002), 157. See also Vadim Volkov, "The Political Economy of Protection Rackets in the Past and in the Present," *Social Research* 67, no. 3 (Fall 2000): 1–35.

preferences and normative worldviews. It is marked by noticeable oscillations driven by the interactions of what Michael Mann terms "multiple overlapping and intersecting sociospatial networks of power," and thus it is pulsating with "the central problems concerning *organization, control, logistics, communication*—the capacity to organize and control people, materials and territories."[11] The interplay of such multiple networks of power and the fracturing of the sociospatial capacity for organization previously monopolized by the party-state lend sociological meaning to claims about the existence or absence of a state shorn of "a general organizing will."

The state-centered approach does not necessitate the repudiation of another assumption, namely that the most important and consequential manifestations of elite domination in a post-Communist setting will be more or less intimately linked to the exercise of political power. But it does not treat it as a given that behind such acts of state-rooted power lies the intent to reaffirm the political primacy and organizational superiority of the state. In a provocative study, Hector E. Schamis demonstrated how economic actors who lobby for "more marketization and less government" wind up triggering a reassertion of state power.[12] Employing a similar sensitivity to paradoxical developments but reversing the analytical perspective, I will show how state agents may exercise public authority in ways that obliterate or scatter the very logistical resources that states need in order to maintain their institutional hegemony. An illuminating distinction introduced by Poggi may help illustrate this point. Poggi distinguishes between two mechanisms for reasserting power. Strong elites may perpetuate their privileged positions through "unperturbed continuation of established arrangements." For organized actors who run states, to draw on this mechanism of power would mean to maintain an organizational status quo in which the institutional hegemony of the state is secured and to use existing state apparatuses to enforce policies from which they benefit. Power, however, may be wielded in a different fashion, which Poggi labels "aoristic." Aoristic mechanisms of power work through the disruption of continuities, the demolition of institutional settings, and the smashing of existing political routines—through "the unlocking of situations, rather than the unperturbed continuation of established arrangements."[13] The simultaneous

---

11. Michael Mann, *The Sources of Social Power* (Cambridge: Cambridge University Press, 1986), 1:1–3, emphasis in original.

12. Hector E. Schamis, *Re-Forming the State* (Ann Arbor: University of Michigan Press, 2002).

13. Gianfranco Poggi, *Forms of Power* (Cambridge: Polity, 2001), 13–14. Poggi refers to one of the forms of past tense in the Greek language, the aorist, which described "one-off

exercise of both forms of power is at work behind the dialectic of institutional presences and absences. What is particularly important is that among the consequences of aoristic elite power may be the destruction of the preconditions for regularized reproduction of state structures. Put differently, among the analytical scripts that a state-centered interpretation should conjure up is the distinct possibility that the deployment of the mechanisms of state-rooted power may result in the nonreproducibility of state structures. The assumption that logistically well-endowed networks wish to retain their dominant positions is fully compatible with the proposition that their strategies will disrupt the rhythm of remaking state structures—a rhythm that would typically be taken for granted under conditions of "normal" stateness.

What would induce powerful agents entrenched in the state to prefer aoristic rather than continuity-friendly mechanisms of power? This question can be answered only after a careful examination of the incentives that mold the political calculus of such agents. It would be unwarranted to define this structure of incentives exclusively in terms of stable rules and reliable enforcement practices—rather, it emerges amid the dynamic interplay of the competing "sociospatial networks of power" invoked by Mann and the vibrations of "the web of political relations" discussed by Tilly. This thicker, more robust understanding of what "the pursuit of self-interest" might mean and bring about can only be grounded in careful explorations of the historico-institutional context.

Such explanations do not necessarily involve new substantive fields of research. Sometimes the state-centered research agenda is augmented through the refocusing of analytical questions that have been popular with students of post-Communist politics. For example, the issue of how party and state separated after four decades of symbiosis has been discussed only in terms of how this process altered the party; in chapter 2, I reverse the question and ask: How did this separation affect the state? Sometimes a state-centered research agenda requires the amplification of well-known explanatory paradigms. For example, a huge literature examines how assorted Communist cadres converted their political power into economic influence and privilege and how this process shaped emerging social and economic landscapes; in chapter 3 I raise the issue of how such "conversions of power" reconfigured state structures and the domain of stateness. Sometimes the state-centered approach calls for novel conceptualizations—for example, of what we mean when we say that "the winners" who amassed assets and power during the early

---

actions which occurred in the past but broke its continuity." The other form is the perfect past, which refers to things that have happened in the past but which in a sense continue to exist in the present.

stages of post-Communist restructuring had a "veto power" within the emerging institutional configurations—a line of conceptual inquiry I follow in chapter 4. And sometimes the state-centered approach challenges us to reorder our analytical frameworks. As I suggest in chapters 5 and 6, this approach should compel us to recognize that "state-building" encompasses two dimensions—the creation of new institutions and the reorganization of existing ones—whose interrelatedness and separateness should be scrutinized. What is important to grasp, therefore, is that the study of state transformation from a state-centered perspective is not inspired by a firm belief that behind the bewildering complexity of observable phenomena there unfolds a master process that students of post-Communism have inexplicably ignored. Rather, it is informed by the realization that through the recalibration of existing research agendas we may reach conclusions that are analytically more enriching.

I embrace a set of claims in the light of which the phenomena I explore appear empirically intertwined and analytically related. I contend that transformative processes in early post-Communism were characterized by a general directionality toward weakening of available state structures. These processes were propelled and conditioned by such factors as struggle for redistribution of state-held logistical resources, the structurally determined nature of post-Communist entrepreneurship, and the location of society's productive assets within webs of institutionalized relations. They inevitably affected existing tools of governance: the civil service, administrative agencies in charge of husbanding public resources, parts of the judicial system, and key components of the bureaucratic machinery. Among the visible syndromes associated with such processes were lack of information about what was to be found where in the public domain, reduced levels of monitorability within administrative apparatuses, scarcity of logistical resources, and the repeated stripping of the state not only of its financial and economic capital but also of its social capital—the creditworthiness that makes effective governing possible. The concrete manifestations of this general trend toward fractured stateness may be depicted as inability to design and implement policy, acute organizational incoherence, and lack of infrastructure for salutary state interventions in largely spontaneous processes of social and economic change.

In a sense, then, the story told in this book resembles the scenario depicted by John A. Hall and G. John Ikenberry: "the 'strong' state over time may become enfeebled by its own action and thereby begin to look 'weak.'"[14] But I go beyond the broad outlines of this scenario and offer

---

14. John A. Hall and G. John Ikenberry, *The State* (Minneapolis: University of Minnesota Press, 1989), 13.

specific insights and hypotheses about state weakness in early post-Communism. Manifestations of such weakness may be captured only imprecisely and crudely by indexes that convey the idea of declining values of selected, objectively measurable quantitative variables. Instead, we should embrace the commonsensical proposition that state weakness is a relational concept—what it does convey is analytical depictions of observable relations between state and nonstate actors. The inevitable usage of emotion-laden, normative language regarding "the constraints" hampering state action, the "emasculation" of bureaucratic apparatuses, and the "enfeeblement" of administrative agencies should not obscure the fundamental fact that—to quote another prominent student of modern stateness, Anthony Giddens—"one person's constraint is another's enabling."[15] Translated into the language of state transformation, this means that an institutional environment in which certain state structures are weakened is an environment in which assorted agents are empowered. From a state-centered perspective, the inquiry into the causes of state weakness should revolve around questions such as: What is the nature of pro- and antistate coalitions, and what factors precipitate their formation? In what organizational forms do these coalitions crystallize, and what is it that they fight over? How should we interpret their failures and successes? A narrative that takes "state weakness" as its overarching theme should offer context-specific arguments about the reconfiguration of fundamental political relations.

The relational character of state weakness reveals itself in another way: the connectedness between "public" and private agents endures through time, and even their separateness does not lose its interactive character. The relations between state structures and their social others do not end quickly and easily, and even the distances between them—to the extent that such distances are asserted—are dynamically maintained (i.e., reproduced through ongoing interactions) as well as liable to swift "shortenings" (i.e., reengagements of previously detached state and nonstate actors). That is why the proper way to think about state weakness as an institutionally reproducible outcome is in terms of organizational figurations, a term I borrow from Norbert Elias. According to Elias, a knowledgeable student of state formation in Europe, the key dynamic component of these processes was the interaction of "figurations made up of numerous relatively small social units existing in free competition with one another." States are always involved in "networks of interdependencies," and to argue that they are "weak" would specify the outcome

---

15. Anthony Giddens, *The Constitution of Society* (Berkeley: University of California Press, 1984), 176.

of the "free competition" between them as well as the conditions that render this outcome reproducible. I contend that in an intensely statist environment—such as early post-Communism—it is the state-centered perspective that helps us situate such outcomes on a comprehensive analytical map and thus discover the general dynamic that "gives to all individual processes" of organizational changes "their direction and their specific stamp."[16]

From an intellectual standpoint, the state-centered approach is invigorated by the idea that those of us who try to make sense of post-Communism should make up for what Anna Grzymala-Busse and Pauline Jones Luong have singled out as "one of the more curious, and persistent, missed opportunities in comparative politics, [namely] a productive dialogue between scholars of post-Communist transitions and of the state."[17] It is the resumption of such a dialogue that my work on post-Communist state dysfunctionality seeks to ignite. The theme of "stateness" and "state-building," although by no means absent from the literature on post-Communism, has been interpreted in a monophonic manner, and as a result its many analytical dimensions have remained unexplored. Only one important aspect of the state-building process has been discussed, to the marginalization of all others: the formation of *nation*-states. An overwhelming majority of analysts today subscribe to the view that the issues related to state-building in post-Communism are coterminous with the problematic of defining boundaries and creating nations. Perhaps the best illustration of this one-sided interpretation is the contention of Linz, Stepan, and Gunther that "questions regarding stateness are irrelevant to political transitions that occur within established nation-states or state-nations."[18] The major implication of this argument is that outside the context of disintegrating federative and multiethnic states the issue of state transformation should not be broached.

Thus authors who write about Eastern Europe have a restricted understanding of the issues that legitimately belong to the study of state-building. Unfortunately, this trend is paralleled by the tendency of authors who dig deeper into the problematic of state transformation to exclude Eastern Europe.

---

16. Norbert Elias, *The Civilizing Process* (Oxford: Basil Blackwell, 1978), 489.
17. Anna Grzymala-Busse and Pauline Jones Luong, "Reconceptualizing the State," *Politics and Society* 30, no. 4 (December 2002): 529.
18. See Juan J. Linz, Alfred Stepan, and Richard Gunther, "Democratic Transition and Consolidation in Southern Europe," in *The Politics of Democratic Consolidation*, ed. Gunther, P. Nikiforos Diamandouros, and Hans-Jürgen Puhle (Baltimore: Johns Hopkins University Press, 1995), 85. See also Rogers Brubaker, *Nationalism Reframed* (Cambridge: Cambridge University Press, 1996), and Michael McFaul, *Post-Communist Politics* (Washington, D.C.: Center for Strategic and International Studies, 1993).

The patriarch of the study of state-building, Charles Tilly, writing in 1992, noted the collapse of the Soviet empire but insisted that more is to be gained from the study of state making in the third world than from exploiting the peculiar transmutations in the second world. He is yet to formulate a statement about the significance of the East European experience for the study of state making.[19] In a review of the comparative literature on the state Karen Barkey and Sunita Parikh deal with "state-building in the Western world" as well as "the Middle East, Asia, Africa and the newly democratizing countries in Latin America." The post-Soviet region is virtually the only geographical zone not subject to serious consideration. The conclusion is obvious: there simply is no work worth reviewing on the transformation of state structures in Eastern Europe.[20] In a long article on "reflections on stateness in an era of globalization," Peter Evans referred to the rise of "civil society" in Eastern Europe but had no comments to offer regarding the development of post-Communist states.[21] A collection of essays on "the developmental state" features—in addition to the requisite accounts of the Southeast Asian "tigers"—articles on France, Brazil, India, and Finland. However, there is not a word about the problem of post-Communist "development" and the role of the state in it.[22] Finally, a special volume on "state-formation" features an important article on several Soviet successor states (inexplicably, it appears under the heading "Culture in the Modern Western State"), but this article is devoted exclusively to the question of "re-formation of nationality."[23] The inclusion of a piece dealing with this particular subject in a volume on state formation reiterates the impression that the problem of state-building in post-Communism is, for all intents and purposes, identical with the construction of *nation*-states and therefore implies that countries in which "the ethnic question" has lost its saliency do not have a "state-formation" problem.

In sum, the general impression shared by the scholarly community seems to be that whatever is interesting about the former second world has nothing to do with the transformation of state structures, and, concomitantly, the themes informing the literature on modern stateness are

---

19. See Tilly, *Coercion, Capital and European States, AD 990–1992* (Cambridge, Mass.: Blackwell, 1992). Tilly *has* incorporated the East European theme in his study of modern forms of social conflict: *European Revolutions, 1492–1992* (Oxford: Blackwell, 1993).

20. Karen Barkey and Sunita Parikh, "Comparative Perspectives on the State," *American Review of Sociology* 17, no. 3 (1991): 523–49.

21. Peter Evans, "The Eclipse of the State?" *World Politics* 50, no. 4 (October 1997): 62–87.

22. *The Developmental State*, ed. Meredith Woo-Cumings (Ithaca: Cornell University Press, 1999).

23. David D. Laitin, "The Cultural Elements of Ethnically Mixed States," in *State/Culture*, ed. George Steinmetz (Ithaca: Cornell University Press, 1999), 291–320.

not very illuminating in a post-Communist context. This frame of mind accounts for the fact that—as Petr Kopecky and Cas Mudde opined—of all facets of post-Communism, "the record with regard to . . . 'stateness' is probably poorest of all."[24] It is this circumstance that blocks the productive dialogue between those who study post-Communism and those who study the making of modern states. It is this circumstance that I seek to change with this book. Early post-Communism was a period riddled with many of the problems usually associated with moments of fluctuating infrastructures of governance. The state-centered understanding of state weakness thus goes to the heart of the most formidable challenge facing students of post-Communist democracies: they have to examine the metamorphosis of densely structured sociopolitical orders that are immensely complex while assuming that all actors involved in the drama are at square one. To exaggerate the impact of the collapse of the system would amount to disregarding the intricate, sprawling institutional legacy of Communism; to claim that post-Communism is simply a transformative episode in the evolution of modernized social systems would denigrate the very real sense in which basic issues related to the functioning of the state were up for grabs. We shall see that the structural and institutional legacies of state socialism indeed constituted a propitious environment for the aggravation of serious symptoms of nonreproducibility of state organizations. And the diminished usability of administrative and bureaucratic apparatuses was a consequence of context-specific manifestations of state-rooted elite power.

The Dominant Explanatory Paradigm: A Policy-Centered Approach

I hope that this book will fill a yawning lacuna in the ongoing conversations about what happened after the collapse of state socialism and that it will bring to the foreground contextual and analytical issues that are beyond the reach of current debates about post-Communist politics. That such a lacuna exists, and that such issues have been consistently disregarded, is perplexing. Given that by the late 1990s the incapacity of state institutions and administrative apparatuses had become one of the leitmotivs in the literature on post-Communism, one would expect that the analytical and empirical issues related to this unexpected development would stimulate plenty of empirical research, generate competing hypothesis, and stir up intellectual debates. A survey of this literature

---

24. Petr Kopecky and Cas Mudde, "What Has Eastern Europe Taught Us about the Democratization Literature?" *European Journal of Political Research* 37, no. 4 (June 2000): 528.

will fairly quickly reveal, however, that a rather simple, parsimonious explanation dominates scholarly explorations of state weakness. To distinguish this hegemonic explanation from my state-centered approach, I dub it a policy-centered approach. At its core lies the contention that the problems afflicting post-Communist states were caused by the policies pursued by newly empowered reformers. In the aftermath of the collapse of one-party regimes, these reformers were overwhelmed by a neoliberal passion. Once catapulted into power, they began to design and implement policies inspired by a neoliberal blueprint permeated by a strong antistatist, pro–free market animus. It was the ideologically driven reformers that proceeded to "dismantle" the state in order to open room for "markets." They were first abetted and then pushed relentlessly by various representatives of international financial institutions that made the flow of much-needed financial assistance contingent on strict conformity with the devoutly laissez-faire orthodoxy. In the wake of the neoliberal onslaught East European societies found themselves afflicted by a series of potentially avoidable crises. A Polanyian "great transformation" was reenacted by pro-Western elites and millions of citizens, only recently victimized by radical revolutionaries pursuing their utopia, were once again forced to pay the exorbitant price attendant to the ideological pet projects of woefully incompetent leaders.[25] In sum, the state was weakened because this is what local neoliberal zealots and their international capitalist mentors wanted.[26]

---

25. The controversial work of Karl Polanyi has been widely advertised as the key to understanding the conundrums of post-Communism; for a representative collection of articles developing Polanyian themes, see *The New Great Transformation?*, ed. Christopher Bryant and Edmund Mokrzycki (London: Routledge, 1994). See also Michael Burawoy, "Transition without Transformation," *East European Politics and Societies* 15, no. 2 (Spring 2001): 269–90.

26. A short list of authors who have depicted "promarket reformers" as the main actors and culprits in post-Communism includes Stephen F. Cohen, *Failed Crusade* (New York: W. W. Norton, 2001); Adam Przeworski, *Sustainable Democracy* (Cambridge: Cambridge University Press, 1995); Richard Whitley, "Transformation and Change in Europe," in *Industrial Transformation in Europe*, ed. Eckhardt Dittrich, Gert Schmidt, and Whitley (London: Sage, 1995); Alice Amsden, Jacek Kohanowicz, and Lance Taylor, *The Market Meets Its Match* (Cambridge: Harvard University Press, 1994); Michael Burawoy, "The State and Economic Involution," in *State-Society Synergy*, ed. Peter Evans, Research Series No. 94 (Berkeley: University of California, International and Area Studies Digital Collection, Research Series #94, 1997); Jacek Kohanowicz, "Reforming Weak States and Deficient Bureaucracies," in *Intricate Links*, ed. Joan Nelson (New Brunswick, N.J.: Transaction, 1994); Guillermo O'Donnell, "The State, Democratization and Some Conceptual Problems," *World Development* 21, no. 8 (1993): 135–1369; David Stark, "Not by Design," in *Strategic Choice and Path-Dependency in Post-Socialism*, ed. Jerzy Hausner, Bob Jessop, and Klaus Nielsen (Aldershot, England: Edward Elgar, 1995); Claus Offe, *Varieties of Transition* (Cambridge: MIT Press, 1996); Kazimierz Poznanski, "Building Capitalism

Why and how this interpretation of the causes of decay of post-Communist state structures acquired a hegemonic status in the literature to the point where it is endorsed by authors who otherwise have next to nothing in common—for example, neo-Hegelians like Francis Fukuyama, analytical Marxists who are also virtuosos of game-theoretical modeling and macro-empirical research like Adam Przeworski, admirers of the Soviet regime who lament its collapse like Jerry Hough, and idiosyncratic prophets of the anti-Enlightenment who are keen to put their fin-de-siècle gloom on public display, like John Gray—is a topic that is interesting in itself.[27] It is fairly easy to demonstrate, however, that the policy-centered approach to the study of post-Communist state institutions suffers from several serious defects: factual inaccuracy, neglect of historical and institutional context, and implausible assumptions about elite behavior.

Factual Inaccuracy

Arguably the most disturbing aspect of conventional wisdom on the causes of state weakness in post-Communism is that its parsimony is bought at a very high price: utter disregard for well-known facts about post-Communist politics. The claim that in the aftermath of 1989 neoliberals came to power all over Eastern Europe is wrong. Leaving the controversial Russian case aside, during the first half dozen years of post-Communism—the period when the symptoms of state decay were most visible—Poland was the *only* country where a handful of intellectuals who had actually read Friedrich von Hayek and embraced his ideas about the state and the market enjoyed their fifteen minutes of fame.[28] To what extent these intellectuals possessed the wherewithal to establish a putative hegemony in the post-Communist intellectual milieu—where vehement Catholics, socialists, and trade unionists were also remarkably active—is debatable. One thing is clear, however—in the early to mid-1990s Poland with its visible and influential cohort of

---

with Communist Tools," *East European Politics and Societies* 15, no. 2 (Spring 2001): 320–55; Peter Reddaway and Dmitri Glinski, *The Tragedy of Russian Reforms* (Washington, D.C.: United States Institute of Peace, 2001); Peter Stavrakis, *State-Building in Postcommunist Russia*, Occasional Paper No. 254 (Washington, D.C.: Kennan Institute for Advanced Russian Studies, August–October 1993).

27. See Francis Fukuyama, *The End of History* (New York: Free Press, 1992); Adam Przeworski, "The Neo-Liberal Fallacy," *Journal of Democracy* 3 (1993): 45–59; Jerry Hough, "Russia—On the Road to Thermidor," *Problems of Post-Communism* 41, nos. 2–3 (1994): 26–31; John Gray, *Enlightenment's Wake* (London: Routledge, 1995). For a more comprehensive treatment of this topic, see Venelin I. Ganev, "The 'Triumph of Neo-Liberalism' Reconsidered," *East European Politics and Societies* 19, no. 3 (Summer 2005).

28. On neoliberalism in Poland, see Jerzy Szacki, *Liberalism after Communism* (Budapest: Central European University Press, 1994).

neoliberals was the exception, not the rule. In some countries, such as the Czech Republic, stylized neoliberal rhetoric masked a pragmatic attempt to initiate incremental and tentative economic change.[29] In other countries, such as Hungary, neoliberal ideas, even though discussed, were never considered seriously in the process of policymaking, and a preference for gradualism—as opposed to radical economic reforms—was shared by virtually all key players.[30] And elsewhere it would be hard to identify the "neoliberals" who supposedly targeted state structures for destruction in the early and mid-1990s. Who were the brave knights of neoliberalism in Meciar's Slovakia? Who were the crusaders of monetarism in Iliescu's Romania? Who were the fans of the International Monetary Fund among Ukrainian post-Communist elites? Who were the "promarket Bolsheviks" in Tujman's Croatia? Unless neoliberalism is depicted as a mysterious force that works its "evil" magic apart from human intent and action, the developments that engulfed these countries during the last decade of the previous century cannot in any meaningful way be characterized as a pursuit of a neo-liberal agenda. Put differently, the crucial fact that critics of neoliberalism cannot account for is that the atrophy of state agencies was readily observable in countries whose governments resolutely opposed radical reforms. Lamentably, then, the policy-centered approach is marked by a brisk circulation of several catch-phrases—"shock therapy," "IMF-imposed austerity programs," "Washington consensus"—and the conspicuous absence of any empirical research on the specific causes of the crisis of stateness in Eastern Europe in the 1990s.

Historical Context

The dominant paradigm is strikingly insensitive to peculiarities of historical context. Over the last several decades, various "economic reforms" have been implemented throughout the world, and the ways in which such reforms have affected state structures have been closely examined. One of the major insights to come out of this literature is that abstract and general statements about the impact of promarket policies are likely to be rather crude and misleading. This insight is cogently summarized by Guillermo O'Donnell: "States are interwoven in complex and different ways in their respective societies."[31] This attitude

---

29. For more on the strategic use of neoliberal rhetoric by Vaclas Klaus in pursuit of non-neoliberal political objectives, see the fascinating analysis by David Stark and Laszlo Bruszt, *Postsocialist Pathways* (Cambridge: Cambridge University Press, 1997).

30. Janos Kornai, "Paying the Bill for Goulash Communism," *Social Research* 63, no. 4 (Winter 1996).

31. Guillermo O'Donnell, *Counterpoints* (South Bend, Ind.: University of Notre Dame Press, 1999), 134.

underpins O'Donnell's own explorations of how economic policymaking has shaped state structures in Latin America; similar ideas have also guided some of the best-known studies of the dynamic evolution of state structures in other parts of the world, for example, Joel Migdal's inquiry into state-society relations in Africa and Peter Evans's analysis of "state embeddedness" in Brazil, India, and South Korea.[32] Unfortunately, it is precisely on questions pertaining to context, state-society relations, and modes of embeddedness that mainstream explanations of state weakness in post-Communism are disturbingly silent. The salient features of the historical setting—the institutional legacy of the centrally planned economies, the political mechanisms for asserting power inherited from the one-party system, the specificity of social and economic structures—are, for the most part, left unexamined. Although the impacts of neoliberal reforms are repeatedly discussed, the emphasis invariably falls on their *generic* consequences, on the impact these reforms are likely to have irrespective of time and place. Occasional disclaimers notwithstanding, the dominant paradigm embraces uncritically the tabula rasa premise—that is, the notion that after the implosion of Communist regimes "the slate was wiped clean"—and therefore persistently accentuates the causal primacy of policies and decisions made *after* 1989. If some aspects of the institutional legacy of socialism are relevant to the discussion of the malfunctioning of the state, we are not informed what they are and how they matter.[33] If there are structural attributes of the state that render it vulnerable irrespective of the policy preferences of new leaders, we are not told what these attributes might be. And if there is something about the post-Communist social milieu that militates against effective governance, this "something" is not discussed.

In the absence of contextual interpretations, analytical work is assigned to misleading metaphors. No single factor has inflicted more damage to the study of post-Communist states than the widespread use of the metaphor of "withdrawal," that is, the general contention that in the former Soviet satellites the state has "withdrawn" from the economy or from society. Why should we assume that—as the metaphor clearly suggests—"state presence" is a matter of "either/or," and not of "more" or "less"? If the metaphor refers to a de jure situation, does reality correspond to what the laws prescribe? And if the metaphor depicts a de

---

32. See Joel Migdal, *Strong Societies and Weak States* (Princeton: Princeton University Press, 1988), and Peter Evans, *Embedded Autonomy* (Princeton: Princeton University Press, 1995).

33. For an excellent defense of the general analytical position that valid answers to important questions about post-Communism should be "largely historical-institutional in nature," see Bunce, *Subversive Institutions*.

facto status quo, then what factors "pushed" the state aside? To this list of general analytical concerns, an array of empirical questions may be added. If a state-owned enterprise is registered as a limited company and the Ministry of Industry possesses the majority of shares, has the state withdrawn from it or not? If the state no longer distributes outputs but determines the prices of various "inputs," does that mean that uncontrolled market forces are allowed "to take over"? If subsidies are slashed but major state-owned companies are granted access to state-subsidized credits, can we assert that the state's regulatory presence has evaporated? As long as scholars attribute explanatory significance to misconceived metaphors such as "the withdrawal of the state" scholarly exchanges will generate lots of polemical heat regarding the normative appeal of certain policies—and little analytical insight as to why and how state structures have devolved in post-Communism. In sum, policy-centered approaches proceed in an unabashedly a priori fashion, with state weakness deducted from the immanent logic of the neoliberal Weltanschauung. Analyses of the decay of state structures in the former Soviet world have taken the form of reexamination of the first principles of theoretical economics—an intellectually exciting approach that, however, permanently marginalizes fact-centered explorations of particular post-Communist places and institutional settings.

Assumptions about Elite Behavior

Finally, the blame-the-neoliberals paradigm proceeds on the basis of two easily identifiable and yet questionable analytical premises. First, that political elites in the former Soviet world are motivated exclusively by their ideology. Second, that these elites possess the power to implement any policy they deem appropriate, and that therefore important outcomes such as the decay of state power directly reflect, and should be perceived as a consequence of, formally enacted reform measures. These premises provide a shaky analytical grounding for explorations of institutional change in particular and post-Communist politics more generally.

To begin with, the proponents of the view that post-1989 East European politics reflects deeply held neoliberal values rarely go beyond textual analyses of official policy statements made by both IMF officials and local politicians. That behind the ideas expressed in such statements may lie other, more pragmatic, or self-interested motives, is not an argument that has been consistently examined. Specifically, that antistatist, promarket declarations, especially by East Europeans, may not be an expression of sincere beliefs or internalized ideological commitments has not been seriously explored. David Stark was one of very few scholars willing to take such statements with a grain of salt; in a relatively early article, with admirable perspicacity, he warned analysts not to take East European politicians at their word and to explore what "real preferences" may be hidden behind policies presented to the public as "IMF-sponsored programs."[34] Notably, however, the suggestion that post-Communist leaders may be opportunistic tacticians who say one thing while trying to get money from Westerners, and then do something completely different when they make decisions regarding the distribution of public resources, has rarely been pursued. And it is easy to see why. If references to constellations of interests and self-serving modes of elite behavior are allowed to adulterate the purity of the dominant explanation, then its core hypothesis—that a set of policies inspired by a "neoliberal blueprint" is the motor behind the major institutional developments that recast post-Communist states—will have to be abandoned for more variegated research on the precise role and impact of diverse factors that have little do to with official policymaking and ambitious ideological visions.

Most important, the dominant paradigm has failed to eliminate a potent alternative explanation of the dynamic undergirding post-Communist politics—namely, that power holders are motivated by *interests*, and not *ideology*.[35] Scholars who have chosen to do "fieldwork" instead of analyzing policy documents and macroeconomic data have repeatedly demonstrated that what lurks behind putative "market reforms" is the rather easily detectable interests of strategically located elite networks. The level and scope of privatization, for example, was determined not in accordance with the shibboleths of neoliberalism but with very concrete electoral considerations in mind.[36] Once in power, parties were much more concerned with constructing and maintaining networks of clients than with the implementation of ideological blueprints.[37] And the process of "deregulation" was molded to fit the preferences of particular constituencies, not as an overarching laissez-faire vision.[38] Undoubtedly,

---

34. David Stark, "Path Dependence and Privatization Strategies in East Central Europe," *East European Politics and Societies* 6, no. 1 (Winter 1992): 52.

35. For an excellent analysis of the problems inherent in ideas-centered accounts of elite behavior that a priori dismiss the relevance of interests, see Sheri Berman, *The Social Democratic Moment* (Cambridge: Harvard University Press, 1998), esp. chap. 2, "Evaluating the Role of Ideas."

36. See, for example, Roman Frydman, Andrzej Rapaczynski, and Joel Turkewitz, "Transition to a Private Property Regime in the Czech Republic and Hungary," in *Economies in Transition*, ed. Wing Thye Woo, Jeffrey D. Sacks, and Stephen Parker (Cambridge: MIT Press, 1997), 41–102.

37. See, for example, Anna Grzymala-Busse, "Political Competition and the Politicization of the State in East Central Europe," a paper presented at "The Postcommunist State" conference, Yale University, April 2001.

38. Krassen Stanchev, "The Path of Bulgarian Economic Reform," *East European Constitutional Review* 10, no. 4 (Fall 2001): 56–61.

the quest for alternative explanations of state decay in post-Communism is compatible with the commonsensical assumption that the role of elite action is worth investigating. But even when such an assumption is embraced, the overuse of the term "neoliberal elites" may prove to be rather unenlightening. *What* these elites should be called—how they should be characterized analytically—cannot be answered simply by references to the putative appeal of imported ideologies. Hence any credible explanation of state weakness in post-Communism will have to revolve around a contextual interpretation of the dynamic and consequences of self-interested elite agency.

The second analytical premise—that proreform elites possessed full power to sculpt their environment in accordance with their vision—is even more problematic. The dominant narrative about the collusion of local free marketeers and their foreign economic advisors conveys the impression that politics in post-Communism is nothing more than a unidimensional, monocausal affair featuring a small, all-powerful group of decision makers whose policies are the sole factor shaping the socioeconomic environment. Certainly, this imagery implicitly justifies the attention accorded to IMF recommendations and economic experts' advice, as well as the exclusion of all problems related to implementation. And yet, the overreliance on the "missionary zeal of reform elites" as an explanatory factor is a dubious heuristic strategy. Even if it is demonstrated that such a "zeal" actually existed, how it was translated into concrete policies and how such policies worked out in practice would still be far from clear. In a deservedly celebrated essay Martin Kahler pointed out that it would be implausible to expect that elite-led attempts to dismantle state structures in order to stimulate the growth of markets would result in spectacularly successful "state withdrawal." Kahler introduced his much-discussed concept of "the orthodox paradox" to bring into sharp relief that such "orthodox" promarket policies are bound to encounter resistance from various incumbents and are therefore likely to result in only minimal "scaling down" of the state.[39]

There are solid reasons, therefore, to expect that policy measures intended to disassemble capacious state edifices might fizzle out rather than accomplish their objectives. But it bears emphasizing that in a post-Communist context the proposition that observable effects can be linked by clear causal chains to the intent of policymakers is even more problematic. What Stephen Holmes said about Russian politics may easily be applied to the region as a whole, at least during the early stages of the post-Communist transformations: "To watch Russian politics is to

---

39. Miles Kahler, "Orthodoxy and Its Alternatives," in *Economic Crisis and Policy Choice*, ed. Joan M. Nelson (Princeton: Princeton University Press, 1990), 54.

observe a football game through a soupy fog where you can make out the teams only faintly and in outline, where you are unsure who has the ball or which way he is running, and where you strongly suspect there are other players on the field whose intentions are perhaps sinister but in any case unknown."[40] Given the general opaqueness of the political domain, disarmingly simple claims about single-factor causality are bound to be an analytical scaffolding too brittle to sustain a serious interpretative structure.

More generally, among the undisputable virtues of the social science literature one should count the suspicion with which claims that "blueprints" designed and promoted by intellectuals are the main cause of social and economic change have usually been met. Those who believe that the analysis of post-Communist politics is undistinguishable from a critique of neoliberal ideology should perhaps think through the implications of William Scheuerman's observation that "any attempt to deduce complex, real-life institutional trends from the alleged contradictions of a particular intellectual system should meet with a healthy dose of skepticism."[41] It is also worth remembering that George Steinmetz has a point when he ridicules "the professional narcissism" of "academic analysts who assume that forms of writing that . . . resemble their own are more causally efficacious."[42] And it would be prudent not to forget the wise warning of a foremost student of social turbulence, Sidney Tarrow: "simply because we *see* them making decisions," Tarrow asserts with regard to attention-grabbing public figures, does not mean that their decisions "must be given *causal* primacy."[43] Once it is recognized that to single out the officially stated intent of formally empowered policymakers is hardly the most enlightening analytical approach, however, the malfunctioning of the post-Communist state will appear as a much more complex phenomenon in which various social, institutional, and organizational factors are involved. The unilateral *actions* of democratically elected neoliberals would appear less important than the web of formal and informal *interactions* between strategically located elites and the historico-institutional setting of which these webs are an essential component.

---

40. Holmes, "What Russia Teaches Us," 24.
41. William Scheuerman, *Liberal Democracy and the Acceleration of Time* (Baltimore: Johns Hopkins University Press, 2004), 119.
42. George Steinmetz, "Introduction: Culture and the State," in *State/Culture*, ed. Steinmetz, 18.
43. Sidney Tarrow, "Mass Mobilization and Regime Change," in *Politics of Democratic Consolidation*, ed. Gunther, P. Nikiforos Diamandouros, and Hans-Jürgen Puhle (Baltimore: Johns Hopkins University Press, 1995), 205; emphasis in original.

It is hard to avoid the conclusion that the dominant explanation of the causes of state weakness in post-Communism cannot survive an even moderately careful scrutiny. The policy-centered approach to the problem of state decay in post-Communism leaves unanswered important questions regarding the factors undermining the coherence of the state apparatus, the transformative dynamics that cause massive loss of state capacity, and the institutional developments and political tactics that render particular state structures dysfunctional. It almost seems as if the *problematique* of state degeneration has been appropriated by warring ideological factions in Western academia, where no-holds-barred clashes over the virtues and vices of neoliberalism are a permanent fixture of the intellectual landscape. A lamentable corollary of this tendency is that the scholarly debate about this aspect of post-Communist politics has come to resemble an exchange of "Persian letters" a la Montesquieu: analyses of far-off places mask polemical arguments tossed at opponents at home. This unsatisfactory state of affairs can only be improved if the quest for alternative explanations of post-Communist state weakness is relaunched, and it is to such an alternative explanation that this book is devoted.

The Hypotheses-Generating Study: Defense of a Method

In an insightful book on post-Communist politics in Russia, Mary McAuley rightly urges students of post-Communism to think of their task as *"changing the mainstream, creating a new intellectual agenda, not simply adopting mainstream concerns."*[44] The mainstream policy-centered approach that quickly gained hegemonic status is clearly ripe for serious, innovative challenges. For those who study the reconfiguration of state structures from a state-centered perspective the task of forging new intellectual armature is a matter of daunting necessity. But what is the best strategy for embarking on such a mainstream-shattering intellectual journey?

My answer is: a hypotheses-generating case study informed by the analytical themes developed in the rich literature on the historical sociology of the modern state. This approach is justifiable *in principle* insofar as loose talk about "state weakness" and "lack of capacity" are largely undecipherable in the absence of concrete, important, and theoretically engrossing vignettes elucidating the political realities behind such terms. This approach is also justifiable in terms of the troublesome blind spots

---

44. Mary McAuley, *Russia's Politics of Uncertainty* (Cambridge: Cambridge University Press, 1997), 7; emphasis in original.

in the literature on post-Communism: neglect of transformative dynamics autonomously generated within the state domain and lack of comprehensive understanding of the myriad of factors that constitute the "context" of post-Communist state weakness. It is, finally, justifiable as a promising way of bringing interpretations of post-Communist experiences to bear on ongoing, transdisciplinary conversations about stateness, governance, and the institutional prerequisites of effective policymaking in the modern world.

Admittedly, today a preference for a case study—any kind of case study—is in need of special justification. Thirty years ago the defense of case-centered analytical strategies may have been superfluous: commenting on developments in comparative politics in the mid-1970s, Harry Eckstein pointed out that "it is not much of an exaggeration to say that the case-study literature in the field comes close to being coterminous with the literature as such."[45] Now, however, the situation is radically different. Those who choose to focus on particular cases and geographical areas are accused of "having defected from the social sciences to the camp of the humanists," of "constituting a center of resistance to new trends in the discipline," and sabotaging "the search for theory and . . . the use of rigorous methods for evaluating arguments."[46] And since the legitimacy of case studies as a heuristic tool has been subject to vigorous attacks, scholars venturing into this less than fully reputable pursuit are under enormous pressure to spell out the theoretical implications of their research.

To be sure, case studies are associated with important analytical trade-offs of which no conscientious scholar should be oblivious—and particularly the trade-off between texture and generalizability. Still, this is a trade-off political scientists should accept. A case study is, indeed, a defective launching pad for those who aim at high-flying nomothetic propositions. But it does contribute, in a variety of ways, to the shared scholarly ambition to enhance theory building. A considerable number of seminal writings on post-Communist politics have been consciously designed and carried out as case studies, for example David Ost's analysis of the role of labor in post-Communist politics in Poland, the survey by Akos Rona-Tas of the rise of the private economic sector in Hungary, M. Steven Fish's inquiry into the dynamics of party formation in Russia,

---

45. Harry Eckstein, "Case Study and Theory in Political Science," in *Handbook of Political Science*, ed. Fred I. Greenstein and Nelson W. Polsby (Reading, Mass.: Addison-Wesley, 1975), 80.
46. Robert H. Bates, "Letter from the President," *APSA-CP: Newsletter of the APSA Organized Section in Comparative Politics* 7, no. 1 (Winter 1996): 1, available at http://www.nd.edu/~apsacp/pdf/APSA-CP_7_1.pdf.

and Gerald McDermott's explorations of the restructuring of the public sector in the Czech Republic.[47] Surely, then, the idea that an in-depth exploration of a single case may amplify the analytical dimensions of existing research programs is not alien to the relatively young tradition of studying post-Communist polities.

Another charge leveled at case studies is that they offer nothing more than mere description. And there are case studies to which this label may be rightfully attached. It might be also pointed out, however, that analytical methods in which good description is one of several scholarly objectives unabashedly pursued may expand our intellectual horizons because they may generate—to use a term introduced by Andrew Abbott—"descriptive heuristics." In the context of my state-centered approach, the case study may bring about at least two of the important analytical benefits Abbott associates with descriptive heuristics.[48] First, it will stimulate us to think in new ways about what is in the foreground and what is in the background of scholarly inquiries into the transformation of state structures. The decision to assign certain processes and phenomena to "the context" and turn others into "focal points" can be made only on the basis of comprehensive knowledge about the dynamics and manifestations of institutional change. Case studies are undoubtedly very useful in engendering such knowledge.

Second, the descriptive heuristics might guide us to novel insights about the level at which determining, structure-transforming actions takes place. The very process of "describing" involves decisions about "where" exactly the things and actions that lead to change are located: At the level of individuals? Networks? Policy-making procedures? Democratic governance? Global context? Once again, it seems to me possible to use a case study as a magnifying glass for comprehending what is at stake when we think about levels of analysis, if not in determining the appropriate level itself.

The particular type of case study that I pursue in this book, the hypotheses-generating case study, was introduced in the contemporary comparativist's arsenal by Arend Lijphart, who described that approach as an inquiry that "starts out with a more or less vague notion of possible hypotheses" and whose objective is "to develop theoretical generalizations

---

47. David Ost, *The Defeat of Solidarity* (Ithaca: Cornell University Press, 2005); Akos Rona-Tas, *The Great Surprise of the Small Transformation* (Ann Arbor: University of Michigan Press, 1997); M. Steven Fish, *Democracy from Scratch* (Princeton: Princeton University Press, 1995); Gerald McDermott, *Embedded Politics* (Ann Arbor: University of Michigan Press, 2002).

48. Compare Andrew Abbott, *Methods of Discovery* (New York: W. W. Norton, 2004), 138–39.

in areas where no theory exists yet."[49] Consequently, I offer generalizations that might be further refined through testing. One generalizable observation is that the first free democratic elections had a more serious impact on state institutions than on postauthoritarian societies. Another generalization presented for consideration is that the survival of institutions "engineered from above" in the early post-Communist period depends on how seriously these institutions interfere with the dominant predatory projects of local elites. Yet another generalizable proposition spelled out in this case study is that varying modes of exercising veto power will affect in different ways the emerging institutional configurations of democratic governance. Once these empirical and analytical clues are incorporated in existing research programs, they may render more productive and rigorous further comparisons between cases.

A hypotheses-generating case study is also a useful instrument for drawing analytical maps that illustrate the salience and hypothesized significance of specific factors implicated in the reconfiguration of state structures at a particular time and place. At present, such maps are not in circulation: the only answer to the question "What is it about post-Communism that explains state weakness?" that is currently available is "the ideas of neoliberal policymakers." A case study of a particular country—particularly a country where the "zero hypothesis," namely that neoliberal hegemony causes fluctuations of stateness, might be swiftly and unequivocally discarded—may sensitize us to the availability of other analytical venues worth exploring. As Eckstein made clear, such an analytical strategy may sharpen our analytical focus: "Unlike wide-ranging comparative studies, case studies permit intensive analysis that does not commit the researcher to a highly limited set of variables and thus increases the probability that critical variables and relations will be found."

Or, to quote Lijphart once again, "to analyze a single country diachronically" is a method that "generally offers a better solution to the control problem than comparison of two or more different but similar units at the same time."[50] In other words, if we want to distinguish the truly important factors and mechanisms from conspicuously available but ultimately false analytical leads, a case study is as good a research instrument as any other. With post-Communism specifically, case studies may enable researchers to avoid "conflating too many particular events," to hold "cultural factors" constant, and thus to contribute to our

49. Arend Lijphart, "Comparative Politics and the Comparative Method," *American Political Science Review* 65, no. 1 (Winter 1971): 692.
50. Ibid., 689.

understanding of "processes perennially at the center of social science concerns."[51]

A hypotheses-generating case study is congruent with the general objective of analyzing a phenomenon such as the reconfiguration of state structures and the ensuing hemorrhaging of institutional capacity, a convincing demonstration of what the outcome actually is should be considered as important as explaining it. As Howard S. Becker argues, case studies are necessary for showing "how something got to be the way it is."[52] The reconstruction of events, of course, should be something more than a purely chronological narrative—its aim must be to recapture interactive dynamics as they transpired in a historically structured environment. The hypotheses-generating case study presents a conceptual vocabulary that might frame possible interpretations of fluctuations of stateness. It does not offer a simple one-dimensional story but insists instead that we need to go through a great number of stories in the plural before we get to an analytically stylized story. A case study provides an opportunity to relate facts to concepts, as well as reality to hypotheses.[53] It facilitates the incorporation of intellectual reflections on post-Communist change into topical debates that animate global civil society. Thus it provides remedies to the fallacies debilitating currently hegemonic, neoliberalism-centered approaches that conjure up monocausal chains linking economic ideas to observable institutional realities and rely excessively on imagery rooted in traditional critiques of capitalism.

In sum, case studies, more often than not, display a measure of skepticism about parsimonious models that claim validity that transcends time and space, and evince an informed preference for a healthy eclecticism. As Rudra Sil persuasively argues, "self-consciously eclectic approaches" foster "greater communication and experimentation across a wider range of research communities across the social sciences" and thus allow diverse groups of intellectual collaborators to "articulate potentially significant complementarities between problems, analyses, interpretations, and observational statements that may otherwise remain hidden."[54] Such an approach is not inherently hostile to analytical rigor and theoretical ambition. The case study may stimulate what Diane Vaughn has called

---

51. Ost, *Defeat of Solidarity*, 3.
52. Howard S. Becker, "Cases, Causes, Conjunctures, Stories, and Imagery," in *What Is a Case?* ed. Charles C. Ragin and Becker (New York: Cambridge University Press, 1992), 205–16, esp. 208–9.
53. Michel Wievorka, "Case Studies" in *What Is a Case?* 159–71.
54. Rudra Sil, "Problems Chasing Methods or Methods Chasing Problems?," in *Problems and Methods in the Study of Politics*, ed. Ian Shapiro, Rogers M. Smith, and Tarek E. Masoud (Cambridge: Cambridge University Press, 2004), 307–31.

"theory elaboration"—"the process of refining a theory, model or concept in order to specify more carefully the circumstances in which it does or does not offer a potential for explanation."[55] One way to refine a theory would be to explore and formalize the ways in which quantitatively measured independent and dependent variables relate to one another. An alternative way would be to conduct—let us borrow Georgi Derluguian's memorable metaphor—an "archaeological survey" that begins with the digging of a "cross-cutting trench to expose ... historical layers" and thus to identify "the most promising leads for a more detailed excavation."[56] This is the general thrust of my methodological approach. The state-centered perspective on the state yields important clues as to where and how to dig. Careful examination of a single country that is analytically wedded to the notion of state transformation may solidify the conceptual scaffolding of future research by depicting the dialectics of state presences and absences against a broader analytical background that convincingly links empirical evidence to concrete conceptual debates. Thus the hypotheses-generating case study allows us to approach the complexity of post-Communist transformations without succumbing to the allures of grand theorizing or the simplistic charms of ad-hocishness. Systematized data that elucidates the social and institutional peculiarities of post-Communism as an episode of state transformation is essential for comprehending the theoretical and comparative dimensions of such notions as "state weakness" and "state strength," "institutional continuity" and "institutional change"—categories indispensable for the analysis of institutional developments in post-Communist stateness. This heuristic strategy will not provide a solid fundament for sweeping lawlike propositions about the multifaceted transformation of state structures in the post–cold war era. But I will show how knowledge about post-Communism may be amalgamated into theoretically engrossing reflections on the fragility of modern mechanisms of governance and the logistical problems facing self-governing political communities in various parts of the world.

The Case

The country I have chosen to focus on is Bulgaria. In theory, this choice does not call for a special justification. As Kiren Aziz Chaudhry remarks in her groundbreaking book on state formation in the Middle East,

---

55. Diane Vaughn, "Theory Elaboration," in *What Is a Case?* 173–202, at 175.
56. Georgii Derluguian, *Bourdieu's Secret Admirer in the Caucasus* (Chicago: University of Chicago Press, 2005), 8.

"Saudi Arabia and Yemen are no more and no less 'unique' that France and England; their capacity to inform theory is not circumscribed by their location on the Arabian Peninsula."[57] This proposition should be readily applicable to countries like Bulgaria as well. It is important to note, however, not only what Chaudhry says but that she has to make such a statement in the first place. The inescapable reality of contemporary social science is that, while all cases are officially proclaimed "equally important," unofficial conventions tacitly acknowledge that some cases are more equal than others. When an "out-of-the-way" country such as Bulgaria is selected for a case study, therefore, adventurous scholars are expected to provide an extra rationalization. In defending my choice of Bulgaria, I emphasize the following considerations.

First, shedding analytical and empirical light on this case seems to be a task worthy in itself. No former Soviet satellite in Eastern Europe has posed so many problems for those willing to systematize and explain the outcomes of post-Communist transformations. It is rather easy to unearth from the literature widely diverging, mutually exclusive interpretations of the Bulgarian case. For some scholars, Bulgaria in the 1990s was a case where, due to the peculiar "mode of transition"—a palace coup against an aging Communist despot—democracy failed to take root and the political order retained its distinctly authoritarian character.[58] For others, it was a "backslider," a country that attained a measure of democraticness, then lost some of it, but ultimately remained "too peculiar" to be characterized in any clear-cut manner.[59] And still others declare Bulgaria a success story—a democratizing "over-achiever" whose progress has defied original predictions of imminent fiasco.[60] The attempt to identify the main factors shaping post-Communist processes resulted in a similar confusion. For some, it was the country's presocialist and socialist pasts that molded its post-1989 trajectory.[61] For others, it was the radical reforms allegedly undertaken in the early 1990s.[62] Analysts of the interplay of political and

---

57. Kiren Aziz Chaudhry, *The Price of Wealth* (Ithaca: Cornell University Press, 1997), 29.

58. Carol Skalnik Leff and Gerardo Munck, "Modes of Transition and Democratization," *Comparative Politics* 29, no. 3 (April 1997): 343–62.

59. M. Steven Fish, "The Dynamics of Democratic Erosion," in *Postcommunism and the Theory of Democracy*, ed. Richard Anderson et al. (Princeton: Princeton University Press, 2001), 54–95.

60. Juan Linz and Alfred Stepan, *Problems of Democratic Transition and Consolidation* (Baltimore: Johns Hopkins University Press, 1996), 333–43.

61. Herbert Kitschelt, Zdenka Mansfelodva, Radoslaw Markowski, and Gabor Toka, *Post-Communist Party Systems* (Cambridge: Cambridge University Press, 1999).

62. Kazimierz P. Poznanski, "The Crisis of Transition as a State Crisis," in *Postcommunist Transformation and the Social Sciences*, ed. Frank Bonker, Klaus Müller, and Andreas Pickel (Lanham, Md.: Rowman and Littlefield, 2002), 55–76. Notably, the author does not specify what these purportedly "radical" policies actually were.

economic changes also classify Bulgaria in incompatible ways. According to some, popular reactions to economic crises led to the recrudescence of ethnic passions and other cultural pathologies.[63] According to others, what transpired in the country attests to the fact that sometimes in a post-Communist setting "popular reaction to protracted economic crisis triggered attempts to advance political and economic reforms by newly elected radical governments."[64] Authors interested in institution building and attempts to mimic Western constitutional models also render diametrically opposed verdicts about the Bulgarian case. For some, the course of Bulgarian politics in the 1990s proves that Western practices *can* be successfully transplanted.[65] For others, the course of Bulgarian politics proves that Western practices *cannot* be adequately reproduced.[66]

Arguably, this assortment of irreconcilable opinions may be a sign of serious intellectual engagement with a complex case. Much more plausibly, however, it reflects persistent confusion stemming from ignorance and exacerbated by the desire to make the case fit preconceived explanatory frameworks.

The last point is worth accentuating: at least so far, analytical characterizations of Bulgaria have usually been driven by comparativists' desire to fill a blank spot in a two-by-two chart or to provide an example of a case that stands at the polar extreme of a preexisting continuum. If and when Bulgaria is approached and included in a comparative study, it is with the purpose of making it fit a ready-made framework rather than to explore its problems, paradoxes, and complexities. Interestingly, whereas the list of "Romanian experts" should include the names of such luminaries as Katherine Verdery, Daniel Chirot, Vladimir Tismăneanu, and Ken Jowitt, Bulgaria is yet to attract the attention of authors willing to write career-enhancing monographs. This is the reason why, if and when it is "compared" to other cases, the risk is great that such "comparisons" amount to little more than stereotyping that fits Bulgaria into an ambitiously concocted analytical narrative.[67] This lamentable tendency

---

63. Milada Anna Vachudova and Tim Snyder, "Are Transitions Transitory?" *East European Politics and Societies* 11, no. 1 (Winter 1997): 1–35.
64. Kopecky and Mudde, "What Has Eastern Europe Taught Us?" 526.
65. Albert P. Melone, *Creating Parliamentary Democracy* (Columbus: Ohio State University Press, 1998).
66. Jon Elster, Claus Offe, and Ulrich K. Preuss, *Institutional Design in Post-Communist Societies* (Cambridge: Cambridge University Press, 1998).
67. The preceding book and the article by Leff and Munck, "Modes of Transition and Democratization," for example, contain numerous claims that are demonstrably erroneous. For more details, see Venelin I. Ganev, "The Rise of Constitutional Adjudication in Bulgaria," in *Constitutional Justice, East and West*, ed. Wojciech Sadurski (The Hague: Kluwer Law International, 2002), 163–89.

occludes important questions regarding what exactly transpired when transformative processes engulfed the country in the 1990s—and correspondingly decreases the value of comparative accounts that use Bulgaria as a case.

In this book I illuminate the relevant analytical dimensions of outcomes that social scientists try to comprehend, as well as the major empirical developments that produced such outcomes. It cannot be properly labeled "a political history of Bulgaria after 1989" and therefore I do not feel obliged to explore all aspects of the country's politics in the 1990s. But as I examine the transformation of state structures, I address questions such as: How exactly did the overlapping dynamics of economic and political change affect the quality of governance? Have Western constitutional practices been successfully transplanted to Bulgarian soil? Has Bulgaria become a consolidated democracy?

The focus on Bulgaria, then, is justified because it will set the record straight with regard to an underresearched and underanalyzed case, and it will enhance the heuristic potential of future comparative inquiries.

There are two additional considerations that may be adduced to vindicate the selection. The first is that the Bulgarian case contradicts the hegemonic narrative about state dysfunctionality in post-Communism, a narrative that assigns to neoliberal reformers a causally central role. Simply put, until 1997—during the period when the symptoms of state weakness were most visible—there were *no* neoliberals in power. For the most part, the country was governed by either former Communists or coalition governments in which they retained a strong and uncontested veto power. For a brief, nine-month period, Bulgaria was ruled by an incoherent anticommunist coalition with a "conservative" agenda involving lustration of Communist officials and restitution of pre-1944 property rights. During the first dozen years of its "transition" Bulgaria remained thoroughly dominated by a left-leaning intelligentsia. In large part because of the lack of indigenous dissident traditions, almost all of the country's prominent journalists and newspaper editors, media pundits, TV talk show hosts, and public intellectuals proudly displayed their soft spot for "the good old days under Zhivkov," while bravely exposing the cruelty of markets and relentlessly ostracizing anyone exposed as "anticommunist." They also vigorously criticized U.S. imperialism and Anglo-Saxon capitalism, and rallied behind the unquestioned credo that "the state should take care of all the needs of the people." Whatever the vices of Bulgarian opinion makers, allegiance to "the magic of the market," "free capitalist enterprise," and "economic liberty" were not among them. Furthermore, relations with international financial institutions were initially suspended, then tentatively renewed—but, until 1996, did not go beyond the point of suspended animation. No foreign economic advisors were invited to draft blueprints for shock therapy.[68] No matter what facets of Bulgaria's post-Communist experience one decides to explore, the contention that this facet is shaped by neoliberals may be safely dismissed. Willy-nilly, those who study the logistical incapacitation of state structures in the country will have to depart from well-trodden paths and exercise their imagination (to refer to Eckstein once again) in the quest for alternative explanations.

Moreover, the focus on Bulgaria will help us sort out important questions about what factors are relevant to what aspect of post-Communist developments. What follows from Bulgaria being a relatively poor, ethnically heterogeneous but predominantly Eastern Orthodox Balkan country? This question points to yet another set of issues in the light of which the choice of the country is eminently sensible. Bulgaria belongs to a set of countries whose political misfortunes—including various syndromes associated with state weakness and malfunctioning of bureaucratic organizations—are frequently explained in terms of what might be called a Balkan *Sonderweg*, an explanatory strategy that, to borrow Geoff Eley's characterization, "relentlessly directs attention to the sins of omission of one's national history."[69] But to what extent are *constants*, such as levels of socioeconomic development, culture, and historical tradition useful for those who want to understand the *changes* affecting the infrastructure of governance after 1989? By holding various factors constant within the framework that analyzes the evolution of state structures, I use data from Bulgaria to specify and explain the relevant aspects of post-Communism as a specific *context* in which processes of state transformation unfold.

Finally, a word about the choice of a time frame. Although some of the most important processes I deal with were well under way before 1989, and some of the stories I look into go beyond 1997, I have chosen these two dates, 1989 and 1997, to demarcate the chronological dimension of my analysis. To be sure, such decisions must involve some arbitrariness that no amount of ambitious explaining can offset. And yet, I think that common sense and the general directionality of the transformative processes I analyze are both on my side. Although 1989 certainly did not swipe the slate clean, it was without a doubt a turning point in the sense specified by Andrew Abbott: "What makes a turning point a turning point rather than a minor ripple is the passage of sufficient time 'on

---

68. In 1990 the country was visited by the American entrepreneur Richard W. Rahn, but even though his radical policy proposals generated some publicity, his advice had no discernible effect on political decision making.

69. Geoff Eley, "The British Model and the German Road," in *The Peculiarities of German History*, ed. Eley and David Blackbourn (Oxford: Oxford University Press, 1985), 10–11.

the new course' such that it becomes clear that the direction has indeed been changed."[70] Crucially for my analysis of how state structures were transformed in post-Communist Bulgaria, strategically located state elites realized fairly soon that the direction had been changed and that they would have to reassert their power under an entirely new set of opportunities and constraints. It seems to me that it would be preposterous to deny that there is an umbilical cord connecting such decisions to the shocking domestic and international developments of 1989. The other turning point in Bulgaria's recent political history, 1997, is the year when the political order that emerged under the obtrusive hegemony of the former Communist Party collapsed and the country embarked on a new path of development. Once again, it fairly quickly dawned on everyone, including the strategically located players and social predators, that the direction had been changed. That such a change occurred should not be construed to mean that problems including corruption, elite insouciance, the criminalization of the public sphere, and widespread economic misery were miraculously resolved. Bit it did mean that, in the aftermath of the events I discuss in chapter 5, a state-rebuilding effort was tentatively launched in post-Communist Bulgaria, and this effort encompassed not only the creation of new institutions (such as the Currency Board) but the replenishing of the logistical resources of existing ones. How and why this tentative and partial rebuilding became possible is a line of inquiry that can only be embedded in an analytically sound account of what transpired *before* 1997.[71] Having justified the use of this case in my book, let me confess that I find disturbingly persuasive Jacob Burckhardt's remark that some objects of study exert "an inner attraction which ... alone is capable of repaying every effort to penetrate the mysteries of society."[72] Whether or not my case meets this high-minded criterion is a question which I will not be able to answer definitively. But this book should be considered an effort to transform the case of Bulgaria from an ugly empirical duckling into a graceful analytical swan.

---

70. Andrew Abbott, *Time Matters* (Chicago: University of Chicago Press, 2001), 245.

71. For an analytical interpretation of the post-1997 state-building effort in Bulgaria—one that emphasizes the importance of new modes of corruption and state elites' opportunity to control flows of resources from the European Union—see Venelin I. Ganev, "Ballots, Bribes, and State-Building in Postcommunist Bulgaria," *Journal of Democracy* 17, no. 1 (January 2006): 75–89.

72. Jacob Burckhardt, *The Age of Constantine the Great* (New York: Dorset Press, 1989), 12.

2 The Separation of Party and State as a Logistical Problem

> Who on earth is "the state"?
> MAX WEBER

How did party and state separate in the aftermath of the dramatic events of 1989? In the literature on post-Communism, this question is almost completely ignored. Yet, such a neglectful attitude is unjustified. The separation of party and state was a major, large-scale organizational phenomenon that directly affected the "stateness" of the former Soviet satellites. The undoing of the institutionalized party-state axis sent shock waves through existing apparatuses of governance and diminished the infrastructural capacity of available bureaucratic machineries. It generated a transformative impetus that disrupted mechanisms of control in the public domain and decreased levels of governability in the fledgling post-Communist polities. Scholars who seek to situate the question of state dysfunctionality in early post-Communism in an analytical framework that is sensitive to historical specificity and to local institutional complexities should put the separation of party and state at the foreground of their inquiries.

Current interpretations of the withdrawal of the party from the state should be amplified through the introduction of state-centered analytical concerns revolving around the issue of how the separation affected the state.[1] The reason such a perspective is necessary is that the progressing

---

1. One of the very few scholars who had an inkling of the significance of this issue during the early stages of the post-Communist transformations was Kazimierz Z. Poznanski. In 1992, he wrote that "the disintegration of Communism has meant inevitable weakening of the state, since the Communist Party was also the state." See "Epilogue," in *Constructing Capitalism*, ed. Poznanski (Boulder: Westview Press, 1992), 211. But he never developed this insightful observation into a more elaborate, empirically substantiated argument.

dissolution of party-state linkages was a process with a *dual character*. On the one hand, it shaped the behavior of the *party*, and was thus intimately linked to the democratization and pluralization of post-Communist political contests. Construed as an episode in the transformation of the hegemonic authoritarian political organization, the problem of the withdrawal of the Communist Party from the state lends itself to an easy "operationalization" and may be conveniently compressed into a captivating narrative of how the party sustained its first electoral loss, conceded its defeat, and surrendered its power. On the other hand—and less obviously—this process involved a series of developments that transformed the state structures of incipient democracies. As the party left, what happened to the state?—this is the main question that informs a state-centered approach to the separation.

My answer is that in each country in the former Soviet bloc the separation engendered debilitating logistical shocks that reverberated throughout local institutional landscapes. The end of the party-state regime necessitated the demarcation of two hitherto inextricably linked domains—the domain of state power and the domain of party power—which in turn touched off a process of competitive redistribution of information, institutional wherewithal, and logistical resources. That state structures were reconfigured as departing party cadres strive to retain control over various resources stored in what was hitherto a common power base is a distinct, shared structural feature of the incipient Eastern European democracies. This systematic effort to reconsolidate the power of party cadres precipitated the atrophy of the institutionalized interactions that formed the infrastructural basis of statehood; the dynamic reproduction of party power has as its downside the fracturing of available tools for democratic governance. Empirical evidence related to the separation bears on broader analytical questions regarding the integrity of post-Communist administrative apparatuses, the ability of democratically elected "principals" to monitor incumbent bureaucratic "agents," and the capacity of state agencies to mobilize people and resources in pursuit of policy objectives. The separation is linked, empirically and analytically, to readily observable fluctuations in the institutional capacities of administrative agencies. It does not stand at a tangent to, but is an integral element of, the transformations of stateness in the early 1990s.

In addition to this broader analytical claim, the state-centered perspective may help us formulate and consider a *comparative hypothesis* centered on the outcome of the first multiparty elections and the way in which they shaped post-Communist politics. The intriguing contrast is between cases where the separation of party and state immediately followed this crucial event and cases where this process was considerably prolonged. What exactly are the differences between these two scenarios? From such a comparative vantage point, a close-up look at the Bulgarian case makes a lot of sense. Bulgaria, along with Romania, belongs to a group of countries where a largely unreconstructed Communist Party won the first multiparty elections. In the discourse on post-Communist politics, these countries were subsequently characterized as laggards that failed to make much progress throughout the 1990s. Even if their "falling behind" cannot be seriously questioned, it has never been quite clear to what extent and why the outcome of the first elections shaped in such a dramatic fashion these countries' fate during the first decade of post-Communist transformations. Usually, the "lack of progress" was attributed to various policies pursued by the newly legitimated former rulers—state support for a failing public sector, preservation of state monopolies, the pursuit of fiscally irresponsible programs. My in-depth study of Bulgaria will re-emphasize the importance of the outcome of the first free electoral contest and explain why it proved to be pivotal for subsequent trajectories of post-Communist development. The gist of my argument is that if the separation of party and state is prolonged beyond the first elections, the damage inflicted on the institutional edifice of the state becomes more serious. The largely invisible dynamic attendant to lengthier processes of separation triggers hidden chain reactions that subsequently mold diverging paths of state transformation. Thus comparative inquiries should focus not only on the various ways ex-Communist parties reestablished their presence in multiparty electoral configurations—a topic that has attracted the attention of knowledgeable observers—but should also encompass the different kinds of state structures they left behind.[2]

The blending of the state-centered perspective with a detailed analysis of how party and state separated in Bulgaria thus presents an explanation of state dysfunctionality rooted in an interpretation of the first elections as a transformative event that not only rendered obsolete modes of reproduction of authoritarian power and thus facilitated the advance of democracy but also created a set of logistical circumstances under which the reproduction of state structures was disrupted.[3] This explanation also rests on an empirically grounded account of the nature of the power of the *nomenklatura* and institutional reading of the causes for variation in post-Communist development.

---

2. For an excellent study of the different adaptive strategies of former Communist parties, see Anna Grzymala-Busse, *Redeeming the Communist Past* (Cambridge: Cambridge University Press, 2001).

3. On the significance of events for transformation of structures, see William H. Sewell Jr., *Logics of History* (Chicago: University of Chicago Press, 2005).

Separation and Democratization

The symbiosis of party and state was unambiguously recognized as one of the most important features of Communist political systems in Eastern Europe, a unique characteristic that set them apart from other types of modern nondemocratic regimes.[4] This analytical consensus, however, did not stimulate scholarly inquiries into how the party and the state separated after 1989. One of the unquestioned presuppositions on which current analyses of multifaceted post-Communist transformations rest seems to be that the separation does not pose analytical challenges distinguishable from more general questions regarding the conditions under which the ruling Communist Party will allow competitive elections and, more generally, submit itself to the rules of democratic governance: "The disintegration of the ruling party in Eastern Europe did not involve much of a change in the state apparatus . . . the state taken over by a Leninist party remained intact, now to be governed by parties elected by the domestic population."[5]

The separation is consequently treated as a simple "cut" incised by the scalpel of the first free elections, a discrete episode that laid the basis of democratic political practices. And it cannot be denied that this phenomenon may be construed as an institutional and attitudinal shift that opened political space for the rise of electoral politics. *Institutionally*, the severance of the party-state link indicated that nondemocratic elites gave up the two monopolies they previously enjoyed: the monopoly on all political institutions and the monopoly on all significant political outcomes. And in terms of *attitudinal change*, the separation created propitious conditions for "the transfer of loyalty from dictatorship to democracy" to take place.[6] It is the withdrawal of the party from the state that marks the moment in which the much-desired "devolution of power from a group of people to a set of rules" became a possibility.[7] Within the context of "democratization studies," then, the separation is linked analytically to developments such as domestication of state power, pluralization

---

4. See, for example, Ellen Comisso, "State Structures, Political Processes, and Collective Choice in CMEA States," in *Power, Purpose, and Collective Choice*, ed. Comisso and Laura D'Andrea Tyson (Ithaca: Cornell University Press, 1986), 19–62; Janos Kornai, *The Socialist Economy* (Princeton: Princeton University Press, 1992); Ken Jowitt, *The New World Disorder* (Berkeley: University of California Press, 1992); T. H. Rigby and Ferenc Feher, eds., *Political Legitimation in Communist States* (New York: St. Martin's, 1982); Graeme Gill, *The Collapse of a Single-Party System* (Cambridge: Cambridge University Press, 1994).

5. Ellen Comisso, "Legacies of the Past or New Institutions?" *Comparative Political Studies* 28, no. 2 (1995): 235.

6. See Giuseppe Di Palma, *To Craft Democracies* (Berkeley: University of California Press, 1990), chaps. 3 and 4.

7. See Adam Przeworski, *Democracy and the Market* (Cambridge: Cambridge University Press, 1991), chap. 2. The passage quoted appears on 11.

of the political domain, and consolidation of a democratic normative framework.

But should we conclude that the full significance of this "turning point" is adequately captured by analytical categories depicting the rise of electoral politics and the dynamics of democratic succession in power? At least some authors have argued that analysts should venture beyond the commonsensical separation-as-democratization interpretation and explore more thoroughly the theoretical and comparative aspects of the dissolution of the party-state link. One such work, by Linz and Stepan, contains insightful clues about the mechanisms whereby the divorce of party and state affects the stateness of fledgling democratic polities, but these insights are never incorporated into a broader, theoretically engrossing argument about the significance of this process. In contrast, a second piece by M. Steven Fish, contains an elaborate argument about how and why various modes of separation may be correlated to diverging paths of post-Communist development, but it misinterprets the mechanisms whereby these outcomes are generated. The problem of separation is both understudied and underanalyzed: we know little about the relevant facts, and we do not know what these facts tell us about the process of institutional restructuring in post-Communism.

In their magisterial book *Problems of Democratic Transition and Consolidation* Juan Linz and Alfred Stepan present an ambitious analytical perspective that has expanded the scope of current research agendas on postauthoritarian transformation.[8] One of the more important claims that they advanced is that it is not enough to consider the relation between "separation" and "democratization" on an abstract conceptual level and then identify the exact moment when the bond between party and state becomes unglued. It is also necessary to explore how the "changing of the guards" affects the process of governance during the subsequent period of "transition." More specifically, Linz and Stepan assert that countries where "the distinction between party and state has been virtually obliterated" are likely to experience difficulties related to one of the "interactive arenas" that consolidated democracies need "to have in place," namely "a state bureaucracy that is usable by the new democratic government."[9] Polities that inherit the legacies of one-party totalitarian regimes are particularly vulnerable in this respect: "The dismantling of the party within the state might seriously reduce the efficiency and coordination of the state apparatus

---

8. Juan Linz and Alfred Stepan, *Problems of Democratic Transition and Consolidation* (Baltimore: Johns Hopkins University Press, 1996). For an illuminating and at times critical discussion of the book, see Gerardo L. Munck, "Bringing Postcommunist Societies into Democratization Studies," *Slavic Review* 56 (Fall 1997): 542–50.

9. Linz and Stepan, *Problems of Democratic Transition and Consolidation*, 7, 11. The other "interactive arenas" that they consider are civil society, political society, the rule of law, and institutionalized economic society.

and open the door for clientelistic take-over by the new democrats or by opportunists."[10] Apparently, Linz and Stepan center their concerns—analytical as well as normative—on one specific topic: the "cleansing" of cadres of the old regime from the bureaucratic corps. If this cleansing does not go far enough, then many of those who remain on the payroll of the state may not be loyal to newly elected democratic leaders and may eventually spearhead resistance to sociopolitical reforms. Fledgling East European democracies might encounter the same problems that Detlev Peukert discussed in his study of the collapse of the Weimar Republic—silent sabotage and persistent subversion by a hostile civil service.[11] On the other hand, if the reformers are too brutal, they run the risk of alienating a number of competent administrators who could, if allowed to continue their careers, help bring about democratic reforms.

Linz and Stepan deal almost exclusively with this latter scenario, which features a massive purge unleashed when the ruling party "went out of power, disintegrated or was delegitimized." Their claim is that if and when the party is forced to retreat "in a hurry," then a crucial component of stateness, the "usability of state bureaucracy," is undermined.[12] The alternative hypothesis—the party wins the first elections and is thus granted plenty of time to set the actual "terms of separation"—is not considered at all. Is it plausible to assume that if such a scenario transpires, the stateness problem anticipated by Linz and Stepan will be spared to the novel democracies? Will the administrative apparatus be more "usable" if it remains under the stewardship of the party and, if so, why? Despite the obvious importance of these questions, they are not addressed in the lengthy volume.

The best discussion of the systemic impact of various patterns of separation is to be found in a pathbreaking article by M. Steven Fish. Amassing formidable evidence, he underscores "the supreme importance of a single political juncture: the outcome of the initial elections held during the transition from Soviet-type socialism." After a careful examination and critique of alternative explanations of differences in post-Communist development—explanations that conjure up economic, cultural, and political-institutional factors—Fish demonstrates that "the outcome of the first elections is the best predictor" of subsequent political and economic progress of the respective countries.[13] In countries where the opposition won and took control of the state apparatus, progress was steady and

---

10. Ibid., 63–64, table 4.3.
11. Detlev Peukert, *The Weimar Republic* (New York: Hill and Wang, 1993), esp. chap. 2.
12. Linz and Stepan, *Problems of Democratic Transition and Consolidation*, 11.
13. M. Steven Fish, "The Determinants of Economic Reform in the Post-Communist World," *East European Politics and Societies* 12, no. 1 (Winter 1998): 31, 57.

far-reaching; in marked contrast, during the 1990s countries where the "old guard" clung to power remained ensnared in a vicious circle of social crises and mass impoverishment. Fish's careful research, in a sense, provides a test to the Linz-Stepan hypothesis that a rapid withdrawal of the party from the state may undermine the administrative basis of effective governance. And the hypothesis obviously fails the test. Whatever the dislocations caused by a "hasty" separation, they are dwarfed by the disastrous medium- and long-term consequences of the former Communist Party's continuing hold on power. Eventually, all throughout Eastern Europe non-Communist elites made their way to executive offices, but in the interim various countries appeared to be locked in widely diverging trajectories, best exemplified by developments in Poland and Bulgaria. In 1996, the Polish economy was the fastest growing economy in Europe; in the course of the same year, the average salary in Bulgaria fell precipitously and the economy shrank by 10 percent.[14]

Why did the first elections have such a systemic, long-term effect? A simple economistic explanation readily comes to mind: the elections made possible the launching of promarket reforms in some countries and solidified the status quo in others. As Fish cogently argues, however, this account is too simplistic and misleading. To be sure, the scope of the first wave of reforms may be explained in terms of electoral outcomes. However, why did stabilization and growth persist when reformers were voted out of power during the "swing to the left" in 1993–95, and why this tendency did not transpire or was prone to dramatic reversals in countries where "proreform" governments were eventually installed? This cannot be adequately explained in terms of the relative radicalness of immediate economic policy change in the aftermath of the first elections.[15] What is necessary, Fish points out, is to resist the charms of economic reductionism and explore in more detail the *political effects* of the first elections.[16] And the analysis of these political effects constitutes the core of his explanation of the systemic impact of the first elections.

Fish's argument raises important questions and is illustrative of the common assumptions underlying most of the current research on post-Communism. It is worth considering in some detail. He singles out two "first order political effects" of the elections as particularly important; both effects are directly related to the *problematique* of separation. First,

---

14. For more details, see Venelin I. Ganev, "Bulgaria's Symphony of Hope," *Journal of Democracy* 8, no. 4 (Fall 1997): 139–54.
15. See Fish, "Determinants," 61.
16. For a similar insight—that the analysis of "the political dimensions of economic management" is indispensable for the comprehensive understanding of varying responses to roughly similar economic problems—see Peter A. Hall, *Governing the Economy* (New York: Oxford University Press, 1986), 4–5.

he underlines the impact of the elections on Communist elites. A decisive defeat in the first multiparty elections and the retreat from the state precipitated a "reformation" of the former Communist parties, while victorious former Communist parties generally "remained wedded to tradition." Second, Fish focuses on the evolution of *non-Communist elites*. Former opposition leaders who triumphed in the first elections and ascended to positions of power soon *"became politicians* and were therefore capable of constituting at least a substantial part of a *new political class*."[17] Thus the outcome of the first elections molded in a rather dramatic fashion the attitudinal and ideological dispositions of political elites: in some countries the challenges of restructuring were confronted by governments composed of reformed Communists, now Socialists, and a rising non-Communist "political class," whereas others remained fatally dependent on the shaky leadership of barely disguised Communists and immature dissidents. These immediate results were later magnified by what Fish labels "the second order effects" of the elections, and among those the level of political stability and the degree of openness of the political system loom particularly large.[18] It is the author's contention that societies where the former Communists lost the elections are markedly more stable and open.

The correlation established by Fish cannot be disputed—in fact, it should be considered one of the most solid and interesting empirical findings to come out of the voluminous literature on post-Communism. Countries in which the first elections brought about the separation of party and state obviously stood a much better chance of extricating themselves from the ruins of socialism than countries in which the separation did not occur until a later moment. Fish's *explanation* of the impact of the first elections, however, is problematic. Let us start with the first-order political effects. Fish correctly points out that the evolution of the former Communist parties yielded a plethora of political organizations, some of which embraced European-type social democratic values (Hungary), while others remained wedded to a faceless and inert traditionalism (Romania), and still others displayed more than a residual commitment to ambitious "socialist projects" (Bulgaria). In sum, there can be no question that the variation in behavior that Fish invokes does indeed exist.[19]

---

17. Fish, "Determinants," 62; emphasis in original.
18. In addition to these political second-order effects, Fish also considers two economic factors, "development of independent loci of economic power in society" and "macroeconomic performance"; see "Determinants," 63–65.
19. For good analyses of the party systems emerging in Eastern Europe, see Gordon Wightman, ed., *Party Formation in East-Central Europe* (Aldershot, England: Edward Elgar, 1995), and esp. Herbert Kitschelt et al., *Post-Communist Party Systems* (Cambridge: Cambridge University Press, 1999), and Grzymala-Busse, *Redeeming the Communist Past*.

This is not the case, however, with Fish's second "first-order" effect, namely the evolution of non-Communist elites. Unfortunately, this area of study is still clogged with stereotypes that purport to distinguish between Westernized and backward national cultures and is rarely refreshed by empirical research. Disappointingly, Fish does not adduce any evidence to substantiate his claim that "major differences" between different countries are easily noticeable—and it is hard to derive that evidence from the literature either. Fish never explains what he means by "a political class," but if the definition provided by the foremost authority on the subject, Gaetano Mosca, is taken as an interpretative guideline—"the political class performs all political functions, monopolizes power and enjoys the advantages that power brings"[20]—an unbiased observer will be compelled to recognize that by the mid-1990s a non-Communist "political class" had emerged in *every* post-Communist country.[21] In each state there were hundreds of non-Communist activists elected and reelected to national parliaments, appointed to strategic executive positions, and engaged in policymaking. In every national political arena it was now easy to spot professional politicians who had embraced "politics as a vocation," and everywhere they wore suits, used cellular phones, and displayed a propensity to indulge in the simple pleasures of incumbency—in other words they had learned "how to enjoy the advantages that power brings." Moreover, even if we concede that common sense and not conceptual niceties help us recognize a political class when we see one, a careful survey of specific case studies reveals that similarities in political conduct are much more striking than alleged differences. For example, Polish elites, whom Fish apparently perceives as a mature "political class," have been characterized as "institutional nomads" who "take over institutions or create institutions for the sake of expediency, use them and abandon them."[22] Conversely, in countries that remained under the domination of ex-Communists, dissident politicians have made remarkably successful

---

20. Gaetano Mosca, *The Ruling Class* (New York: McGraw-Hill, 1939), 50.

21. In the absence of clearly articulated criteria for distinguishing between the behavior of "politicians" and the supposedly inferior conduct of "dissidents-turned-democrats," attempts at classification will inevitably be marked by an unacceptably high degree of arbitrariness. For an attempt to clearly spell out "the indicators of the quality of the political class," see Juan J. Linz, "Some Thoughts on the Victory and Future of Democracy," in *Democracy's Victory and Crisis*, ed. Axel Hadenius (Cambridge: Cambridge University Press, 1997), 421.

22. A. Kaminski and J. Kurczewska, "Institutional Transformation in Poland," in *The Transformation of Europe*, ed. Matti Alestalo (Warsaw: IFIS Publishers, 1994), quoted by Jacek Wasilewski, "Elite Circulation and Consolidation of Democracy in Poland," in *Postcommunist Elites and Democracy in Eastern Europe*, ed. John Higley, Jan Pakulski, and Wlodzimierz Wesolowski (New York: St. Martin's, 1998), 165. See also Eduardo Guerrero, "Sociedad civil," *Politica y gobierno* 5, no. 2 (1998): 381–422.

careers: for example, Emil Constantinescu (president, 1996–2000), Andrei Plesu (foreign minister, 1997–99), and Corneliu Coposu (a prominent parliamentary leader) in Romania. The same holds true for some influential members of the Bulgarian non-Communist political elite: Zhelyu Zhelev (president, 1990–97), Petar Stoyanov (deputy minister of justice, 1991–92, and subsequently president, 1997–2002), Ivan Kostov (chairman of the Union of the Democratic Forces, minister of finance, 1991–92, and prime minister, 1997–2001) have all made widely recognized contributions to the development of Bulgarian democracy. There is no evidence that the outcome of the first elections had such a dramatic impact on the formation of political elites in various countries as Fish suggests. Differences between groups of politicians within individual countries seem much more pronounced than the alleged cross-country variation invoked by Fish.

The same criticism may be leveled against Fish's main "second-order effects," namely "openness" and "stability." Insofar as the former is concerned, throughout the 1990s patterns of government interference with freedom of speech were very similar throughout the region.[23] For example, attempts to subdue the state-run electronic media to the whims of ruling majorities erupted in both Hungary and Bulgaria.[24] And "libels against the president," a proscription that imposes tangible limits on freedom of expression, are prosecuted and punished both in the Czech Republic and Romania.[25] As for "stability," the problem is with the method of measurement employed by Fish to substantiate his claim that important differences between countries exist. The only evidence he presents is derived from a risk assessment study—it is widely known that such studies are based on narrow economic considerations and "measure" the policies of particular *governments* rather than the characteristics of the *political system* as a whole. Fish never discusses other measures routinely used in similar comparative projects—such as executive turnover and average government tenure. According to such criteria, in the early and mid-1990s Romania was in fact more "stable" than the Czech Republic and governments in Bulgaria were as stable as those in Poland.[26]

---

23. The obvious exceptions are Serbia and Belarus, where authoritarian practices of suppressing political freedoms continued throughout the 1990s.

24. On the Hungarian case, see Patrick H. O'Neil, "Hungary: Political Transition and Executive Conflict" in *Postcommunist Presidents*, ed. Ray Taras (Cambridge: Cambridge University Press, 1997), 212; on Bulgaria, see "Bulgarian Update," *East European Constitutional Review* 5 (1995) and 7 (1998).

25. On the Czech Republic, see "Czech Update," *East European Constitutional Review* 3 (Spring 1994): 8; on Romania, see "Romania Update," *East European Constitutional Review* 4 (Winter 1995): 21.

26. Joel Hellman, "Winners Take All," *World Politics* 50, no. 1 (January 1998): 213. By the end of 1996 there had been one executive turnover in Romania and two in the Czech Republic; the average tenure in months was fourteen in Poland and thirteen in Bulgaria.

Overall, then, Fish does not provide a convincing account of the significance of the first elections; the diverging patterns of the evolution of ex-Communist parties is the only "variation" of an important variable that he establishes unambiguously. Some of the most interesting questions raised by Fish's empirical findings, therefore, remain unanswered: Why did the first elections generate long-term difference in post-Communist development in political systems whose level of "openness" and "stability" did not vary markedly? Why did the elections lead to the emergence of patterns of better governance in some countries and not others, even though the "quality" of the "political class" was not distinctly different? Why was the fate of "reforms" so different in countries whose "outward" democratic attributes were similar?

The current literature does not offer convincing answers to these paradoxes, because the problem of separation and its logistical impact on stateness is either ignored, treated in a cavalier manner, or inadequately explained. One question in particular has been systematically overlooked: How does the separation affect the functionality of state structures?

I will try to answer this question by presenting empirical evidence from Bulgaria. I agree with Fish that the first elections had a momentous impact that transcended the concrete outcomes of the voting and the domain of electoral competition more generally. I agree with Linz and Stepan that the separation had direct bearing on the process of governance in post-Communism. But, unlike them, I link the problem of separation directly to this specific feature of the post-Communist political condition, the unraveling of the institutional bases of governance.

Party and State in Bulgaria, 1989-91

The most conspicuous feature of the Bulgarian post-Communist transformation is that the former Communist Party preserved its nearly absolute grip on power until the beginning of 1992, and generally retained its hegemonic position in national politics—on both the central and especially the local level—until 1997. The "conjuncture" which, as Fish has persuasively argued, decisively shaped the course of the Bulgarian transition was the first multiparty electoral contest held in June 1990, in which the former Communists (whose party was renamed the Bulgarian Socialist Party, or BSP) won 211 seats in the 400–member Great National Assembly.[27] Until the end of 1990, the BSP's control over all branches

---

27. The Great National Assembly was convened to draft and adopt a new constitution, but it also performed the functions of a regular legislature, including the installation of and control over the Council of Ministers.

of power was absolute and undivided.[28] In early 1991, some portfolios were conceded to the opposition, but the BSP possessed veto power over all decisions regarding personnel changes on all levels in the bureaucracy, and it could easily block efforts to restructure the state apparatus. In other words, for more than two years after the palace coup that removed aging General Secretary Todor Zhivkov from power, the domination of former Communist cadres was challenged but never seriously imperiled.

Throughout the early stages of the Bulgarian post-Communist transformations, the dominant political figure was Andrei Lukanov. He was indisputably the most powerful party member among the highest ranking state officials, and the most influential and knowledgeable state official among the party leadership.[29] Lukanov was an archetypical representative of the nomenklatura, and a close-up look at his strategic behavior as a post-Communist leader may help us comprehend the dimensions and manifestations of nomenklatura power.

Lukanov had impeccable Communist credentials. Born in Moscow of Bulgarian parents in the 1930s, he frequently boasted that he was "a third-generation Communist." By the early 1980s, Lukanov was considered the éminence grise behind a rising faction of allegedly proreform cadres within the Communist Party. Unlike the rest of the leaders of the anti-Zhivkov clique, whose previous involvement in economic policy-making was marginal, Lukanov had spent his entire career as a highly privileged appointee in the strategic executive branches related to foreign export, foreign trade, and international finance.[30] In the mid-1980s, he was directly involved in the preparation of Decree No. 56, which legalized certain kinds of private business activities and sought to introduce

---

28. The only decision-making site over which the BSP lost control in the mid-1990 was the presidency. However, at that time the presidency was a new institution, with ill-defined prerogatives. The capacity of Bulgaria's first non-Communist president, Zhelyu Zhelev, to shape the policies of the executive branch was practically nonexistent. For a detailed analysis of the Bulgarian presidency, see Venelin I. Ganev, "Semi-Presidentialism in Bulgaria," in *Semi-Presidential Regimes in Europe*, ed. Robert Elgie (Oxford: Oxford University Press, 1999), 134–58.

29. Lukanov should be considered a representative both of the state and of the outgoing authoritarian regime. On the importance of this distinction for the study of democratic transitions, see Robert M. Fishman, "Rethinking State and Regime," *World Politics* 42 (April 1990): 422–40. In many ways, my analysis confirms Fishman's hypothesis that "where a distinction [between party and regime] is not easily drawn . . . special problems are likely to emerge in the process of democratization," 434.

30. The most prominent among them were Petar Mladenov, Zhivkov's foreign minister, who initially succeeded Zhivkov as general secretary and was later elected president; Alexander Lilov, whose specialty was Marxist-Leninist ideology and who subsequently became the BSP's chairman; and Gen. Dobri Dzhurov, who had been serving as a minister of defense for more that twenty years.

"market elements" into the management of state-owned enterprises.³¹ In his capacity as leading reformer, Lukanov presided over the Zhivkov regime's hesitant attempts to introduce "market socialism."³² During the same period, he occupied simultaneously a number of key positions: he was chairman of the Foreign Currency Commission of the Central Committee of the Communist Party; leading member of the Governmental Commission on Foreign Currency Issues; and chairman of the Governmental Commission on Scientific-Technological Cooperation, which made all decisions regarding Bulgarian investments abroad. In addition, he became minister of international economic relations and first deputy prime minister. In March 1990, he was appointed prime minister by the last Communist parliament.

Adamantly opposed to what he derisively called "Western economics," Lukanov pledged to resist "the restoration of capitalism" in the country.³³ He repeatedly denounced "shock therapy" as a cruel and doomed reform strategy and vowed to pursue "a social-democratic alternative" that would embody "the socialist ideals" of the former Communist Party.³⁴ On various occasions Lukanov and his ministers condemned "neoliberalism" as an "inhuman ideology" that masks the ugly face of Western imperialism. Lukanov's intellectual guidance clearly left its imprint on the BSP's categorical position on the issue of economic change throughout the 1990s, namely that fostering markets is tantamount to "social sadism."³⁵

Consistent with this position on domestic issues was Lukanov's boldest move on the international arena: in the spring of 1990 he declared a moratorium on Bulgaria's foreign debt payments, a decision that endeared the government to the hard-core Communist electorate but instantly made the country a pariah in world financial markets. Defying routine practices followed in similar situations, Lukanov did not notify

---

31. The original text of the decree is published in *Durzhaven vestnik* (State Gazette) No. 4/1989.

32. On Lukanov's career before 1989, see revealing details in Rumen Bikov, Margarit Mitzev, and Nacho Nachev, *Ikonomicheskata kriza v Bulgaria* (The Economic Crisis in Bulgaria) (Sofia: Sv. Georgi Pobedonosetz, 1992).

33. Compare Andrei Lukanov, *Lukanov za krizata* (Lukanov on the Crisis) (Sofia: Hristo Botev, 1992).

34. See Andrei Lukanov, *Sotzialnata demorkatzija* (Social Democracy) (Pleven: Severno Eho, 1992).

35. See, for example, Alexander Lilov, *Dialogut na tsivilizatziite* (The Dialogue of Civilizations) (Sofia: Zahari Stoyanov, 2004); Zhan Videnov, *Otvud politicheskija teatur* (Beyond the Political Theater) (Sofia: Hristo Botev, 1998); Velko Vulkanov, *Na kolene pred istinata* (Kneeling before Truth) (Sofia: Bulvest 2000 [1996]). Alexander Lilov was chairman of the BSP (1990–91) and the party's main ideologue after 1989; Zhan Videnov was chairman of the BSP (1991–96) and prime minister of Bulgaria (1995–97); Velko Vulkanov was the BSP's candidate for president in the 1992 elections.

Bulgaria's creditors in advance of his radical act, and neither did he seek restructuring or rescheduling of the payments (a fax was simply sent to a few major Western banks on a Sunday afternoon).[36] Up until the very end of his tenure as prime minister—he was forced to step down when mass protests against his inefficient government engulfed the country in November 1990—Lukanov refused to launch even incremental and tentative "proreform" policies.[37]

Did Lukanov's conspicuous opposition to neoliberal policy recommendations mean that his goal was to ensure the functioning of existing economic structures, oppose change, and solidify the status quo? An answer along these lines is usually offered by scholars all too eager to pinpoint "the progress" of post-Communist countries along a reform–no reform continuum. And, indeed, from a certain perspective it may appear that the government did nothing, that it resolutely refused to implement any promarket policy measures and remained implacably hostile to so-called Western experts. But such depictions of the politics of Lukanov's government are inaccurate and misleading. In fact Lukanov and his ministers undertook a series of steps that reshaped dramatically the institutional and economic landscape of the emerging Bulgarian democracy. Exploring those steps brings us back to the question of separation and its most important cumulative effect: the weakening of state institutions and the fracturing of the infrastructure of governance.

Before I embark on a more detailed survey of Lukanov's institutional reforms, let me reiterate a central idea that informs the state-centered analytical approach: during the process of separation, governmental agencies on all levels are in a precarious position. What resources the "state" will control is an issue to be resolved by multiple actors—operating both in the central administration and in numerous localities—whose optimal strategy for accumulating wealth is to steal as many state assets as possible. What instruments of governing the "state" will possess is a question to be decided by elites whose future power will be proportional to the institutional and organizational wherewithal they can extract from the amorphous state-party amalgam. The state's capacity to enforce rules and impose sanctions is determined by agents whose main strategic concern is that in the near future state power may be used by newly installed

---

36. See *Banker* 47/1998, 7–9. The default is also discussed in detail in Krassen Stanchev, ed., *Anatomia na prehoda* (Anatomy of the Transition) (Sofia: SIEMA, 2004).

37. After his ouster, Lukanov became a member of the BSP parliamentary faction. In 1996, he was assassinated in Sofia. Preliminary police findings suggest that Lukanov might have fallen victim to factional struggles within the BSP—the consensus among political observers and investigative journalists is that he was most likely murdered by a small faction of the Orion group. As of this writing, however, the ongoing investigation of Lukanov's death has not produced definitive results.

governments to thwart both their "local" schemes for quick enrichment and their dominant position in society in general.

It is against the background of this institutional configuration that Lukanov's team exploited the unique opportunity to set unilaterally the terms of the party-state divorce. I will deal with three types of policy measures initiated by this group of cadres: deliberate dismantling of mechanisms of control, informalization of discretion, and deinstitutionalization of information. They have a direct bearing on some of the most persistent questions in early post-Communism: Why was it so difficult for elected politicians to monitor lower-ranking state officials, and in particular the performance of managers in state-owned enterprises? What were the structural preconditions for the widespread siphoning of assets from the public domain, and what patterns of embezzlement were observable? Why were extant instruments of governance in post-Communism invariably found to be seriously defective, and why was the capacity of democratically elected officials to enforce regulations in the economic domain so severely constrained?

Dismantling the Mechanisms of Control

With the start of the half-hearted economic reforms in the early 1980s, managerial discretion in the daily operations of state-owned enterprises inevitably increased, and the party-state relied on a special institution to monitor the conduct of state officials in the economic sectors—the Committee for Party and State Control.[38] As the name indicates, this was an institution with a mixed legal status, staffed by both party and state officials and empowered to question managers both in their capacity as state agents and party members.[39] The committee was specifically designed as a monitoring institution charged with the collection of information about mismanagement and embezzlement in the economic sector. (Regular police work, including political repression and the investigation of crimes such as murder, rape, and theft was carried out by the police and state security.) The committee built up branches throughout the country and maintained offices in each regional center. The local committees built up mechanisms for monitoring state-run enterprises and collected data on abuses of power, and embezzlement in particular. Wrongdoers were tracked down and information was regularly passed on to the central executive organs as well as the *prokuratura* (the East European institutional equivalent of the district attorney's office).

---

38. See also Marvin R. Jackson, *Bulgaria's Attempt at "Radical Reform"* (Cologne: Bundesinstitut for ostwissenschaftliche und internationale Studien, 1988).
39. On this institution in a Soviet context, see Jowitt, *New World Disorder*, 142.

One of the notable initiatives of Lukanov's government was to push through the last all-Communist parliament (which was not disbanded until June 1990) a decree abolishing the committee. Assembled documentation about embezzlement, corruption, and other similar crimes disappeared.[40] As a result, "the center" lost a useful instrument for monitoring the management of the state economy.

This move was paralleled by the breaking up of various units within the internal ministry and the security services that were primarily charged with overseeing the conduct of managers of state property. It was Lukanov who orchestrated the exodus of a large contingent of state security officials and made sure that after a series of reorganizations of the security services former cadres reemerged in "civil society" as duly licensed "protection agencies." When they left, these cadres took their know-how, along with a number of incriminating documents; newly appointed officials had to rebuild investigative mechanisms from scratch. The normal functioning of crucial departments in law-enforcement agencies—and specifically those in charge of investigating economic crimes and overseeing Bulgarian investments in foreign countries—was thus interrupted.[41] The newly fashioned protection agencies worked in close collaboration with the BSP, and the bosses of the thriving underworld were among their most notorious clients.[42] A development that Vadim Volkov has described as "privatization of the power ministries"—or the conversion of the Communist state's coercive and information-gathering capacity into a privately controlled asset available to strategically located political and economic entrepreneurs—was basically complete before Lukanov left office.[43] Various components of the law-enforcement mechanisms on which the incipient Bulgarian democracy had to rely were thus pulverized from within by incumbents leaving the state.

Informalization of Discretion

The institutional aspect of discretion—or discretion conceived as an element of conducting policy in a rule-structured environment with a view to achieving institutionally defined goals—is eclipsed by strategic self-interest, or calculating actions, by incumbents who are trying to maximize their chances of survival in a radically changing environment. Discretion usually means is the prerogative of officials to make decisions

---

40. On the importance of this institution and the significance of its abolition, see Bikov et al., *Ikonomicheskata kriza*, 8.

41. See ibid., 122.

42. See Jovo Nikolov, "Organized Crime in Bulgaria," *East European Constitutional Review* 6 (Fall 1997): 80–84.

43. Compare Vadim Volkov, *Violent Entrepreneurs* (Ithaca: Cornell University Press, 2002), 127.

without consulting their superiors. Agents with discretion are expected to abide by general guidelines, but they do not have to follow direct orders from above; their decisions are reviewed and possibly reversed only under exceptional circumstances, and they are not subject to daily monitoring. Strictly speaking, discretion is a legal term that may be analyzed as "weak," "strong," or even "Herculean."[44] What I want to underscore is something different. As the process of separation got under way in Bulgaria, strategically located cadres began to exercise their official prerogatives exclusively for the benefit of their informal associates. In a fairly closed system of economic contacts, those with discretion communicate with agents they already know—and in an authoritarian one-party system these agents will be, without exceptions, party members. At a time of massive transfer of state-owned assets, on the aggregate this informal element crystallizes into a consistent social pattern of redistribution that benefits strategically located party cadres. The process of separation was thus marked by a struggle for control over resources, and the persistent efforts of incumbents to carve out domains of private power directly undermined the organizational integrity of public agencies.

Several strategies for increasing "discretion" were employed by Lukanov's government in 1990. Perhaps the most important was the Decree of the Council of Ministers No. 111 of November 14, 1990, which gave the minister of economy and planning the authority to "release resources, materials, and foods from the state reserve." The state reserve was, legally speaking, a gray area where lots of resources were stockpiled and monitoring was completely lacking. During the Communist era, there was some collegiality in making these decisions, presumably making monitoring easier (especially post hoc, that is, by politicians who succeeded the incumbents). At this time, however, discretion was unequivocally put in the hands of a single ministry that the BSP controlled completely. Not surprisingly, over the next years the state reserve was depleted. Oil, metals, grain, food—everything was exported abroad by shady trading companies affiliated with BSP leaders. For example, the grain amassed in the state reserve was exported by close associates of future BSP prime minister Zhan Videnov, and various metals were sold abroad by business partners of Krassimir Premyanov, chairman of the BSP's parliamentary faction.[45] When the BSP finally stepped down in 1997, all warehouses where the national reserve had been kept were looted.

---

44. On the legal meaning of discretion—and what is has to do with Hercules—see Ronald Dworkin, *Taking Rights Seriously* (Cambridge: Harvard University Press, 1977), 31–39.
45. Information about these affairs is available in various issues of *Kapital* newspaper, available at www.capital.bg. See, for example, *Kapital*, October 25, 1995; November 10, 1996; and January 27, 1997.

Two other decrees also provided windows of opportunity for siphoning off state property—Decree of the Council of Ministers No. 74/90 and Decree of the Council of Ministers No. 129/90.[46] They granted to two strategic institutions—the Ministry of Internal Affairs and the Ministry of Defense—the right to sell and lease property and assets "that need to be replaced" or are "no longer needed." Immediately, various officials in these institutions engaged in entrepreneurial schemes whereby army-controlled resources were transferred to private "businesses" or joint ventures. The decrees did not establish any procedures for monitoring the discretionary acts relating to disposal of assets. Future governments were deprived of the opportunity to exercise control over management of property in two of the most important state institutions, to which large portions of the national budget were allotted.

At the same time, a process of "selective privatization" began to gain speed. For a variety of reasons, privatization did not become an issue in Bulgaria until 1993, and all branches of the economy remained dominated by the state. All, that is, with one conspicuous exception: transportation, especially the fleet of trucks.[47]

The value of trucks and other means of transportation as a logistical resource can hardly be overestimated. The ability to carry things quickly between destinations is a crucial prerequisite for success in all spheres of competitive social encounters. As Susan Strange points out, "The question of how people and goods get from one place to another is always a highly political matter. Markets obviously play a part . . . but states also play a part. What choice is made for the running of a transport system substantially affects who gets what in the way of benefits and opportunities."[48] This observation is especially pertinent in the post-Communist context, and the importance of having means of transportation has not escaped the attention of the more perceptive analysts of late socialism. Jadwiga Staniszkis reports that the struggle between authorities and homegrown entrepreneurs for control over trucks has been one of the most significant processes accompanying the birth of what she calls "political capitalism" in Poland.[49] In Bulgaria, the struggle was over before it even began. By means of several political decisions the state rapidly lost is dominant position, and BSP-affiliated companies quickly filled the lucrative niche. First, a regulation of the Ministry

---

46. See *Durzhaven Vestnik*, Nos. 60/90 and 101/90, respectively.
47. See Atanas Gotchev, ed., *The Competitiveness of Bulgarian Export Industries* (Sofia: Albatross, 1997), 46.
48. See Susan Strange, *States and Markets* (New York: Basil Blackwell, 1988), 137; emphasis added.
49. See Jadwiga Staniszkis, *The Dynamics of Breakthrough in Eastern Europe* (Berkeley: University of California Press, 1991), 41.

of Transportation was issued in late 1989 allowing state managers in trucking companies to sell at second-hand prices state-owned vehicles and farm machines. Soon thereafter thousands of vehicles were sold at very low prices, depleting the state fleet.[50] Then the entire international transportation sector was decentralized and privatized: out of the existing twenty-nine trucking companies, 240 regional and seventeen thousand private companies emerged, virtually all of them owned by former nomenklatura.[51]

At least two long-term economic effects may be traced back to this development. First, the treasury lost a considerable amount of revenue. The industry has a great profit potential in that it provides service to destinations that major West European companies consider risky (such as Russia, the Middle East, and Iran). Approximately 40 percent of all trucking services, measured by tons per kilometer, are sold on the lucrative international market. Second, the rapid rise of a private transportation fleet created a private competitor that invariably outbid the state during periodic struggles over fuel, a scarce and valuable resource. In the early 1990s, during the prolonged UN-imposed Yugoslavian embargo, ambulances and fire engines were frequently forced into idleness from empty gas tanks, while thousands of privately owned trucks shuttled between Bulgaria and Yugoslavia, bringing their owners enormous profits.[52] The privatization of the means of transportation was an ingenious strategy: as the Communist Party was getting ready to surrender "the kingdom," it appropriated all "the horses"—a tactic whose foresight Richard III would have certainly appreciated.

Deinstitutionalization of Information

Another interesting pattern that took place during this period was the systematic rechanneling of sources of information. In his analysis of the rise of the colonial state in India, Sudipta Kaviraj points out that "British administrators brought with them an entire cognitive apparatus from modern Europe, especially mapping and counting" and produced "an image of India as a geographic and demographic entity which far surpassed in tangibility and precision the hazier notions with which people transacted business in earlier times."[53] In post-Communist Bulgaria the reverse process took place: the capacious structures involved in the

---

50. See Roman Frydman, Andrzej Rapaczynski, and John S. Earle, eds., *The Privatization Process in Central Europe* (Budapest: Central European University Press, 1993), 35.
51. Gotchev, *Competitiveness*, 46.
52. See also Nikolov, "Organized Crime in Bulgaria," 80–84.
53. Sudipta Kaviraj, "Crisis of the Nation-State in India," in *Contemporary Crisis of the Nation State?* ed. John Dunn (Oxford: Blackwell, 1995), 117. His broader idea is that the primary object of scholarly investigation should be the emerging "social ontologies";

convoluted procedures of "economic planning" were turned into empty shells and the parameters of the national economy were covered by clouds of ambiguity. Deinstitutionalization of information implies that information is no longer available to the state institution that initially collected it but only to party-appointed incumbents and their informal associates.

At least two extremely important repositories of information were first transferred to the Council of Ministers and later effectively dissolved. It is not known what happened to the information, but there is little reason to doubt that it has been appropriated by the incumbents. The first that was transferred from the Central Committee of the Communist Party to the Council of Ministers was the Institute for Social Governance. It was the repository of various data assembled through sociological surveys, opinion polls, model testing, as well as the largest social science library in the country, which had been assiduously assembled during prolonged book-buying sprees in London.[54] When the institute was transferred to the jurisdiction of the Council of Ministers, it was renamed the Institute for State and Economic Management of the Council of Ministers.[55]

The other information repository was the Center for Information Technologies and Automated Systems, which was, likewise, transferred from the Central Committee to the Council of Ministers. It collected and stored information about the economic infrastructure, exports, and business contacts abroad, as well as the computerized data base about the economy in general. Its functions were described in the respective governmental ordinance as "information and technological services; consulting in the sphere of information technologies; computerization of governance."[56] By the end of 1990 both institutions were effectively eliminated and their archives and stored data had disappeared.[57]

One puzzle that calls for an explanation here is why Lukanov and his clique had these repositories of information moved to the Council of Ministers before appropriating them. Prima facie, the most plausible hypothesis is that it was a preemptive move by Lukanov intended to keep prospective rivals within the party away from the sensitive data. Although evidence about intraparty rivalries during this early period is

---

I am reluctant to use that phrase to describe what went on in Bulgaria after 1989, but certainly his focus on "the new realities of governing" in postcolonial India is an analytical strategy that scholars of post-Communism might follow.

54. Interviews with Ognjan Shentov and Tihomir Bezlov, Center for the Study of Democracy, Sofia, June 1995.
55. *Durzhaven Vestnik*, 9/90, Governmental Ordinance 2/90.
56. Ibid., 32/90, Governmental Ordinance 21/90.
57. Interviews with two former high-ranking officials at the Ministry of Trade and Tourism, summer 1997. Both of them requested to remain anonymous.

sparse, it is reasonable to assume that the prime minister preferred to have the information in the hands of a government he controlled completely rather than leaving it with the party apparatus, where it could be accessed by other party functionaries.

Another important institution that evaporated was the special department in the Ministry of Foreign Trade that monitored the operation of offshore companies and foreign subsidiaries of Bulgarian firms, Zadgranichni druzhestva or Companies Abroad. At least one of the members of the government that succeeded Lukanov's attempted to recover some of that information, but he soon discovered that all documents were gone, including all information about bank accounts, business documents, and auditing protocols.[58]

The deinstitutionalization of information accompanied the early efforts by the BSP government to "restructure" the economy. The pattern was clear: existing institutions were abolished, assets were transferred to new legal entities, but the information stored at "the center" vanished. Immediately after the November coup in 1989 the Council of Ministers passed Order (*razporezhdane*) on the Closing Down of Associations. These associations were the megastructures of the Bulgarian economy, huge conglomerates in which a considerable part of the nation's productive capacities were concentrated. They included Communications; Construction and Construction Industry; Industry for Man (Communist newspeak for the consumer industry) National Agrarian-Industrial Union; Forests and Timber Industry; Heavy-Machine Building; Transportation, Agricultural, and Construction Technologies; and Metallurgy and Mineral Resources.[59] The first issue was determining the legal status of "tangibles," the assets possessed by the associations. The order stipulated that "all rights and liabilities of the abolished associations are automatically transferred" to several ministries.[60] Given the size of the organizational changes unleashed at that moment, as well as the complexity of sorting out conflicting claims over assets, this process resulted in administrative confusion and extremely high transaction costs. But it bears emphasizing that at least some effort was made to structure this process.

The second issue was determining what would happen with the "intangibles" of these associations, such as information and data-collecting mechanisms. The order did not address this, and what in fact happened was that the heads of the respective accounting departments of the associations were ordered to bring their records to the Council of Ministers . . .

---

58. See Bikov et al., *Ikonomicheskata kriza*, 122.
59. See *Durzhaven vestnik*, 92/89.
60. See Article 2 of the order.

and it soon disappeared. It is not possible to determine exactly when that happened, but the operation was completed before the formation of the new cabinet in December 1990.

The same scenario was repeated in November 1990. Only days before submitting his resignation, Lukanov signed Decree No. 110, Decentralization and Demonopolization, which abolished a large number of the so-called economic unions (*stopanski obedinenija*) in the agricultural, food processing, and commercial sectors of the economy.[61] The ministries of agriculture and trade were ordered to register each subsidiary of the larger unions as a new, separate firm (Article 2). As in the case of Order No. 16, the managers of the central offices of the unions had to bring their archives and documents to the Council of Ministers, and when a new government was sworn in a month later, everything had already vanished. In 1997, a high-ranking government official told me that he still lacked information about various basic parameters of the sectors he was supposed to "govern" (for example, the volume of agricultural trade and the productive potential of the food processing industry). His attempts to retrieve the lost information were unsuccessful.[62] In short, many of the lights of the old regime were turned off, and the economy sank into a semidarkness that future rulers found extremely hard to penetrate.

It would be naive to believe, however, that the information was actually lost. Rather, it was "reappropriated" by those who had access to it, those who also had plans about how to use it in the future.

One tentative conclusion that may be drawn from these episodes is that the distinction between "centralization" and "decentralization" may not be invariably useful in determining the relative strength of "the center" and the periphery. This distinction may lead us to believe—and often does indeed indicate—that when "centralization" is the order of the day the power of central authorities tends to increase and that during campaigns for "decentralization" the opposite tendency transpires. But it is possible to conceive of situations where *both* "centralization" and "decentralization" enhance the power of the same strategically located elites at the expense of the state. Insofar as Order No. 16 terminated the autonomous existence of associations and reintegrated them in the respective ministries, it must be considered a centralization-boosting measure; Decree 110, in contrast, provided for the creation of numerous units where few monopolistic structures existed before and should therefore be categorized as a form of decentralization. But in

---

61. *Durzhaven vestnik*, 93/90.
62. Interview with Alexander Tassev, deputy minister of trade and tourism, Sofia, summer 1997.

both cases the most enduring effect of organizational restructuring was the transfer of logistical resources from the state to an emerging rival set of networks. In addition to underscoring the obvious—namely, that analysis of legal documents must be supplemented by a closer look at the dynamics of their implementation—the deinstitutionalization of information shows how hard it is to draw a line between "bad governance" and "subversion of the state" in the haze of post-Communist politics.

A detailed inquiry into the politics of the last all-Communist governments that steered the Bulgarian state in 1989–91 warrants several general conclusions. First, this period, usually depicted as an interlude between the past that had not really gone away and the future that has not yet arrived, was in fact eminently important. During the first fourteen months after Zhivkov's ouster, Lukanov and his ministers made and implemented a series of decisions that reshuffled in a rather dramatic fashion the institutional framework that would be used in post-1989 Bulgaria. Although it is technically true that no reform was implemented, the revamping of existing structures was remarkably speedy: key institutions disappeared, a new mode of managing state assets arose, and the main information flows on which the process of governance relies were rechanneled. The proverbial status quo, of which the ex-Communists were allegedly so enamored, was reshaped with resolve. Second, the popular view that extant state apparatuses were ferociously assaulted by radical neoliberal reformers who wanted to scale back the state is misleading—in fact, the evidence suggests that such assaults were engineered by departing Communist cadres. Third, my survey of Lukanov's policies illuminates the *nature* of the changes unleashed by party officials. Obviously, they had no preference for "marketization," and the fostering of market institutions was certainly not a goal to which they accorded high priority. What they did, however, was redefine, with rigor and dispatch, their own position vis-à-vis the state agencies under their control. As the de facto control over publicly owned assets shifted from state to party officials, the institutional mechanisms that ensured the monitoring of these assets were destroyed and administrative agencies were stripped of their access to information about the economy.

The cumulative effect of the changes triggered by the party's withdrawal from the state was that state structures lost much of their capacity to implement reform programs and monitor performance in the public sector. This was the result of both the structural characteristics of the post-Communist political condition and the conjunctural impact of the first elections, which allowed the party to dictate the terms of its withdrawal.

Separation as Defection: Theoretical and Comparative Implications

During the momentous first months after 1989, the question of who on earth is "the state"[63] did not generate much discussion—after all, everyone knew that there was not much difference between "the Communists" and "the state." As my exploration of the separation of party and state demonstrates, however, strategically located cadre elites had to cope with two distinctly different logics: the logic underpinning their self-interested attempts to preserve their dominant positions, and the logic of maintaining the robustness of state structures. The clash between these logics explains why the withdrawal of the party from the state diminished the administrative capacity of bureaucratic apparatuses and decreased levels of governability in the democratizing polity. The separation of party and state brings into sharp relief a formidable challenge facing students of post-Communist democracies: they have to examine the metamorphosis of densely structured sociopolitical orders that are immensely complex, while having to assume that all actors involved in the drama are at square one. How do patterns of governance change when the authority of the party-state is decoupled into "party authority" and "state authority"? What criteria for legitimacy prevail when state officials are faced with competing demands for loyalty?[64] What is an instrument of governance and what is an organizational resource to be used by private agents?

Refracted through such analytical concerns, the severance of the state-party nexus emerges as an episode illustrating what Michael Mann calls "the dialectics of state/society relations." Mann's principal insight is that organizational dominance of the state is not a static equilibrium occasionally disrupted by foreign invaders or armed revolts of oppressed masses. Rather, it is a necessarily precarious arrangement that may rapidly unravel if and when powerful groups launch an offensive to claim state-accumulated resources. The dialectic discussed by Mann plays out in the following way: the more successful a state organization is in extracting resources from society, the stronger the state domain is; with the strengthening of the state domain the logistical power of insiders grows; the greater the logistical power of insiders, the easier it is for them to

---

63. Max Weber, "Suffrage and Democracy in Germany," in *Political Writings* (Cambridge: Cambridge University Press, 1994), 104.

64. As Graeme Gill correctly points out, the problem of conflicting demands coming from "party" and "administrative" bosses could arise under Communism as well: *Collapse of a Single Party System*, 7–8. Given that the party and the state made up one huge network, however, this predicament was rarely if ever related to either/or questions, as it suddenly was after Communist rule.

evade sovereign control and abandon the state domain with impunity. Or, in Mann's words:

> If the extraction of resources from society is successful, it increases both the infrastructural and the despotic power of the state. But is also increases social infrastructural resources in general. The logistical constraints mean that the new infrastructures cannot be kept within the body politic of the state. Its agents continually "disappear" into civil society, bearing the state's resources with them.[65]

Whether or not this is a pattern running through history and observable in Mesopotamia as well as Rome, Egypt as well as the British Empire, is a debatable proposition.[66] But Mann's analysis does provide a vantage point from which to probe the reconfiguration of state structures in post-Communism. Historically, Communism was a process of successful extraction from the population, and it did result in the creation of a gigantic state-controlled public domain. It is precisely this domain that was targeted by the agents of the "body politic of the state" as they began to "disappear into civil society." And, given the institutional symbiosis of party and state, it is not that difficult to identify these "agents"—strategically located nomenklatura.[67] Steven Solnick has persuasively argued that the general uncertainty surrounding the collapse of one-party regimes induced street-level functionaries to behave in a self-interested manner.[68] Similar patterns of behavior transpired in the highest decision-making bodies and crucially shaped policies designed at the very top of the state pyramid of power. Conceived as a historically specific manifestation of the "state/society dialectic," the separation was the dynamic factor that drained state structures of their functional capacity.

In a post-Communist setting the seemingly perplexing Weberian question of who on earth is "the state" should not motivate us to deal exclusively with the formal positions of identifiable actors, the scope of their lawful authority, and the legalistically drawn boundaries dividing those who are "out" of the state from those who are "in." Rather, it should push us to consider the domain of post-Communist stateness as the site of multiple interactions between competing networks. I want to suggest that losses of administrative capacity may be linked to the reconsolidation

---

65. See Michael Mann, *States, War and Capitalism* (Oxford: Blackwell, 1988), 23.
66. Mann himself seems to believe so—he proceeds on the basis of the ahistorical assumption that the evolution of society is driven by "the growth of human beings' capacity to organize." *States, War and Capitalism*, 9.
67. In that regard, my findings are fully congruent with the analysis of elite transformation presented in Iván Szelényi, Gil Eyal, and Eleanor Townsley, *Making Capitalism without Capitalists* (London: Verso, 1998).
68. Steven Solnick, *Stealing the State* (Cambridge: Harvard University Press, 1998).

of the power of the nomenklatura and that the fracturing of mechanisms of governance is the aftereffect of the recombination of the resources that ensured the party's dominant role. To figure out who the state is one needs to reject the notion of a consolidated unitary entity and explore instead a multiplicity of agents deliberately creating numerous institutional ambiguities in their pursuit of context-specific opportunities.

The main analytical insight that the state-centered perspective yields is that the separation has a dual character. On the one hand, it involves cutting the party down to size, or, to use the felicitous expression of Slovenian scholar Ivan Bernik, "transforming the Party into a party."[69] This is the process of separation as it appears under the rubric of democratization: the pluralization of the public sphere, the rise of electoral politics, and the acceptance of the principles of democratic governance. From this vantage point, the withdrawal of the Communist Party reduced the *despotic power* of the state, or "the range of actions which the elites are empowered to undertake without routine, institutionalized negotiations with civil society groups."[70] Understandably, studies of the separation have so far focused exclusively on this issue—on how the party's capacity to repress dissent and crush political opponents began to decrease with the advance of democratic practices in Eastern Europe. And, indeed, the contention that the dismantling of the party-state colossus reduced the repressive potential of post-Communist states and made the ascent of pluralist democracy possible cannot be denied.

On the other hand, the dissolution of the party-state connection undercut the capacity and coherence of state structures and thus had a powerful impact on the *infrastructural power* of the state, or "the capacity of the state to actually penetrate civil society and to implement political decisions throughout the realm."[71] The study of post-Communism should therefore proceed on the assumption that the physiognomy of the new democracies will be determined not simply through "the removal" of despotic elements but also by the fluctuations of the infrastructural power of post-Communist states—and the withdrawal of the party from the state is the analytical focal point on which these two interpretative themes converge. The most fascinating conclusion to which this line of inquiry leads is that the separation is an instance of defection of strategically located elites from the state. The claim that democracy has been

---

69. See Ivan Bernik, "The Forgotten Legacy of Marginal Intellectuals," in *Transition to Capitalism?* ed. Janos Matyas Kovacs (New Brunswick, N.J.: Transaction, 1994), 210.

70. I borrow this definition of "despotic power" from Michael Mann; see his "The Autonomous Power of the State," in *States, War and Capitalism*, 5. (This seminal paper was originally published in *Archives Européennes de sociologie* 25, no. 2 [Fall 1984]: 185–213.) See also Michael Mann, *The Sources of Social Power*, vol. 1 (Cambridge: Cambridge University Press, 1986), 169–70.

71. Compare Mann, "Autonomous Power," 5.

"accepted" by former Communist rulers is perfectly compatible with the observation that at the same time these rulers were subverting the infrastructure of governance. Acceptance of democracy, defection from the state: this is the best way to characterize the behavior of the high-ranking cadres of the ancien régime.

It is precisely the organizational and institutional implications of the separation that are obscured if the phenomenon is reduced, à la Linz and Stepan, to the problem of replacement of one set of officials with another. From a state-centered perspective, what was at stake at this particular juncture was not only the appropriate method for recruitment of civil servants but also what the scope of the state's logistical control was going to be. Moreover, the reconfiguration of state structures proceeded in a largely sub-rosa fashion. That retreating authoritarian elites tried to shape the postauthoritarian environment is not in itself very surprising. For example, Stephen Haggard and Robert R. Kaufman have shown that military rulers who seriously contemplate relinquishing their power may chose to negotiate over "the terms of withdrawal" and articulate the general norms of a newly ignited democratic political game.[72] In the same vein, Delia M. Boylan has examined "the insulation incentive," the motivation behind Pinochet's use of institutional reform in order to put key sites of strategic decisions (such as the Central Bank) beyond the reach of democratic policymaking.[73] As a rule, however, strategic behavior in a non-Communist context aims to structure the formal aspects of the transition, such as the legal rules that define the political, institutional, and budget prerogatives of the military and constitutional provisions that regulate political competition and decision making. In contrast, Communist elites in Bulgaria used the separation to reshape the institutional arena by stripping state institutions of their resources and by reducing levels of governability. Their "preemptive strikes" targeted not the emerging rule-structured arena of democratic politics but the capacity of state structures.

The analysis of the dual character of the separation, then, is essential to understanding the transmogrification of state structures during the early stages of post-Communism. But it may also help us come to grips with some comparative riddles that Fish glosses over in his analysis of the dynamic of post-Communist change. Why did the first elections seemingly lock up various countries in diverging trajectories of development even though—contrary to what he asserts—these countries appear to be

---

72. Stephen Haggard and Robert K. Kaufman, *The Political Economy of Democratic Transitions* (Princeton: Princeton University Press, 1995), chap. 4.

73. Delia M. Boylan, "Preemptive Strike," *Comparative Politics* 30, no. 4 (July 1998): 443–62.

equally democratic? Why do some states prove to be less successful in solving the arduous tasks of socioeconomic restructuring even though their political systems are no more unstable than those of states that have somehow engineered major breakthroughs?

The analysis of the separation presented in this chapter suggests a state-centered answer to these comparative questions. If the opposition succeeds during the first electoral campaign the separation becomes an interparty affair. As the Communist Party withdraws, a countervailing interest emerges in the state. The state ceases to be an abstraction, and people of flesh and blood—and interests—come to occupy important offices in the administration. The phenomena that I analyzed above—the dismantling of mechanisms of control, informalization of discretion, and deinstitutionalization of information—will inevitably gain some momentum, but their scope will be limited. In contrast, if the Communist Party or its successor wins the elections, the separation is an intraparty affair—sociologically speaking, there is no one to defend the interests of the state during the period of separation. If the separation is a quick one, the retreating party is confronted by the power of an opposing interest; if the new elections did not trigger an "infusion" of new social forces into the administration, then party elites will be restrained solely by their perceived obligations to the "the state" as a legitimate abstract idea.[74]

Moreover, the state-centered approach reveals that the difference between a "fast" and "slow" separation is not only a matter of siphoning off "less" or "more" resources from the public domain but also of the magnitude of the damage inflicted on the infrastructure of governance. A quick separation means that the party will hijack primarily material objects, tangible assets, and that the infrastructure of governance will be afflicted by a relatively mild form of "informalization of discretion." This process was easily observable throughout Eastern Europe—by appropriating cars and computers, money and apartments, the nomenklatura ensured for itself the status of a thriving social group under the "new" conditions.[75] Rarely, indeed, has Fortuna been more benevolent to former princes so visibly deprived of *virtù*!

However, when the appropriation of tangible assets husbanded by the state is accompanied by a more thorough dismantling of mechanisms of control and deepening of the process of deinstitutionalization of information, then the effectiveness of the institutional tools of democratic

---

74. Or, as the authors of a book on "Kremlin capitalism" put it, the only constraints that party officials faced were "moral scruples and how much [they] dared do blatantly in front of the rest of [their] team"; see Joseph R. Blasi, Maya Kroumova, and Douglas Kruse, *Kremlin Capitalism* (Ithaca: Cornell University Press, 1997), 34.

75. Compare Solnick, *Stealing the State*.

rule—the ability of public authorities to organize citizens, assets, means of communication and transportation in pursuit of legitimate policy objectives—will be severely curtailed. A prolonged separation is bound to escalate into a drawn-out competition over the very sources of social power, defined by Mann as "the organizational means for attaining human goals."[76] Moreover, it might be assumed that this is a zero-sum game: logistical power amassed by converters is power lost by concrete state agencies. The very status of the state as a dominant societal organization will thus be radically undermined.

While it is comforting, indeed, to view democratic elections as a mechanism that will sooner or later bring the Fortinbrases of democracy on the scene, by the time they make their appearance the already "rotten" institutions of their state may have reached a condition of terminal decay, and thus the order "Take up the bodies!" will not be carried out.[77] To see why, we should perhaps remember one of the most ancient techniques employed in the fight between states and unruly social actors. Throughout the ages, rulers engaged in struggles with various societal competitors have found an ingenuous way to solidify their position: castration. This was a widely used method to prevent state servants from defecting from the state and establishing roots in society.[78] The state-centered approach to the separation suggests that a similar scenario transpired in the immediate aftermath of 1989, but the roles were reversed: it was state servants, reasserting their power at the moment of survival, that incapacitated their sovereign. Students of East European transitions should come to grips with the image of a "castrated state" not as a Freudian nightmare conceived in the surreal mists of post-Communism but rather as the cornerstone of a sound analytical strategy. In Bulgaria, the debilitating impact of the separation was almost instantly amplified by newly emerging forms of elite agency that further contributed to the process of reconfiguration of state structures.

76. Mann, *Sources of Social Power*, vol. 1, chap. 1.
77. See *Hamlet*, Act 5, Scene 2.
78. See Mann, *Sources of Social Power*, 1:170; Shmuel N. Eisenstadt, *The Political System of Empires* (Glencoe: Free Press, 1963).

3 Conversions of Power

> VLADIMIR: Haven't they?
> ESTRAGON: What?
> VLADIMIR: Changed.
> ESTRAGON: Very likely. They all change. Only we can't.
>   SAMUEL BECKETT, *Waiting for Godot*

The separation of party and state and the defection of powerful elites dramatically reduced the usability of existing institutional tools of governance in post-Communist Eastern Europe. It would be plausible to argue, however, that the decrease in administrative capacity attendant to the end of Communist rule may be a necessary price to pay for the accomplishment of worthwhile objectives—such as the advancement of political pluralism, which cannot be achieved without diminishing the hegemonic stature of the state. Moreover, there is no a priori reason to believe that the consequences of the separation will be long lasting. It is fairly easy to think of historical cases in which the organizational disarray caused by radical political change was rather rapidly superseded by a period of intense institution building and the creation of robust bureaucratic structures—Theda Skocpol's account of the aftermath of "social revolutions" is perhaps the best known example of how radical political changes eventually result in *stronger*, not weaker, states.[1] The empirical finding that the separation of party and state affected the organizational capacity of existing governmental agencies in negative ways simply reaffirms the validity of a general proposition that few knowledgeable readers would dispute—that during times of massive political and economic dislocations the ability of state agents to exert control over polarized and mobilized societies diminishes. But this argument does not prejudge the issue whether the logistical

---

1. Theda Skocpol, *States and Social Revolutions* (Cambridge: Cambridge University Press, 1979).

traumas inflicted during the separation of party and state are a transient damage remediable through the state-building efforts of newly empowered elites or the first act of a protracted drama in which the chronic crisis of stateness is the main plot.

In this chapter, I will explain why the "quick resuscitation" scenario conjured up by Skocpol did not materialize in Bulgaria in the early 1990s. My analysis will revolve around one specific phenomenon which is always mentioned but rarely discussed in depth: the conversion of political power accumulated under the old regime into economic influence in post-Communism. That strategically located nomenklatura cadres were able to use their political influence for economic benefit is by now well documented in the literature on post-Communism. Nevertheless—and this is the novel argument presented in this chapter—the transformative dynamics and institutional consequences of this process have not been fully examined. To the list of topics traditionally covered in analyses of conversions(Who were the actors most likely to benefit from this process? How much assets did they acquire? Will they become a "capitalist class"?), I will add several conceptual and empirical issues related to the transformation of state structures in early post-Communism: How is the boundary separating the domain of "political power" from the sphere of "economic power" actually drawn? What are the types of state-held capital appropriated by those who convert their power? How do conversions reshape the structure of basic social relations in which the functioning of law-enforcement mechanisms are embedded? I will show that the conversion is a sui generis example of entrepreneurship that necessarily reconfigured key state structures, added momentum to the trend toward institutional anomie, and made the rapid replenishment of the logistical power of the state extremely difficult. It has frequently been argued that the multiple "transitions" unfolding in post-Communism—to democracy, a market economy, and the European Union—generate "transition costs" and it is incumbent upon analysts to understand how these costs are distributed.[2] In a similar vein, I will demonstrate that conversions generated "conversion costs," and these costs had to be absorbed by the infrastructure of governance.

The Conversion Thesis

The argument that well-positioned cadres were able to "convert their political power into economic power" runs through numerous accounts of post-Communist political and economic change. Although explicit definitions of "conversion" are difficult to come by, it is not hard to distill the

---

2. The problem of "transition costs" is discussed at various junctures in Claus Offe's *Varieties of Transition* (Cambridge: MIT Press, 1997).

analytical essence of the idea the term seeks to convey: the metaphor encompasses a set of practices (from single "hits" to more or less institutionalized interactions) that allow certain elites to redeploy various assets that they controlled during the Communist era into a new institutional context and thus preserve their dominant position. That an account of this phenomenon should figure prominently in any serious analysis of modes of change in post-Communism is by now widely recognized. It would be hard to imagine an interpretative framework purporting to capture the salient features of post-Communist politics—who got what, when, and how—in which the problem of conversion is left unmentioned.

To some extent there is a divergence of opinion when it comes to assessing the desirability and necessity of the general trend toward re-empowerment of strategically located members of the Communist nomenklatura. The reasons why such a development may be considered risky and potentially dangerous are obvious: the continuing domination of nondemocratic, secretive and unscrupulous elites threatens to derail democratic and economic reforms. Some authors have argued, however, that conversions of power are conducive to, rather than incompatible with, the progress of such reforms. Tatyana Vorozheikina, for example, maintains that nomenklatura-driven "accumulation of capital" is necessary if capitalism is to "take off."[3] Jadwiga Staniszkis has insisted that, overall, conversions have resulted in more rational utilization of resources in the hand of relatively experienced economic agents.[4] And the always provocative Elemer Hankiss has opined that granting former elites the opportunity to benefit from privatization might have been the price to be paid for the peace of the transition: "The ruling elite would have dug in its heels ... if it had not discovered a chance of escaping ahead, a chance of converting the power it had in the *ancien regime* into a new sort of power which would be workable and valid in the new system to come."[5] In other words, the conversion may fall within that category of unintended consequences in times of massive political change which Raymond Boudon characterizes as "undesired, but desirable": even though no one quite intended to unleash the process, and even though it has engendered some perverse effects, overall society is better off as a result.[6]

3. Tatiana Vorozheikina, "Clientelism and the Process of Political Democratization in Russia," in *Democracy, Clientelism, and Civil Society*, ed. Luis Roniger and Ayse Gunes-Ayats (Boulder: Lynn Rienner, 1994), 114.
4. Jadwiga Staniszkis, *The Dynamics of the Breakthrough in Eastern Europe* (Berkeley: University of California Press, 1991).
5. Elemer Hankiss, *East European Alternatives* (Oxford: Clarendon Press, 1990), 233.
6. Raymond Boudon, *The Unintended Consequences of Social Action* (New York: St. Martin's, 1982), 5.

This interesting debate about the desirability of conversions notwithstanding, the bulk of the studies that explore this phenomenon have been empirical and not normative in nature. These studies proceed on the basis of two reasonable assumptions that are rarely articulated and almost never questioned. The first assumption is about what might be called the repertoire of conversion. Most observers imply that this repertoire consists exclusively of botched privatizations and illicit acquisitions of property rights. Conversions are depicted as coterminous with large-scale, corrupt sales of public assets. For example, in a study of Russia's emerging banking sector Juliet Johnson defines "nomenklatura privatization" as "the way in which those in positions of economic and political power in the Soviet system took advantage of economic decentralization by appropriating state resources for themselves."[7] Along the same lines, Frydman, Rapaczynski, and Earle refer to "the process of unsupervised and uncontrolled conversion of state property into private ownership by the members of the communist elite" and call this process "spontaneous privatization."[8] Olga Kryshtanovskaya and Stephen White's research on post-Soviet elites led them to conclude that the ascent of these elites was solidified by means of what they call "privatization of the state by the state," or a process whereby "public officials, using their formal powers, privatize those sections of the state for which they themselves are responsible."[9] Michael McFaul, an insightful analyst of conversion in Russia, opined that the essence of this process is "the allocation of first property rights." He convincingly demonstrated that the most visible winners during the first round of this allocative process were enterprise directors, who were in a position to make a first step—a huge first step, in fact—toward the acquisition of private property rights.[10] The tendency toward enrichment of the former cadres transpired irrespective of the carefully prepared plans for privatization; it was a largely illicit undercurrent that constantly imperiled the carefully crafted schemes for equitable distribution of state-owned resources. That is what motivated Nicolas Spulber to characterize conversions of power as "prikhvatizatzija"—"a blend of the terms *privatizatzija* and *khvatat* ('privatization' and 'to grab'), hence 'grabitization.'"[11] The conversion of power is presented as a rational

---

7. Julia Johnson, *A Fistful of Rubbles* (Ithaca: Cornell University Press, 2000), 36.
8. Roman Frydman, Andrzej Rapaczynski, and John S. Earle, eds., *The Privatization Process in Central Europe* (Budapest: Central European University Press, 1993), 183.
9. Olga Kryshtanovskaya and Stephen White, "From Soviet *Nomenklatura* to Russian Elite," *Europe-Asia Studies* 48, no. 5 (1996): 721.
10. Michael McFaul, "The Allocation of Property Rights in Russia," *Communist and Post-Communist Studies* 29, no. 3 (September 1996): 287–308.
11. See Nicolas Spulber, *Redefining the State* (Cambridge: Cambridge University Press, 1997), 120.

response to microincentives inherent in a situation where the idea of private ownership is valorized and large-scale privatization is simultaneously sanctioned by elites who possess de jure decision-making power, informally carried out by elites with de facto control over state-owned resources. In sum, the conversion is seen as a process inextricably linked to—and perhaps even coterminous with—massive transfers of assets between two more or less clearly demarcated domains within the polity: the domain of "political power," where those who convert were initially entrenched, and the domain of "the market and private property rights," where they reemerge as formidable players.

The second assumption that runs through the literature on conversion is about the effects of this phenomenon: the conversion is important because it revamps the socioeconomic landscape and reorders social hierarchies. From the dominant analytical perspective the process of transforming political power into economic advantage precipitates the formation of new social roles associated with capitalism, as well as the stratification of the hitherto flattened socioeconomic setting. A typical assertion regarding the effects of conversion stipulates that as many officials "turned their political capital into economic capital, converting skills and connections acquired under the old system into marketable assets under the new one," they "redefined themselves as capitalists."[12] Notably, in the late 1980s and early 1990s there was a debate as to who exactly would eventually occupy these newly created social roles. Some scholars, such as Victor Nee, predicted that the old elites would be fairly rapidly pushed out and new elites would assert themselves.[13] Others, like Vitalii Naishul, hypothesized the opposite, namely that the new roles would be played by old cadres.[14] By the late 1990s, this debate was resolved in favor of the Naishul hypothesis. As Iván Szelényi and his collaborators have established, it is elites embedded in the structures of the ancien regime—elites who possessed "political capital [defined as] that type of social capital which is institutionalized through the practices of the Communist Party"—who almost instantly occupied positions of economic power and social prestige.[15] Or, as the author of an exhaustive survey of the corporate sector in Hungary summarized his findings, "Power

---

12. Joan Nelson, Jacek Kochanomicz, and Kalman Mizsei, "The Transition in Bulgaria, Hungary, and Poland," in *A Precarious Balance*, ed. Nelson (San Francisco: Institute for Contemporary Studies, 1994), 23–24.

13. See Victor Nee, "A Theory of Market Transition," *American Sociological Review* 54 (October 1989): 663–81.

14. See Vitalii Naishul, "Liberalism, Customary Rights, and Economic Reforms," *Communist Economies and Economic Transformation* 5, no. 1 (1993).

15. Iván Szelényi, Gil Eyal, and Eleanor Townsley, *Making Capitalism without Capitalists* (London: Verso, 1998), 22.

accumulated during state socialism is converted into assets of high value in a market economy" and therefore, for better or worse, "the first shall last."[16] Scholars who have conducted empirical research on conversions in the former second world tend to accept the proposition that the conversion is first and foremost a "historically contingent process of class formation" whose true significance lies in its impact on the social and the economic domains.[17]

The dual focus on privatization and the socioeconomic ramifications of conversions has resulted in research projects that are intellectually stimulating and theoretically engrossing. At the same time, the unquestioned acceptance of the analytical assumptions underpinning such projects has had a somewhat constraining effect.[18] More specifically, current interpretations of conversion rest on a one-sided view of the nature of post-Communist entrepreneurship, a view that fails to depict the essential ties between the rise of entrepreneurial behavior and the reconfiguration of the state domain. To illustrate this point—and to suggest ways in which the dynamic and effects of conversions may be more comprehensively grasped—it is useful to turn to Joseph Schumpeter, one of the foremost students of entrepreneurship. Schumpeter maintained that entrepreneurship consists of two specific functions, one of which is widely recognized, and the other inexcusably neglected. The recognized, popular function is "carrying out of new combinations" with available resources.[19] The underappreciated one is "withdrawal of resources from their previous employment."[20] From a historical and analytical perspective, this second function, "the withdrawal," is probably even more interesting than the first. Schumpeter, somewhat iconoclastically, argues that it is the method of withdrawal that distinguishes capitalism from socialism: whereas under capitalism the withdrawal is carried out by individuals exercising property rights, in socialism it is executed by civil servants

---

16. Akos Rona-Tas, "The First Shall Be Last?" *American Journal of Sociology* 100, no. 1 (July 1994): 45–65. See also Catalin Augustin Stoica, "From Good Communists to Even Better Capitalists?" *East European Politics and Societies* 18, no. 2 (May 2004).

17. Szelényi et al., *Making Capitalism without Capitalists*, 68.

18. For a somewhat similar attempt to expand the problematic of conversion, see Joel Hellman, "Breaking the Bank," PhD diss., Columbia University, 1997. Hellman asserts that the conversion argument leaves unanswered the question of *why* conversion took place in the first place. Hellman then constructs a model that explains why bureaucrats respond to the reduction of the sphere of central planning by capturing residual rights of control over the assets in their domain.

19. See, for example, *The Theory of Economic Development* (New Brunswick, N.J.: Transaction, 1983), 65–66.

20. Ibid., 95. For a typical example of a scholarly paper that discusses Schumpeter's concept of "the entrepreneur" without ever broaching the problem of "withdrawal," see Edward A. Carlin, "Schumpeter's Constructed Type—The Entrepreneur," *Kyklos* 9 (1956): 27–41.

exerting their public authority.[21] Although many will find this contention objectionable, the insight that inspired it is eminently sound: without a thorough, empirically grounded account of how resources are withdrawn, analyses of the nature and impact of entrepreneurship will be incomplete. More broadly, what Schumpeter alerted his readers to is that, while it is essentially true that in every historical situation, entrepreneurs are individuals who "move things around," the sociological meaning of the term "moving things around" varies in different historical contexts, and hence "reliable propositions about economic change, and, therefore, about entrepreneurship" may be generated only if researchers pay close attention to historical detail and contextual peculiarities.[22]

Once the withdrawal of resources is posited as an analytical problem, the relevance of state-centered approaches becomes indisputable. Where do the resources that are being converted in post-Communism come *from?* In early post-Communism, resources were withdrawn from the domain demarcated as the state—because there was nowhere else they could be withdrawn from. Of course, in every post-Communist country in the early 1990s there were countless grassroots economic agents who pooled family resources and launched their own businesses—a process whose cultural, economic, and political significance can hardly be overestimated. Nevertheless, in the immediate aftermath of 1989, the redeployment of resources held in the immense public domain and previously guarded by the party-state was the most significant form of entrepreneurship—this is precisely the development that the term conversions of power seeks to capture. Even though conversions are invariably depicted as a form of extraction from the public domain, the statist implications of this process have not been thought through. Analytical studies of post-Communist conversions of power examine in detail how resources are redeployed in the pursuit of personal wealth and status, but such studies routinely fail to follow Schumpeter's advice and consider the implications of the withdrawal. It is these implications that are in the foreground of my analysis. Rather than dealing with the *economic power* that was acquired through conversion and the characteristics of the emerging *socioeconomic domain*, I wish to explore how the conversions affected various *attributes of statehood* and the dynamic relations in which *state structures* were embedded. Is it reasonable to assume, for example, that the demarcation of a "political" and "economic" fields is institutionalized enough to justify repeated references to "transfers" of capital from one to the other, and if there

---

21. See also Schumpeter, *Theory of Economic Development*, esp. 116.
22. Joseph Schumpeter, "Comments on a Plan for the Study of Entrepreneurship," in *The Economics and Sociology of Capitalism*, ed. Richard Swedberg (Princeton: Princeton University Press, 1991), 408, 414.

is no clear boundary between the two domains, then how is it possible for elites to redefine their roles? The undisputed cogency of the imagery of "grabbing" notwithstanding, what was it exactly that those who converted were doing in order to accomplish their objectives? How did conversions of political power into economic power restructure organizational contexts within which processes of governance unfolded?

With such analytical concerns in mind, I will scrutinize several cases of conversion that had a profound impact on Bulgarian politics and society in the early and mid-1990s. These stories provide new material in support of the argument that the repertoires of conversions are more variegated, that they encompass modes of agency that transcend the narrowly defined problematic of privatization of the economy (such as strategic shifting of the boundaries that separate state and nonstate domains, and skillful utilization of what I, borrowing from William H. Sewell, call "the polysemy of resources"), and that they target a wider array of resources than is habitually presupposed. I also draw on the Schumpeterian insight that the question of how forms of entrepreneurship revamped the immediate institutional context precede—logically and chronologically—the question of how such patterns of behavior precipitated social and economic changes. In this chapter my unifying theme is that, at least in the short and medium run, modes of elite agency associated with conversions directly affected the capacity of the state to maintain an institutionalized order in which transactions could take place, and thus increased levels of social anomie. Under the structural conditions of post-Communism, the surfeit of opportunities for conversion rendered much more difficult the task of constructing the institutional basis of effective democratic rule. In sum, I wish to situate conversions on an analytical terrain where broader issues related to the historical specificity of post-Communist entrepreneurship, the microdynamics propelling institutional change, and the aggregate attributes of the infrastructure of governance intersect. What brings these stories together is the insight that when thinking about conversions of power after 1989, we should go beyond the *generic* scenario of how the powerful became rich and look into the *unique* and mutually reinforcing dynamics of economic change and state restructuring in a concrete historical context.

The Case of the Crafty Minister, or the Polysemy of Assets in Post-Communism

Let us examine the assumption that conversions consist of the transfer of resources between two more or less clearly demarcated domains, "the state," where political power is paramount, and "the market," where economic power is crucial. To begin with, the assumption conveys the questionable impression that in early post-Communism something that might be meaningfully called "market domain," or "market power," or "economic power" actually existed. If there was no clearly demarcated market sphere where economic power reigned supreme, then what exactly was political power being converted into? The notion of "transfer" between different arenas of power is conceptually misleading and empirically inaccurate. On many occasions, what in fact happened was strategic manipulation of the invisible boundary that supposedly separates the two domains. It is precisely the ability to move this boundary on an ad hoc basis and to reap the attendant benefits that is the most spectacular manifestation of elite power in early post-Communism. Such moves damaged the institutional fabric of the state and made it open at countless points to predatory forays. In addition, the conversions increased levels of uncertainty for all economic agents and thwarted the creation of stable regulatory frameworks. There are perhaps good theoretical reasons why the boundaries between "public" and "private" domains should be deliberately or spontaneously blurred.[23] Post-Communist experiences suggest, however, that such blurring may be, and is, used as a strategic device that aggravates the dysfunctionality of state apparatuses and thus makes the pillaging of public domains easier.[24]

I wish to consider the case of an off-budget fund, and therefore a few preliminary words about these funds are in order. These funds can be seen as "discretionary tools of governmental policy that can direct scarce resources" toward industrial sectors and social groups favored by the administration.[25] It is a well-established proposition in the literature that such funds are generated by the desire of executive officials to expand the scope of their discretionary power. The operation of the funds is not subject to prior legislative approval. Theoretically, officials at the Bulgarian Ministry of Finance were required to collect information about their activities and parliament-authorized audits are possible; in practice, nothing of the sort happened prior to 1997.

After 1991, an unprecedented number of off-budget funds were created in Bulgaria. As the former Communists reconsolidated their power in late 1992, they channeled 100 percent of the revenues from privatization into off-budget funds (in comparison, the proreform government that came to power in 1997 put only 15.8 percent of the privatization

---

23. For an enthusiastic endorsement of the notion that the boundaries between the public domain and its surroundings should be constantly blurred, see David Stark and Lazslo Bruszt, *Postsocialist Pathways* (Cambridge: Cambridge University Press, 1998).

24. See also Venelin I. Ganev, "Notes on Networking in Postcommunist Societies," *East European Constitutional Review* 9, nos. 1–2 (Winter–Spring 2000): 101–7.

25. John Waterbury, *Exposed to Innumerable Delusions* (Cambridge: Cambridge University Press, 1993), 199–201.

revenue in off-budget funds).[26] The government's discretion for raising money for the funds was broadly defined, running the gamut from "selling information about the functioning of the fund" to "donations."[27] Also, a considerable portion of the international aid given to the country, including loans from the European Union, was placed in the funds.[28] By the mid-1990s, there were more than twenty-four thousand bank accounts in the country that serviced such funds; during certain years, the funds outspent the parliament-approved budget by one-third![29]

The off-budget funds have been understudied and rarely appear on the analytical radar of scholars transfixed on various "blueprints for privatization," macroeconomic data and microanalysis of the strategies employed by individual state-owned enterprises (SOEs). Looking at these off-budget funds gives us a glimpse of how a considerable part of the state's resources are managed, and of patterns of action usually covered by the veil of the tantalizingly abstract expression "restructuring of the state sector."

The central character of the story is Kliment Vuchev. In February 1995, he was appointed as a minister of industry in the socialist government of Zhan Videnov. A former member of the nomenklatura, Vuchev was adamantly opposed to privatization and the expansion of the private sector. He championed the position that preserving the state sector intact is the best way to perpetuate the accomplishments of socialism.[30] He was an ardent supporter of the state sector of the economy and began his tenure by urging SOEs not to repay their debts to commercial banks.[31] He spent his entire career in the state sector and firmly believed that it was destined to dominate Bulgaria's economy. On various occasions, he expressed his hostility toward private businesses and entrepreneurs. All privatization projects in his ministry were put on hold and, instead, a sustained effort to recentralize the industrial sector was undertaken. Vuchev attempted to restore the principle of central coordination and control in the state

---

26. See Krassen Stanchev and Luisa Perrotti, *The Role of the Core Executive in the Privatization Process—Country Report: Bulgaria* (Sofia: Institute for Market Economics—OECD/Sigma World Bank Project, 1999), 7–8. I wish to thank Mr. Stanchev for providing me with a copy of this report.

27. See, for example, the special Ordinance (No. 136 of July 4, 1995) for the establishment of the Fund for Development of Industry, published in *Durzhaven Vestnik*, June 11, 1995: 11–12.

28. See, for example, the bulletin of the Central Bank regarding the creation of the Fund for Reconstruction and Development, *Bulgarska Narodna Banka—Informatzionen Bjuletin*, November 1, 1991, 16.

29. See *Banker*, March 1, 1999, 2–3.

30. Interview with V. P., a political advisor to Zhan Videnov who wishes to remain anonymous, Sofia, June 1996.

31. See *Kapital*, April 9, 1996, 24–25.

industrial sector through the creation of several large consortia presided over by himself.[32]

One of Vuchev's main projects was the inauguration of the Industry Fund (hereafter referred to as "the fund"). The fund was set up in late 1995. Its original budget was 1,096.5 million lev; in June 1996, it was increased to 1,754.5 million lev.[33] (In contrast, the fund that the ministry set up to assist private entrepreneurs was only 48 million lev, twenty-two times less than what was allotted to the state sector.)[34] Officially, the fund's main purpose was to finance the reconstruction of the state sector and to extend interest-free loans to SOEs. Unofficially, it was also expected that the fund would subsidize money-losing state enterprises without increasing the budget deficit.

How was the money raised? There is ample evidence that intimidation of directors of SOEs was the main tactic. It was made clear to the directors of the largest SOEs that they would either participate in the campaign or lose their jobs. Likewise, the director of MDK, Bulgaria's largest copper mine, initially contributed "only" twenty million leva. When informed that his position was in jeopardy, he promptly doubled the "voluntary" contribution and kept his post. The director of another large metal-producing company, Elatzite, acted in a similar manner. The story of the director of Stomana, one of Bulgaria's largest steelworks, is quite interesting in this respect. Initially, the director refused to make the requested "contribution" to the fund; later he paid a minimal sum. Soon thereafter he was dismissed and his successor promptly contributed 25 million leva to the fund.[35] The pattern here is not hard to detect: through pressure and threats, cash-hungry enterprises were forced to commit considerable financial resources to an administratively generated campaign.

Among the contributors were Kremikovtzi (Bulgaria's largest industrial enterprise), Himko (the largest chemical plant), Pharmacy (the largest pharmaceutical company), and several SOEs belonging to the military-industrial complex. Many military plants were forced to chip in. Vuchev vowed that he would attract private investors to the fund,

---

32. The main instrument in this respect were the eight large consortia, which together served as a vehicle for transmitting Vuchev's commands to virtually the entire state-owned industrial sector; see "Interview with Kliment Vuchev," *Foreign Broadcasts Information System*, January 23, 1996, 8–11.

33. When the fund was set up, the exchange rate was $1 to 70.1 leva, which means that the fund began with a capitalization of $15.5 million; at the time of the increase, the exchange rare was $1 to 143 leva, which means that the dollar value of the fund declined to $12.3 million. Still, the amount of money amassed by the fund was considerable.

34. "Interview with Vuchev," 8.

35. *Kapital*, September 11, 1996, 11–12.

but this never materialized. Among the 229 founders of the fund, 217 were SOEs, one was a state-owned bank (Balkanbank), and two were state-owned insurance companies. Clearly, the participation of private entrepreneurs was purely symbolic.

The fund did not possess a sophisticated structure. It was registered as a limited company in accordance with the commercial code. Vuchev became executive director of the fund, and a couple of close associates from the Ministry of Industry, including his secretary, were appointed deputy directors.

In 1996, as Prime Minister Videnov moved to privatize some SOEs and close down a limited number of money-losing factories, Vuchev refused to carry out government instructions. When it became clear that the minister of industry's sabotage was becoming a formidable obstacle to Videnov's attempt to change the image of his government, Vuchev was dismissed (on June 10, 1996, only days after the capital of the fund was increased).[36]

When the newly appointed minister, Ljubomir Dachev, tried to find out what is going on with the money in the fund, he discovered something rather startling. Vuchev was registered as director of the fund not in his capacity of minister of industry but as a private citizen. Legally, the fund was not run by the ministry but by Vuchev. Recognizing the legal obstacles surrounding his effort to access the fund's documentation, Dachev tried to persuade influential cadres in the former Communist Party (the BSP) that they should pressure Vuchev to relinquish control over the fund. When the BSP government finally fell in 1997, Edit Getova, the newly appointed deputy minister of industry, tried to file a suit against Vuchev, but the courts dismissed her case, arguing that a duly registered company run by a private citizen cannot be forced to comply with the orders of the ministry. Vuchev's position seemed well fortified behind legal formalities. There were no legal links between the fund and the ministry. The resources accumulated in the fund "exited" the domain of the state. From a domain governed by a state official, the fund was transformed into a business estate run by a private entrepreneur.

Perhaps not surprisingly, the fund never fulfilled the tasks originally assigned to it. Despite the fact that—in accordance with the charter of the fund—numerous SOEs requested loans, only twenty-four projects were considered. And in only four cases were preliminary steps toward providing loans taken. None of the projects were ultimately financed.[37] Instead, the fund acted as a trading company and, hardly surprisingly, all its undertakings turned out to be unmitigated disasters. Through

---

36. For details, see "Bulgarian Update," *East European Constitutional Review* 5, nos. 2–3 (Spring–Summer 1996): 5.

37. For more details, see *Kapital*, August 23, 1997, 15.

deals with a nebulous Singaporean firm and a fictitious Russian holding company, the resources were siphoned off. One of the deals involved nonferrous metals, another concerned oil deliveries. In both cases, deliveries were symbolic, only a fraction of what the fund was supposed to receive for its money (in the case of the Russian oil, only five hundred of the contracted 6,200 tons were actually delivered). In both cases, payments were made in advance, and there was no effort to sue for breach of contract undertaken by Vuchev in his capacity as a director. Attempts by future governments to trace the money and recover at least some of it were futile; Vuchev always responded that losses were due to "commercial risks."[38]

I will not question the solid consensus in the literature, which posits that what was converted were assets "belonging" to the state. My story is precisely about one of the numerous state officials who, to use Steven Solnick's apt characterization, rushed to claim assets under their control on such a large scale that "they are not merely stealing resources from the state . . . they [are] stealing the state itself."[39] The shrinkage and depletion of the state-controlled domain is my main focus. At the same time, I question some of the assumptions of the dominant approach to conversions.

One such assumption is that conversions of power are somehow constrained by "asset specificity," the availability of alternative uses of particular assets.[40] Solnick, for example, defended the following argument: nonspecific assets, such as money, can be easily and costlessly redeployed; in contrast, it is much harder to "convert" goods and services that are highly specific to the environment in which they are ordinarily used. He also asserted that "bureaucrats who shuffle money around will by definition be in a better position [to convert their power] than a railwayman [who] cannot easily divert significant railway assets—or himself—to alternative uses." In other words, information about "asset specificity" would allow us to determine in advance the sites of conversion, map the soft loci in the state, and predict the likely targets of predatory action.[41] In Solnick's reading, the state-controlled domain would appear as a checkerboard on which problematic spaces coexist side by side with safe havens that appear impervious to "conversion."

---

38. Even though none of the other funds has been as well researched as this one, there is direct as well as circumstantial evidence that this pattern is typical. It is easy to observe, for example, in the attempt to form a Bulgarian-Ukrainian bank with the resources of the Fund for Reconstruction and Development in 1996.
39. Steven Solnick, *Stealing the State* (Cambridge: Harvard University Press, 1998), 7.
40. He borrows the concept from Oliver Williamson, who uses it in his theory of transaction-cost economics. See Oliver Williamson, *The Economic Institutions of Capitalism* (New York: Free Press, 1985), 52–56.
41. See Solnick, *Stealing the State*, 30–32.

The problematic nature of this view becomes clear when we examine a bit more carefully the evidence pertaining to Solnick's sole example of "specific assets"—the railroads. Here is one among many interesting stories about the Russian railway system in the post-Communist period:

> As a recent scandal revealed, high-ranking officials of the Ministry [of Railroad Transport] used their influence so that part of the rail network and stock was sold to a private company whose owners were wives, nephews, and sons of those ministry officials. The private company was given preferential treatment in fulfilling contract work for the ministry and controlled 90 percent of the profitable Western-sector routes. It had exclusive rights to export coal and many other perks. Hundreds of millions of dollars were made and divided up, much of it bypassing the treasury.[42]

Obviously, Solnick's prediction is wrong: despite the ostensible "specificity" of assets, the railway system in Russia—as well as elsewhere in the post-Communist world—was subject to large-scale "conversions" and "appropriations." What does the fact that conversions of even "environment-specific assets" proceed with relative ease say about conversion as a post-Communist phenomenon?

The Vuchev story demonstrates that in the context of studies of conversion, "asset specificity" might not be so important. Resources rarely have unambiguous meaning; their properties are only partially "set" in objective reality, which in turn means that an array of resources may be interpreted in varying ways. Or, to use the term coined by Sewell, for a student of post-Communist conversions, it is the notion of "the polysemy of resources," not "asset specificity," that should guide research and analysis. Sewell does not deny that resources have physical properties that are real and therefore not alterable through human effort. But he also acknowledges that "the activation of material things as resources, the determination of their value and social power, is dependent on cultural schemas that inform their social use." And how these resources will be used is ultimately a matter of human agency: "Agency . . . is the actor's capacity to reinterpret and mobilize an array of resources in terms of cultural schemas other than those that initially constituted the array."[43]

Those who convert power act precisely as agents who "reinterpret" resources and disrupt cultural schemas that may stabilize forms of economic exchange (such as the schema that rests on the understanding

---

42. Vladimir Brovkin, "Fragmentation of Authority and Privatization of the State," *Demokratizatzija* 6, no. 3 (Summer 1998): 507.

43. See William H. Sewell Jr., "A Theory of Structure," *American Journal of Sociology* 98, no. 1 (July 1992): 12–18.

that the legal boundaries between the public and the private domain are fairly well demarcated).

Theoretically, there are reasons to celebrate the dexterity and entrepreneurial drive of those who are able to find alternative ways to mobilize resources. In a post-Communist context, however, such activities subvert authoritative definitions of what is public and what is private and thus exponentially increase the risks inherent in economic transactions. As a result of Vuchev's entrepreneurship, the public domain was deprived not only of tangible assets but also of stable interpretative frameworks that may structure the behavior of public and private agents.

Moreover, the Vuchev case also exposes the limitations of conventional accounts that depict conversion as a transfer of resources from the "political" and "economic" domain to that where there are "rights to private property." It suggests that the major institutional mechanism underpinning conversion is the constant shifting of the "line of difference" separating state and nonstate domains. Conversion is enacted as the ascribed "identity" of strategic actors is selectively redefined. At times, they don the garb of agents of the state, and the next moment they appear as participants in market-type exchanges. It is not the movement of resources in a marketlike medium, but the effects generated in institutional "spaces" that make conversion possible.

This process is by no means unique to post-Communism. It has been analyzed, for example, by Stephen Krassner in his study of the notorious Aramco case, in which U.S. government officials used a private corporation for state purposes they suspected Congress would refuse to endorse.[44] One difference, however, is obvious. In the Aramco case, as Timothy Mitchell argues, "the fact that Aramco can be said to lie outside the formal political system . . . is essential to its strength"; in other words, actors could enjoy the benefits they strove for only if they could be perceived as permanently "residing" in the nonstate domain.[45] In post-Communism, the pattern of "shifting boundaries" is more complex: actors revive their strength when they are able to define themselves at times as belonging to the realm of politics and at other times as private actors. This is how essential advantages are reaped; this is the key to the successful reproduction of conversion. There is no movement of resources that begins "inside" and ends "outside" the state; it is the opportunity to shift back and forth that matters. Keeping the boundary between "political" and "economic" orders fuzzy is essential for conversion.

---

44. See Stephen Krassner, *Defending the National Interest* (Princeton: Princeton University Press, 1978), 212.

45. Timothy Mitchell, "The Limits of the State," *American Political Science Review* 85, no. 1 (March 1991): 77–96.

"Political power" is employed not only to redirect resources but also to redefine the boundaries of the state domain. And "economic power" may not be coterminous with the acquisition of property rights but with reaping the ad hoc–created advantages that appear on both sides of the elusive divide.

More broadly, while conversion may entail large-scale depletion of the public domain, the emergence of "economic power" as a coherent alternative coordinating principle is far from certain.[46] The relation between self-interested exercise of political power and the spread of market-oriented behavior is much more tenuous than is usually implied, and therefore the argument that conversion eventually crystallizes into market-driven profit making is in need of revision. That is why the outcomes generated by conversions are not readily captured by categories that presuppose the existence of Western-type markets in the respective states. If the nature of the "economic power" wielded by those who convert remains opaque, what is beyond doubt is that these actors energetically revamp and reorganize, and ultimately precipitate the liquefaction of, the tools of governance, such as off-budget funds and state-run financial structures more generally.[47] The conversions do not entail the replacement of state-centered mechanisms of allocation of resources by market-centered coordination of autonomous economic activities, but they do involve the engineering of various withdrawals of "uncaged" public assets and the compromising of the institutional integrity of the state domain.

The Orion Case

Current understandings of the types of resources—or capital—being withdrawn from the state is unjustifiably circumscribed. Conversions may involve not only economic but other forms of capital as well. In the aftermath of such withdrawals from the state, the dynamic relations between governmental agencies and mobilized social constituencies become marred by distrust and suspiciousness, which in turn considerably reduces the chances that potentially salutary policies may accomplish their objectives.

The story that brings these analytical points into sharper relief is about a failed bank, the Bulgarian Agricultural and Industrial Bank (BAIB).

---

46. Szelényi at al. seem to share a similar intuition; they assert that more often than not those who convert power are motivated by consumerist considerations rather than entrepreneurial ambition and that "even if they come to constitute a capitalist class it is likely to be a *rentier* class": *Making Capitalism without Capitalists*, 173.

47. On "liquefaction of structures," see Roberto Mangabeira Unger, *Social Theory* (Cambridge: Harvard University Press, 1990), 46–47.

That institutions usually designated as "banks" tend to dissipate into thin air is a fact with which all East Europeans were forced to come to grips during the first decade of "reforms." Not surprisingly, the perennial crisis of the banking sector was a major theme in studies of early post-Communist politics. So why add yet another story to this body of literature? There is something unusual about the rise and fall of this particular bank. Neither was its operation based entirely on "insider networking," nor was its demise caused primarily by "financial" reasons. The bank certainly served as a conduit for personal enrichment of power holders, but the peculiar twists and turns that marked its short history provide a good opportunity to introduce several issues that are either obscured or ignored by the proponents of the conversion argument.

The Bulgarian Agricultural and Industrial Bank was the brainchild of a small circle of collaborators that came to be known in Bulgaria as the Orion circle. The core members of the Orion circle were former employees of the Bulgarian secret services. Roumen Spassov was the official owner of Orion's first legally registered company, Orion Commerce. His father served for several decades as a deputy minister of internal affairs.[48] Roumen Spassov worked for the same ministry in the 1980s. Krassimir Raidovski, another leading Orion member, was an officer at the Intelligence Department of State Security; in the 1980s, he was the leader of the Bulgarian counter-intelligence ring in Greece. Mikhail Danov was also affiliated with State Security; in the 1980s he took an important position in Kintex, Bulgaria's largest arms-trading company; after 1989, he worked as a financial manager of Duma, the newspaper of the former Communists. The remaining members of the Orion group were Veska Medzhidieva, who was married to Roumen Spassov; Nikolai Krivoshiev, a businessman exporting agricultural products; Ljubomir Kolarov, a member of the Supreme Party Council of the Bulgarian Socialist Party (BSP); and Zlatimir Orsov, a BSP deputy and an influential member of the parliamentary committee on agriculture. Over the years, this group of personal friends was involved in various business ventures. They trusted one another and shared the ambition of turning themselves into big-time capitalists.[49] Nevertheless, they remained outsiders and could not gain a foothold in the state-owned sector of the economy. Compared to the sprawling network commanded by conglomerates like Multigroup (more on this in the next chapter), the connections of Orion were relatively limited. Prior to 1994, they operated primarily as

---

48. In this capacity, he was in charge of the concentration camp system in Bulgaria in the late 1950s and the early 1960s. After 1989, an attempt was made to subject him to investigation for the crimes committed during his tenure, but this effort soon fizzled out.

49. For more information about the business ventures of Orion prior to 1994, see *Demokratzija*, December 14, 1995, 7; and *Kapital*, February 5, 1996, 23.

"an unruly coalition," a loose clustering of elites, "neither institutionalized nor otherwise formally recognized, who cooperate to pursue or control wealth and other resources" and whose "territorial base is primarily regional or local rather than national."[50]

At some point in 1994, the Orion group got in contact with Zhan Videnov, an up-and-coming young BSP politician. Although the exact circumstances surrounding the beginnings of this relationship are not clear, by the second half of that year Mikhail Danov used his contacts in Germany to arrange a quasi-official preelectoral visit for Videnov there, and Krassimir Raidovski organized a similar visit in Greece. Given the paucity of European contacts of the adamantly anti-Western Videnov, the help of the former intelligence officers must have been quite valuable.[51]

After the 1994 elections, the political fortunes of Orion changed dramatically. BSP won an absolute majority in the new parliament, and Zhan Videnov was elected prime minister. He did not forget his trustworthy collaborators. Krassimir Raidovski was appointed director of the Press-Center of the Council of Ministers. There he controlled the flow of information from the cabinet to the public and, even more importantly, to the prime minister. Ljubomir Kolarov was appointed chairman of the Committee on Mail and Long-Distance Communications, and Mikhail Danov became director of the Bulgarian Telephone Company. Orion became directly involved in the processes of governance. In fact, it was marketed as the emblem of the team of young professionals and experts who allegedly reinvigorated the aging former Communist Party.

Arguably the most ambitious project launched by the Orion circle once it made its breakthrough in the state apparatus was the creation of the BAIB. The bank was registered with the court on October 10, 1994; there is plenty of evidence suggesting that the money necessary for the application was procured through loans from the State Savings Bank. The granting of a license, however, raised some concern about foul play, and the prosecutor general ordered an investigation into the legality of the registration.

Meanwhile, the newly registered bank existed in a state of suspended animation until April 1995 when Veska Medzhidieva was appointed chief executive officer and Mikhail Danov became chairman of the board of directors. Immediately, a large-scale money-raising campaign was launched. This campaign was born out of the collaboration between BAIB and an organization called the Union of the Agricultural Cooperatives in Bulgaria

---

50. See Katherine Verdery, *What Was Socialism, and What Comes Next?* (Princeton: Princeton University Press, 1996), 192–93.

51. As Videnov himself points out in his memoirs, see Zhan Videnov, *Otvud politicheskija teatur* (Beyond the Political Theater) (Sofia: Hristo Botev, 1998), 118.

(UACB). The UACB was dominated by the Bulgarian Socialist Party, but it also commanded considerable support in the countryside. It brought together peasants who were reluctant to venture into private farming and were willing to continue their participation in agricultural cooperatives even after these cooperatives were disbanded in 1992.[52] This idea undoubtedly enjoyed some popularity. The UACB may be considered, therefore, as a mass organization that covered the entire country, had grassroots support, and represented a genuine social interest. The plan that the leaders of the UACB and the BAIB hammered out was simple: to pool the privatization vouchers of the members of cooperatives—along with any other money the farmers could scramble together—into several investment funds, to deposit the money of the funds in BAIB, and then to use them to acquire SOEs related to agricultural activities (mills, canning factories, and the like).[53] With a view to accomplishing that goal, the leadership of UACB sent letters to all the members, urging them to deposit all the money they had in the BAIB.

Soon thereafter, large sums of money collected by the UACB were channeled into the BAIB. In most cases, members of the cooperatives were convinced to turn in their vouchers to the chairmen of the cooperatives, who in turn deposited them in the bank. The bank was persistently presented as a tool that "the government" would use to help cooperative farms. On several occasions, the minister of agriculture, Svetoslav Shivarov, attended meetings of the bank's shareholders.[54] Meanwhile, a simple message was repeatedly articulated by members of the Orion group, that they represent the government, and therefore whoever is against them, is against the prime minister.[55] From the very beginning, the bank's existence was presented as serving an important social goal. Zlatomir Orsov, a leading member of the Orion circle, described the BAIB's and UACB's commons objectives in the following way: "The agricultural cooperatives will become owners and will manage the enterprises related to their business. If this opportunity is squandered, they will be forever exploited by intermediaries and speculators."[56] Somewhat

---

52. On this, see Gerald Creed, *Domesticating Revolution* (University Park: Pennsylvania State University Press, 1998).

53. Mass privatization in Bulgaria was slated to begin by June 15, 1996. Vouchers were to be distributed to all Bulgarian citizens: they would have to pay a minimal sum—five hundred levas—to obtain a voucher worth fifty times more. Vouchers then could be "invested" in "investment funds" that were authorized to take part in auctions and buy state-owned enterprises.

54. See *Kapital*, April 15, 1996, 23.

55. See, for example, the newspaper articles translated in *Foreign Broadcast Information Service*, January 19, 1996: 5–12.

56. See *Kapital*, June 12, 1996, 27–28.

paradoxically, this private bank was cast as a bulwark against capitalism. It was also presented as an element of a broader governmental BSP-sponsored plan to reverse the downward trend in agriculture that took place after 1989. This strategy was appealing, because it held the promise that the farmers would be relieved of the necessity of engaging in intractable financial dealings and so could attain a measure of control over their future amid the tribulations of market transformations.

In places where persuasion did not work, intimidation and threats were employed to force peasants to turn over their vouchers. Overall, however, the campaign proceeded with some measure of enthusiasm: UACB's activists regularly deposited everything they had in the bank. "We find it somewhat difficult to collect cash in order to participate in the fund," one of these chairman confessed when interviewed about his experience. "But we will find it somehow . . . what is demanded of us is to collect the vouchers of the cooperative and participate in the fund."[57]

Meanwhile, the investigation initiated by the prosecutor general yielded interesting results: forty-seven of the shareholders who signed the BAIB's charter turned out to be fictitious legal entities. Based on that evidence, the Supreme Court annulled the registration of the bank and ordered its liquidation.[58]

At this point, something quite remarkable happened. Orion member Zlatimir Orsov engineered the passage through parliament of an amendment to the Commercial Code, which allowed the shareholders of a company subject to liquidation to merge with another company. The thinly veiled idea was, of course, for the BAIB to "merge" with another institution and thus to continue its legal existence.[59] This maneuver affirmed the perception of the farmers that "the leaders of the state are with us" and allowed the campaign to continue unabated.

Soon thereafter, however, the attempt to engineer a merger and retain the banking license fizzled out. Meanwhile, Videnov's government found itself embroiled in various controversies, and the prime minister was forced to resign in December 1996.[60] This marked the end of Orion's political dominance. Immediately, it became clear that all the money collected by the BAIB in collaboration with the UACB had disappeared. The farmers lost everything they had deposited in the bank. The most prominent members of Orion, including Roumen Spassov, Veska Medzhidieva, and Nikolai Krivoshiev, emigrated to South Africa, where they now live

57. See *Kapital*, November 12, 1996, 23–24.
58. See *Demokratzija*, April 20, 1996, 3–4.
59. See Article 270a of the Commercial Code, *Durzhaven Vestnik*, June 1, 1996, 3.
60. For a detailed account of the events that led to the resignation, see Venelin I. Ganev, "The (Ir)Relevance of Postcommunist Constitutionalism," in *Institutional Engineering in Eastern Europe*, ed. Jan Zielonka (Oxford: Oxford University Press, 2001), 186–211.

the life of wealthy retirees.[61] The others slipped into obscurity; even though there are outstanding arrest warrants for several Orion leaders, all of them have been able to avoid unpleasant confrontations with the criminal justice system.

Before we reflect on the implications of this story for the study of post-Communist conversions, let us consider the importance of its ending. The fact that those most actively engaged in conversion wound up in a distant foreign country brings into relief the deficiency of a rarely articulated preconception in the analysis of conversions—that those who convert will acquire economic power in the same state where they possessed political power. This need not be the case. If converted assets reemerge, it is unlikely to happen in the market economy of the respective country but through selective plug-ins in the expanding global system of "flexible accumulation."[62] As Vladimir Shlapentokh acidly noted, the West has proven to be very hospitable to the post-Communist nouveaux riches and readily procures the *krysha*, or "roof," that they need in order to begin a postconversion life.[63] Conversions are therefore not a component of a larger movement toward capitalism; they are a manifestation of the capacity of strategically located elites to engage in self-seeking pursuits under specific structural conditions.

But the deeper relevance of the Orion story lies elsewhere: it demonstrates that what the state is deprived of as conversions flourish is not simply financial resources but other forms of capital as well. Was the Orion saga a simple case of deception, whereby a group of mendacious entrepreneurs mislead naive citizens? Was it a manifestation of the notorious gullibility of backward Balkan peasants? Or was it a sign of bewilderment generated by the shock following the confrontation with intractable "market mechanisms"? The answers to all these questions is no. This story reveals as much about how governmental authority is exercised by those who convert power as it does about financial theft. That is why it brings into sharp relief the statist implications of conversions of power. A comparison with another deceit par excellence may be helpful: the Romanian Caritas case, so wonderfully analyzed by Katherine Verdery.[64]

Caritas was a typical pyramid or Ponzi scheme that paid enormous dividends to some depositors with money collected from other depositors. Soon after it was launched in 1992, Caritas became a truly mass

---

61. See *Sega*, September 7, 1997, 10–11. Attempts to extradite members of Orion and indict them with embezzlement were unsuccessful.

62. On "flexible accumulation," see David Harvey, *The Condition of Postmodernity* (Cambridge, Mass.: Blackwell, 1990), 147.

63. On the West as a *krysha*/roof, see Vladimir Shlapentokh, "Early Feudalism," *Europe-Asia Studies* 48, no. 3 (1996): 405.

64. See Verdery, *What Was Socialism*, 168–203.

phenomenon: between two million and four million participants (that is, between 10 and 20 percent of the Romanian population) entrusted their savings to Ioan Stoica, the chairman of Caritas. Of course, this incredible popularity did not forestall the imminent collapse of the pyramid: on May 19, 1994, it was finally closed down, and Stoica had to serve a prison term.

The differences between BAIB and Caritas are important for a proper understanding of post-Communist conversions. The first, and most obvious difference, was that the central government was not involved in the pyramid scheme run by Ioan Stoica. Although he enjoyed a warm rapport with Georghe Funar, the mayor of Cluj (the Transylvanian town where Caritas's headquarters were located), his "business" initiatives were not endorsed by the central government. On the contrary, the opposition of Romanian president Ion Iliescu was vocal and unrelenting. In fact, it was a series of comments by the president that precipitated the inexorable fall of the pyramid scheme. In contrast, in the Bulgarian case the government was perceived as enthusiastically endorsing the project. Second, whereas Caritas was open to all, the BAIB was designed with a specific organized group in mind. It drew on the shared interests and perceptions of an identifiable set of social agents—peasants interested in cooperative farming. Finally, as Verdery points out, what motivated millions of Romanian citizens to invest their money in Caritas was "faith." This is how they came to terms with "the abstract sphere in which money circulates and multiplies without clear agency." In comparison, the Orion project was much more concrete and rational—what the peasants expected to get was not magical multiplications of their investments, but machinery, tools, fertilizers, seeds, and other goods and services related to their productive activities. In fact, the initiatives of the UACB display at least some of the attributes that, according to M. Steven Fish, characterize a "mature" post-Communist civil society: aggregation of interests (in this particular case, the interests of cooperative farmers); representation of interest (through the activities of UACB, an organization that has local branches all over the country); articulation of interest (devising a plan for a meaningful participation in the upcoming privatization).[65] What made the plan particularly appealing is that it appeared as an offer of assistance by the state. Neither the goals nor the means were defined in an abstract fashion. On the contrary, "privatization" and "agricultural reform" were the contextual background against which conversion got under way.

---

65. M. Steven Fish, *Democracy from Scratch* (Princeton: Princeton University Press, 1995), 53–54.

If this is not simply a case of mass deception, neither is it a case of run-of-the-mill conversion. The elements of conversion are all there: a group of power holders uses their power to initiate a series of transactions so that a large amount of money falls into their hands. Arguably, the most interesting aspect of this story is that the hijacking of assets was preceded by a stage of visible, albeit limited, grassroots mobilization, a pulling together of dispersed resources held by numerous societal agents. At first glance, this seems like a series of transactions unfolding in the domain of civil society. Neither the bank nor the farmers' union was "state owned." But the relations between them were mediated by the state, and the state provided the assurances that motivated the farmers to enter the game. Symbolically and rhetorically, the state was involved, providing the credibility that made cooperation possible.

The other interesting aspect of this episode is that this conversion scheme was, uncharacteristically, outward oriented. Rather than working within the hermetically closed domain of administrative discretion, the Orion circle sought to exploit possibilities outside the formal boundaries of the state, probably because Orion had relatively weak positions in the state-owned sector of the economy. And, in many respects, the group displayed entrepreneurial acumen. The campaign they designed and carried out at least in part responded to a genuinely felt social need. They utilized grassroots mobilization. And their strongest tool was that they could market their project as an offer for cooperation with the state. The theme that they raised was quite important: the adjustment of farmers to the emerging market mechanisms.

What does this story tell us about conversion? Some modes of conversion routinely involve what might be called embezzlement of the social capital of the state. This description draws on Pierre Bourdieu's analysis of "social capital," which he defines as "relations of mutual acquaintance and recognition . . . which entitles [the agent] to 'credit' in the various senses of the word."[66] Just like every other agent, the state possesses social capital, and its social capital (which is quite distinct from its capacity to exert coercion) is the willingness of its citizens to enter into collaborative medium- and long-term relations with state agencies. Just like other forms of capital, social capital may be embezzled when it is employed not in accordance with the rules regulating its usage. This is precisely what happened when Orion used the rhetoric of governance and state-provided assistance to mobilize and then gain access to the resources of a large number of Bulgarian farmers. In the case of the BAIB the conversion

---

66. See Pierre Bourdieu, "Forms of Capital," in *Handbook of Theory and Research for the Sociology of Education*, ed. John G. Richardson (Westport, Conn.: Greenwood, 1986), 248–49.

did not involve the removal of assets from the state's domain. Rather, it involved the collection of "credit" supposedly on behalf of the state. The result was the depletion of the social capital of the state.[67]

Such forms of conversion affect not so much the functioning of state institutions as the relations between state agents and mobilized social constituencies. The embezzlement of the state's social capital creates formidable obstacles to cooperation between state agencies and organized societal constituencies in post-Communism. To comprehend the importance of this finding, we only need to recall that reforms of the kind contemplated in countries like Bulgaria throughout the 1990s cannot be implemented in the absence of such collaborative efforts—or, as an astute observer put it, "An aggressively reformist state requires not merely acquiescence, but also cooperation [as] post-Communist citizens are being asked to adapt their behavior to new and complicated rules of the game."[68] Once disengagement becomes a preferred mode of action, social actors and organizations "undertake evasive strategies of political withdrawal rather than engage in ambitious efforts at structural transformation."[69] The embezzlement of social capital, this specific form of conversion, thus undermines the basis of state-society cooperation. Those who convert not only strip the state of its assets, they deprive it of the opportunity to make allies.

Conversion and the Structure of Creditor-Debtor Relations

One of the immediate effects of the conversions was the historically specific structuring of creditor-debtor relations in early post-Communism. This resonated with specific institutions of governance, such as law-enforcement agencies. In essence, this story follows the typical scenario conjured up in the literature: it involves the appropriation of public assets by powerful individuals affiliated with the former Communist Party. However, the story has several intermediary stages that generated important consequences, which a simplistic view would miss. My broader argument is that conversions of power precipitated the coalescence of

---

67. On the state as a field on which agents struggle to appropriate various forms of capital, see also Loic Wacquant, "Towards a Reflexive Sociology," *Sociological Theory* 7, no. 1 (Spring 1989): 40. For the role of social capital in the process of governance, see more generally Robert Putnam, *Making Democracy Work* (Princeton: Princeton University Press, 1992).

68. See Stephen Holmes, "Cultural Legacies or State Collapse?" in *Postcommunism*, ed. Michael Mandelbaum (New York: Council of Foreign Relations, 1996), 65.

69. See Michael Bratton, "Peasant-State Relations in Post-Colonial Africa," in *State Power and Social Forces*, ed. Joel S. Migdal, Atul Kohli, and Vivienne Shue (Cambridge: Cambridge University Press, 1994), 252.

powerful predatory coalitions that had a strong incentive to disrupt the institutional basis of law enforcement mechanisms. The configuration of creditor-debtor relations, this major artifact of conversions of power, created particular constellations of incentives that rendered assaults on certain state agents very likely and made the blocking of law enforcement a strategic objective that powerful nonstate agents tried immediately to accomplish. The withdrawal of state assets thus led to the permanent incapacitation of key state agencies.

The major actors in this case were Bulgaria's commercial banks. How and when these banks emerged is a crucial empirical question related to post-Communist conversions of power.

The remarkable thing about the banking system in Bulgaria is that it was arguably the first element of the "market economy" to be put in place. Conceived as a functional prerequisite of economic reform, a two-tiered banking system (composed of a central bank and commercial banks) replaced the former centralized and monopolized system in 1989–90. The formation of a banking system passed through two stages. First, the local branches of the Bulgarian National Bank (BNB) were turned into state-owned commercial banks. Then, new banks began to be licensed by the BNB. Here is the number of banks granted licenses in each year: 1990 (61), 1991(8), 1992 (2), 1993 (7), 1994 (10), 1995 (4), 1996 (2).[70]

In other words, by the end of 1991, when the BSP had to temporarily relinquish power, almost 75 percent of the banks allowed to operate in the post-Communist period had already been established. One of the most interesting facts about the early history of the Bulgarian post-Communist banking system was that until 1994 the owners of banks were not required to account for the origin of the money with which they applied for a license. Specifically, they did not have to present proof that the money was not borrowed, not to mention stolen or laundered.[71] The banking system became an unmonitored niche where resources withdrawn from the state were stashed. By the end of 1989, the first year in which market-oriented economic activities were allowed, 92 percent of the capital of newly registered firms was in the fledgling "financial sphere," that is, in newly created banks.[72] What this means in practice is that most of the private banks in Bulgaria were set up with money borrowed from the two state-owned financial institutions, the BNB and the State Savings

---

70. See *Pari*, August 18, 1997, 11.
71. For more details, see "Doklad za prichinite, doveli do kraha na bankovata sistema" (Parliamentary Report on the Causes of the Collapse of the Banking System), *Banker*, May 24, 1999, 4–6.
72. See Vesselin Minchev, "Zashto lesno, kato mozhe da e trudno?" (Why Make It Easy, When It Can Be Difficult) *Ikonomika* 24 (1994), 15.

Bank (where the savings of virtually all Bulgarian citizens were deposited). Agorbiznessbank, Banka Zemedelski Kredit, Purva Chatsna Banka, Biznes Banka—these are some of the banks that operated with state credits that were never returned.[73]

Sensing the danger that this legacy posed to the financial sector, the first parliament in which a volatile non-Communist coalition held a majority of the seats (elected in 1991) passed a law banning former high-ranking Communist officials from occupying leading positions in the banking sector. However, this lustration law was struck down by the Constitutional Court which held that it violated the constitutionally guaranteed right to free choice of profession.[74] Whether or not this law would have been an effective tool for ensuring the stability of Bulgarian banks is open to debate; the fact remains that the country's fledgling financial institutions remained a habitat populated exclusively by members of the former nomenklatura.

Borrowing money from the state was the first part of the simple two-step plan to convert political influence into privately consumed wealth. The second step was enacted when the commercial banks began to give out credits to insiders. In effect, what the commercial banks did in 1991–96 was to create a new kind of creature that came to be known in Bulgaria as a "credit millionaire" and became the emblem of Bulgaria's failed "transition." A credit millionaire is someone or something (a private individual, firm, SOE, organization, even soccer clubs were implicated in this affair) that took millions in loans and never bothered to pay them back. After the 1997 parliamentary elections, the new parliament undertook an investigation, which revealed that the total number of unserviced credits was 10,763, whereas the number of recipients was approximately 3,000, that is, each recipient drew three credits on average. The total sum of money lost is estimated to be 2,745,578,451,000 leva. Virtually all loans were extended to large and small nomenklatura-controlled firms.[75] In the words of Roumen Avramov, "Far from being an institution supporting a market economy, the Bulgarian banking system was turned into a tool that certain individuals, with a remarkable lack of imagination, used to appropriate the money of depositors."[76]

---

73. See *Pulen spisuk na kreditnite milioneri v Bulgaria* (A Complete List of Bulgaria's Credit Millionaires) (Sofia: Izdatelska Kushta Trud, 1998).
74. See Decision 8/1992, published in *Reshenija I opredelenija na Konstitutzionnija Sud* (Sofia: Akademia na naukite, 1993), 120–24.
75. For more details, see *Pulen spisuk*.
76. Roumen Avramov, "Tzenata na stabilizatzijata e ogranichen suverenitet" (The Price of Stabilization Is Limited Sovereignty), in *Ikonomicheska politika* (Economic Politics) (Sofia: Otvoreno Obshtestvo, 1996), 76.

The most important consequence of this mode of withdrawal of state assets is that it structured in a particular way the configuration of creditor-debtor relations. Generally, the conversions in the banking sector made it possible for the strong to exploit the weak. Those who converted power owed money to the state; the state, in its turn, owed money to millions of ordinary depositors who were weak and disorganized. Thus social groups that had converted their power and amassed various assets had no incentive to assist in the survival and strengthening of the state (their creditor). In contrast, the social groups that had an interest in the survival of the state (their debtor) possessed only the diffused power of an unorganized citizenry in a fledgling democracy.

An analytical category introduced by Bruce G. Carruthers, the "Eumenes effect," might help us appreciate the historical distinctiveness and analytical importance of this dynamic configuration.[77] As Plutarch reports, Eumenes was one of Alexander's favorite generals; as a Greek among Macedonian warriors, he found himself in a precarious situation after the death of his mentor. However, he came up with a solution to his predicament: he started borrowing huge sums of money, especially from his most bitter rivals. Suddenly, all-powerful figures in the post-Alexandrian world developed a strong incentive to ensure Eumenes' political and physical survival: keeping him alive was the only way for them to retrieve at least some of their money.

Carruthers uses this simple and powerful story as the analytical cornerstone of his fascinating account of the miraculous "strengthening" of the English state in the second half of the seventeenth century and the emergence of a stock market in London:

> In 1672, there was no stock market in London and England was a weak nation state and second-rate military power. In 1712 ... the shares of many joint-stock companies were traded on an active and highly organized capital market [and] Great Britain had become one of the major military powers in Europe.[78]

The moving forces behind this transformation cannot be comprehended unless the position of the king is adequately understood. During that period, the king became what Carruthers calls "a sovereign debtor." He took loans from virtually all wealthy merchants in the country. The web of interlocking relations between powerful creditors and the sovereign debtor generated the dynamic that produced "the Eumenes effect": the emergence of a strong financial constituency with a stake in the political

---

77. Bruce G. Carruthers, *The City of Capital* (Princeton: Princeton University Press, 1996).
78. Ibid., 8.

survival of the state. The fairly rapid coalescence of a formidable political coalition adverse to centrifugal tendencies in the state and supportive of the expansion of state extractive capacities was made possible by the crucial convergence of interests: "Creditors acquired a vested financial interest in the continuation of the state, government or regime to which it loaned money." Thus, it was the structure of creditor-debtor relations that provided the foundation for state-building. This mode of relationships also triggered the emergence of financial markets and property rights; but its most important effect took place in the process of forging political allegiances and prostate coalitions: "State-building meant cultivating domestic elites as well as enlarging extractive capacity."[79] In his celebrated study of early modern political thought, J. G. A. Pocock makes the same point: "The institutions of the new finance, of which the Bank of England and the National Debt came to be the most important, were essentially a series of devices for encouraging the large and small investor to lend capital to the state, investing in its future political stability and strengthening this by the act of investment itself."[80]

The comparison between post-Jamesian England and post-Communist Bulgaria will surely incur the wrath of the gatekeepers of conventional political analysis, but this comparison brings into relief an important circumstance. As a result of large-scale conversions, the conditions under which Bulgaria began its journey to "democracy and market economy" were entirely different than those in England in the late seventeenth century: the novel financial system was run by powerful elites who had *borrowed* from the state and thus formed a coalition with a stake in *weakening* their "sovereign creditor" by undermining its capacity to regulate and enforce contracts in the banking sphere. The state in post-Communism, then, was not a Eumenes, whom powerful players on the political field had an incentive to protect. Instead, as relations between former cadres/insiders were reconfigured into a web of creditor-debtor relations, an entirely different logic was imparted in the relations between "the sovereign" and its financial "partners." Rather than favoring construction and maintenance of robust state institutions, those who benefited from the conversions in the banking system had an incentive to weaken the state.

An alternative way to convey the same idea would be to invoke Mancur Olson's analysis of the conditions under which the institutional basis of market exchange and the rule of law may be consolidated. The gist of Olson's analysis is the following: "If the average burglar is not as

---

79. Ibid., 9, 26.
80. J. G. A. Pocock, *The Machiavellian Moment* (Princeton: Princeton University Press, 1975), 425.

prosperous or politically influential as his victim, the net force of the private sector is on the side of the law."[81] Leaving aside whether we can meaningfully talk about a "private sector" in early post-Communism, clearly the average burglar-turned–credit millionaire was much more powerful than the average victim. Eventually, predators do have a stake in the emergence of a solid "private property regime."[82] In the short term, however, their interest is in maintaining control over what they have acquired through conversion and in disrupting the infrastructure of law enforcement. Once conversions got under way on a fairly large scale, the subversion of state regulatory functions became an imperative that powerfully conditioned the behavior of strategic elites in post-Communist Bulgaria.

From this theoretical perspective, it becomes easy to make sense of what actually happened in Bulgaria from 1989 to 1997. A number of low-level public officials—particularly tax collectors and those in charge of enforcing financial regulations—were subject to violent attacks and physical intimidation. In an important interview, a former minister of finance referred to the "physical insecurity" of his employees as one of the main reasons why efforts to streamline the banking sector in the early to mid-1990s consistently failed.[83] The rise of powerful debtors who benefited from the conversion thus led to the weakening of the state in the very primal sense of rendering it incapable of ensuring the safety of its civil servants. More generally, the new configuration of power permanently weakened the regulatory capacity of the state. Under formal and informal pressure from powerful debtors, entire investigative units in the Ministry of Internal Affairs specializing in financial crimes were dismantled.[84] If and when elected politicians tried to push prosecutors and magistrates to enforce the collection of debts, their efforts encountered firm, large-scale, and low-visibility resistance.[85] Attempts by officials at the Ministry of Finance to streamline monitoring procedures and impose financial discipline on commercial banks were sabotaged by bureaucrats affiliated with networks of debtors.[86]

---

81. Mancur Olson, "Why the Transition from Communism Is So Difficult," *Eastern Economic Journal* 21, no. 4 (Fall 1995): 442.
82. For an excellent analysis of the concept of "private property regime," see Frydman et al., *Privatization*, 134–48.
83. Interview with former minister of finance Stoyan Alexandrov, *Banker*, July 7, 1999, 1.
84. Edvin Sugarev, *Bankovijat bankrut na Bulgaria* (Bulgaria's Bank Bankruptcy) (Sofia: Fakel Press, 1996), 24–26.
85. Interview with Alexandrov, 2.
86. Interview with Roumen Avramov, deputy chairman of the Bulgarian National Bank, April 12, 1998.

In sum, once political control over the banking sector was converted into de facto acquisition of private wealth, a powerful elite constituency emerged with a vested interest in weakening and undermining the ability of the state to regulate a strategic sector of the economy. The dynamic of creditor-debtor relations, one of the most important artifacts of conversion, permanently undermined the capacity of the fledgling Bulgarian democracy to sustain the viability of structures essential for the maintenance of state control over flows of financials resources.

The story of the Bulgarian banking system and how creditor-debtor relations were structured illustrates the argument that the ramifications of conversion have not been sharply delineated. The imagery invoked in the literature suggests that in the aftermath of the conversion former political elites abandoned their political positions only to reemerge as extremely well-heeled "market players," whose rapport with the state bears a close resemblance to the relations between states and business in Western democracies. In fact, the resources were appropriated by groups that began to behave as political entrepreneurs highly motivated and logistically equipped to disrupt the institutional environment in which they operated.

The Costs of Conversion: A State-Centered View

If there is one general conclusion that may be formulated on the basis of the foregoing analysis, it is that in the literature so far, this theme is treated as a favorite old song: everybody recognizes the first lines and no one cares much about the entire text. The rather familiar refrain of the song refers to "botched privatizations," "corrupt transactions," and "the growing gap between rich and poor." But a close-up reading of all the verses is bound to reveal intriguing subplots, unexpected messages, and overlooked meanings. The state-centered approach makes possible the construction of a more robust narrative on conversions. It suggests that the existing stock of images associated with conversions should be diversified—in order to take into account forms of conversion that cannot be construed simply as assignment of first property rights to politically privileged insiders. Post-Communist entrepreneurship is in fact coterminous with the disorderly withdrawal of resources from the state and is therefore a dynamic factor reconfiguring the state domain. That is why the state-centered perspective should be considered as an invitation to fine-tune certain assumptions currently informing the study of conversions—for example, the notion that conversions principally involve the transfer of resources between clearly delineated spheres (the sphere of political power, where the process begins, and the sphere of economic power, where the process is consummated). Most important, however, the state-centered perspective allows us to examine the costs of conversions and to integrate an empirically grounded exploration of concrete forms of Schumpeterian entrepreneurship into a broader survey of the important factors that militate against the emergence of effective and coherent governmental structures in early post-Communism.

The general argument that as techniques of conversion were applied on a large scale they generated effects that go beyond the redistribution of public wealth and thus triggered important institutional changes that directly and perilously affected the institutional potential of democratic governance may be concretized in two specific claims regarding the crisis of stateness in post-Communist Bulgaria. The first is that conversions constitute a major impediment to "monitorability" within state structures. As a rule, conversions are a form of utilization of decentralized knowledge—it is only actors that have learned what is to be found where and when in the state domain who can engage in conversions. As Charles E. Sabel has argued, however, in bureaucratic structures infected by such self-regarding modes of behavior, attempts to determine whether or not actors entrusted with discretion and decision-making authority will behave in accordance with normative and professional standards will be futile. The more advanced the "learning" of self-interested agents, the more fragile "the stability of relations normally required for monitoring." The reverse side of institutional innovations employed by "converters" is "the breakdown of monitorability" and enduring "threats to the principals' control over subordinate agents."[87] As the Vuchev case demonstrates, the dynamics of conversion stem from the ability of knowledgeable elites to manipulate both their superiors and the normative frameworks that constitute the basis of governance. It is precisely the power to defy the definitions articulated by public policy and to impose alternative "reinterpretations" that manifests itself in the process of conversions. Put differently, before the confrontation with their competitors in the market place, those who converted power revamped their immediate institutional environment; their victories dramatically aggravated the principal-agent problems that incapacitated the fledgling Bulgarian democratic polity.

The second claim is that the hijacking of the political capital of the state renders impossible the generating of "positive synergy" between public officials and organized social constituencies. The term "positive synergy" was introduced by Peter Evans to designate a situation in which a simultaneous empowering of state structures and societies through

---

87. Charles E. Sabel, "Learning by Monitoring," in *Handbook of Economic Sociology*, ed. Richard Swedberg and Neil J. Smelser (Princeton: Princeton University Press, 1994), 137.

mutual cooperation might take place.[88] Conversion affairs such as the collapse of the BAIB demonstrate that one of the lasting aftereffects of the embezzlement of social capital might be the blockage of such opportunities for reinvigoration of state and society. In fact, an argument could be made that this particular mode of conversion through embezzlement of social capital gives rise to a type of state-society relationship that is the exact opposite of the construction of synergy, namely disengagement. Having been involved in concrete projects under the auspices of state agents, social actors may draw the rational conclusion that the risks of vulnerability attendant on exposure to the state may be greater than the rewards of participation.[89]

Conversions precipitate a decline in what students of bureaucracy call the "programmatic capacity" of administrative structures, or the ability of the bureaucracy to carry out programs in accordance with a previously specified plan.[90] In the immediate aftermath of these processes, state structures become unable to win struggles for control over assets and socially accepted meanings, to defend their lower-level state employees against frontal attacks launched by powerful foes, and to form cooperative alliances with social constituencies. The immediate and palpable cost of conversion is the radically diminished functionality of key state apparatuses.

In addition to these more specific conclusions, the state-centered approach to conversions brings into sharp relief the broader historical perspective that the conversion of political into economic power is a sui generis process without much precedent. Mark I. Lichbach and Adam Seligman have demonstrated that in early modern Europe, even though "wealth and religion were fungible into politics, the fungibility in turn of political power back into other forms of power or resources was extremely limited."[91] Along the same lines, Ernest Gellner has argued that while "in traditional societies he who has political power, soon acquires wealth as a consequence," in industrial societies "wealth leads to power, more than the other way around."[92] The reigning consensus is cogently expressed by Pierre Bourdieu: "Economic capital is at the root of all other

---

88. For the distinction between "endowed" and "constructed" synergy, see Peter Evans, "Government Action, Social Capital, and Development," in *State-Society Synergy*, 189–203.

89. See Victor Azarya and Naomi Chazan, "Disengagement from the State in Africa," *Comparative Studies in Society and History* 29, no. 2 (April 1987): 106–31.

90. "Programmatic capacity is the ability of the bureaucracy to carry out programs in accordance with a previously specified plan": Daniel P. Carpenter, *The Forging of Bureaucratic Autonomy* (Princeton: Princeton University Press, 2001), 28.

91. Mark I. Lichbach and Adam Seligman, *Market and Community* (University Park: Pennsylvania State University Press, 2000), 108.

92. Ernest Gellner, *The Conditions of Liberty* (London: Penguin Books, 1994), 74–75.

types of capital."[93] Although this statement has been rightfully criticized for its ahistorical character, it adequately reflects the sensibilities informing the dominant research agendas in contemporary social science.[94] It is obvious that post-Communist conversions of capital differ both from those in traditional society (because they transpire in modern, industrialized, differentiated, urbanized, stratified polities) and from those in Western-type political systems (because, pace Bourdieu, they demonstrate that under certain conditions political and not economic capital may be "at the root of all other types of capital"). My state-centered approach suggests that the most salient peculiarity of this historically constituted mode of conversion is that it generates significant conversion costs. These costs accumulate when resources are withdrawn from the state and ultimately damage the infrastructure of governance. That is why the study of post-Communist conversions of power should encompass both the metamorphoses of elite power and the transformation of state structures after 1989.

Overall, then, the fixation on newly emerging economic elites might have led us all too easily to the assertion that the most important effects of the conversion are to be observed in the social and economic sphere. In fact, the most important fact about post-Communist conversions is that they generate an *asymmetrical effect*. The economic power that they allegedly create may or may not have anything to do with markets and rational capitalist pursuit of wealth. In contrast, the damage inflicted on political power, and public authority more generally, is inescapable, massive, and palpable. In his famous Ninth Thesis on the Philosophy of History, Walter Benjamin describes Paul Klee's captivating painting "Angelus Novus." The face of the angel is turned toward the past, where "he sees one single catastrophe which keeps piling wreckage upon wreckage." This is the angel of history: he is caught in a storm that "irresistibly propels him into the future to which his back is turned, while the pile of debris before him grows skyward."[95] This is how we should picture the retrieving, quite unangelic Communist cadres and the kind of "state" they leave behind. They face the past and that is their power. It is uncertain what this power is converted into. But everyone can see the wreckage inflicted by the silent storms of conversion—a testimony to a situation in which the privileged could change, while countless Vladimirs and Estragons remained stuck in a quagmire of unfulfilled hopes and unrealized expectations.

93. Bourdieu, "Forms of Capital," 252.
94. See, for example, Craig Calhoun, "Habitus, Field, and Capital," in *Critical Social Theory* (Oxford: Blackwell, 1995), 132–61.
95. Walter Benjamin, "Theses on the Philosophy of History," *Illuminations* (New York: Harcourt, Brace, 1968), 257–58.

4 Winners as State Breakers in Post-Communism

> It must be indicative of something, besides the redistribution of wealth.
>   Tom Stoppard's Guildenstern, after betting on "tails" and losing ninety-three consecutive coin tosses, *Rosencrantz and Guildenstern Are Dead*

Amid the turbulence that marked the early stages of post-Communism, various winners emerged on the political scene—powerful groups that occupied strategic positions and established control over vital flows of resources. The relations between these winners and post-Communist states are among the most important dynamic factors driving the restructuring of post-Communist states. An in-depth analysis of these relations, particularly of how they have evolved over time, is indispensable for an adequate understanding of emergent forms of control over resources and the ways in which specific displays of newly acquired power impinge on the effectiveness and coherence of the machinery of government. More broadly, an inquiry into the alchemy of winning may furnish a vantage point for a fresh analytical look at salient aspects of the fluctuations of post-Communist stateness.

A study of the spectacular rise of Multigroup, the most powerful economic conglomerate in post-Communist Bulgaria (1991–97), provides the empirical background connecting the study of post-Communist success to the analysis of the transformation of state structures. As we already saw, a cohort of strategically located agents in post-Communism was able to exploit various lucrative opportunities by raiding a logistically vulnerable public domain. What remains to be examined is the conflictual nature of the relations between such agents and their changing counterparts within the state, the disruptive reversals to which they have been prone, and the institutional consequences of such reversals. The Multigroup story demonstrates precisely the contradictory dynamic that characterized the relationships between winners and the state, specifically how periods of collusion alternate with phases of hostile clashes, and why powerful private actors eventually find themselves ensnared in antagonistic struggles with key administrative agencies. In a detailed examination of these struggles we can focus on the structural context in which they erupt, the strategies employed by rivals trying to outflank each other, and how they reshape the organizational landscape in post-Communism. What is at stake in these conflicts is the redistribution of national wealth—and yet, they differ significantly from redistributive conflicts in societies where powerful actors use state agencies to appropriate assets held by other social groups (class struggle, interest group politics, "patrimonial plunder," for example).[1] The historical distinctiveness of the behavior of successful predatory elites in post-Communism is that they have had an incentive to behave as state breakers, not state makers.

The case study I present here highlights the analytical themes adumbrated in the preceding chapters: the vulnerability of state structures, the impact of strategic elite action on the capacity of administrative apparatuses, and the significance of the sociohistorical context for understanding the transmogrifications of the framework of governance. It supplements the analysis provided so far in previous chapters in two crucial aspects. On an empirical level, it demonstrates that the rapport between state agencies and powerful elites cannot be conveyed in a formulaic manner, because collusion may be quickly followed by rivalry. An up-close look at these alternating phases may help us dissect the dynamic of these relations. On an analytical level, it demonstrates that the power to *establish* control over resources is different from the power to *retain* control. To protect their gains, nonstate elites that benefited from the separation and conversion were sometimes compelled to exercise veto power. The ways in which this veto power was wielded fairly rapidly became a potent factor affecting state institutions. The story of Multigroup illustrates how the logistical conflicts attendant to the separation have evolved over time, and how the effects generated as a result of conversions of power are amplified in a dynamically changing institutional setting.

One particular concept, "The Dorian Gray Effect," will help me present my analytical conclusions in a structured manner. The main idea behind the concept is that we should think in a new way about the challenges involved in post-Communist transformations. Assessing the prospects of

---

1. On "patrimonial plunder," see Paul D. Hutchcroft, "Oligarchs and Cronies in the Philippine State," *World Politics* 43, no. 3 (Fall 1991): 414–50.

reforms, Barry R. Weingast defined "the fundamental political dilemma" of newly emerging politicoeconomic systems: "A government strong enough to protect property rights is also strong enough to confiscate the wealth of its citizens."[2] My analysis brings into a sharp relief another monumental problem: private groups strong enough to resist the government may also be strong enough to undermine the organizational basis of effective democratic governance. It is this aspect of "winning" in post-Communism that the concept of "The Dorian Gray Effect" seeks to capture.

Post-Communist Winning: Analytical Problems and Empirical Ramifications

Several decades ago, Joseph Schumpeter warned that agreement will always elude those who debate the question of "whether social ascent and descent through success or failure in business spells positive or negative social selection."[3] Surprisingly, a consensus has rapidly emerged among the community of scholars studying early post-Communism: it is the "bad characters" that enjoyed a flying start after the implosion of state socialism. "Success" and "winners" are always mentioned in a panoptic antiheroic context: they are corrupt bureaucrats, unscrupulous entrepreneurs, bloody criminals, ominous security cadres, phony bankers.

Scandalized as we are by this monumental example of "negative" social selection, however, we should not allow the question *who* surged ahead eclipse the no less significant question *how* they won their victories and *what tactics* they used to hold on to their ill-gotten spoils. In other words, the institutional implications of the redistribution of power and influence are yet to be fully explored.

Among the writings that focus on the various dimensions of "post-Communist winning," one clearly stands out: Joel Hellman's insightful study "Winners Take All."[4] In this seminal article Hellman presents a fresh perspective on the broad set of problems related to economic reforms, democratization, and social change in post-Communism. Among his important contributions is that he adduces enough empirical evidence to discredit the popular argument that radical reforms are both cruel and

---

2. Barry Weingast, "The Economic Role of Political Institutions," *Journal of Law, Economics, and Organization* 11, no. 1 (Spring 1993): 1–23.
3. Joseph Schumpeter, "Capitalism," in *Essays on Entrepreneurs, Innovations, Business Cycles, and the Evolution of Capitalism* (New Brunswick, N.J.: Transaction, 1997), 201–2.
4. Joel Hellman, "Winners Take All," *World Politics* 50, no. 1 (Fall 1998): 203–34.

foredoomed, whereas "gradualism" is humane and effective.[5] But the significance of his work lies elsewhere: he casts ample light on the political dynamics that allowed winners to amass their wealth and on the nature of the veto power whereby they are able to preserve a status quo advantageous to them. Hellman challenges the view that the *problematique* of "the reforms" should be construed in terms of the policy choices made by key decision makers at crucial political junctures (and specifically in the aftermath of the first free elections). Instead, he argues that processes of change might be more realistically depicted as "a sequence of many distinct choices over time on separate components of an overall reform plan . . . that do not necessarily coincide with the electoral calendar." The "politics of reform," therefore, involve much more than the implementation of internationally approved projects administered with steely determination by local leaders. Shifting the analytical focus that usually guides research on "the political economy of post-Communist transitions," Hellman singles out as key players in this process "the earliest and biggest winners." These groups of actors benefited from the initiation of reforms but later sought "to stall the economy in a *partial reform equilibrium* that generates concentrated rents for themselves." This equilibrium is only maintained because "winners" wield enough power to block attempts to change it—they possess the capacity to block reformist policies and prevent further marketization of the economy. The continuing domination of early winners and their dilatory tactics precipitated "the increasing concentration of rents to winners [which] should entail a corresponding decrease in consumption of the losers." The gist of Hellman's argument is that the behavior of winners constitutes a causal factor that functions independently of both the wishes of elected politicians and the reactions of disgruntled constituencies. A major corollary of this argument is that analytical accounts of the overall dynamic of transformative processes, as well as particular outcomes of these processes, must contain a survey of the strategies of early winners. Thus Hellman recasts the debate about post-Communism—a debate that regularly veers into more or less acontextual discussions of the first principles of political economy—as an inquiry into concrete mechanisms of power that structure the interactions between a complex set of actors operating in the area where political and economic domains intersect.[6]

---

5. See, for example, the essays in Beverly Crawford, ed., *Markets, States, and Democracy* (Boulder: Westview Press, 1995), and the manifesto by Adam Przeworski, Luis Carlos Bresser Pereira, and José Maria Maravall, *Economic Reform in New Democracies* (New York: Cambridge University Press, 1993).
6. Hellman, "Winners Take All," 221–22, 203.

Hellman does not refer directly to the problem of the transformation of state structures in post-Communism. But his basic insight—that the strategies employed by the beneficiaries of the early reforms have something to do with the ills besetting post-Communist societies—may be fruitfully employed in the analysis of the diminished administrative capacity of these societies. Under the specific circumstances of post-Communism the systematic weakening of particular state agencies was bound to become an indispensable element of the strategies whereby "winners" sought to retain their privileged position. In order to substantiate this claim and to flesh out the broader implications of my argument, I will develop two state-centered analytical themes which are treated in a somewhat mechanical and cavalier manner in Hellman's account.

The first theme revolves around the question of how winners manage to maintain the status quo from which they benefit. In an attempt to shed analytical light on this issue, Hellman resorts to the somewhat puzzling expression "implicit veto power": "Indeed, it is reasonable to assume that the winners might have an implicit veto power in the decisions over separate components of economic reform."[7] This notion, however, fails to specify the exact nature of the activities whereby winners vitiate attempts at further reforms: Do they rely on regular political procedures, or other types of strategic interventions? What is it that makes their "veto" effective? How does it affect the overall process of governance?

The second theme addresses the question of why the continuing domination of winners have such disastrous consequences. What is the flip side of post-Communist success?

In a way that is reminiscent of dominant interpretations of conversions of power, Hellman seems convinced that the effect of "winning strategies" will be most acutely felt in the social and economic sphere. The longer societies remain subservient to the stratagems of winners, the more massive the redistribution of resources, and the greater the social and economic costs borne by citizenry. Although it is undeniable that such negative trends are at least partially driven by the logic of "post-Communist success," the exclusive focus on the socioeconomic dimension obscures the fact that the process of societal redistribution is preceded by organizational struggles for control over resources held in the state domain, and that these struggles pit state agents against logistically well-endowed rivals. The very fact that these rivals survived indicates that they possessed power; what that power is and why the manner in which it is wielded is relevant to the analysis of reconfiguration of state structures is what I address in this chapter. In a very real sense, the most enduring

---

7. Ibid., 222.

damage inflicted by winners is the demolition of the administrative tools that make possible state intervention in the process of economic restructuring and the redistribution of resources more generally. Interweaving the themes of "winning" and "state-building" will integrate into a unified analytical framework the interrelated inquiries into the dynamics of economic transformation and the fluctuation of state capacity.

All too often, the activities of "winners" and "losers," "politicians" and "constituencies," "reformers" and "conservatives" are deduced in an a priori fashion from abstract models constructed with other epochs and places in mind. It may be worthwhile, then, to take a closer look at what "winners" actually do. Focusing on a single conglomerate as it develops over time is germane to one of the major goals of my inquiry: exploring the diachronic dimension of post-Communist success stories and detecting changes in the strategies of winners.

Multigroup: Formidable Winner in the Bulgarian Transition

Multigroup was by far the strongest economic conglomerate to emerge in Bulgaria after 1989.[8] An institutional creation conceived behind thick veils of secrecy, it rapidly rose to prominence during the governments of Ljuben Berov (1992–94) and Zhan Videnov (1995–97). There was hardly a branch of the national economy in which Multigroup did not have a stronghold, and the fairly dense web of companies it controlled covered virtually the entire country. An economic giant in an economy of rather modest proportions, it earned a reputation as an all-powerful corporate actor capable of generating profits even in times of acute and enduring economic turmoil. Whatever the magic formulae of "winning" in post-Communism, the managers of Multigroup obviously knew them well.

Despite the pervasive presence of Multigroup in the Bulgarian economy, it would be erroneous to characterize the company as a "financial-industrial group, or . . . organization formed under the aegis of the state, within which industrial enterprises and financial institutions are combined in some form or another for the purposes of coordinated economic activity."[9] De jure and de facto, Multigroup was a private entity—no state agencies took part in its internal decision-making process. The term "elite group," with its emphasis on the role of personal connections and informal

---

8. The following case is based on an exhaustive survey of six leading Bulgarian newspapers—*Kapital, Pari, Banker, Sega, Demokratzija* and *Duma*—and on numerous interviews with investigative journalists and officials, most of whom wish to remain anonymous.

9. Compare Irina Starodubrovskaya, "Financial-Industrial Groups," *Communist Economies and Economic Transformation* 7, no. 1 (Fall 1995): 5–19.

ways of wielding power, seems a more appropriate designation.[10] Multigroup International Holding was established in 1990 in Vaduz, Liechtenstein, and its original capital was set at fifty thousand Swiss francs. The actual owner is not known: according to Liechtensteinian law, a holding may be registered under the names of local lawyers who are not required to disclose the names of their clients. Thus Multigroup is officially registered under the name of an employee of a local law firm. On August 5, 1991, another holding company called Multigroup was set up in Zug, Switzerland. On July 27, 1992, Multigroup Bulgaria was finally registered in Bulgaria; it is owned by the Swiss Multigroup. The Liechtensteinian Multigroup, in turn, owns majority shares in both the Swiss Multigroup and in the holding's subsidiary in Bulgaria.

Who ran Multigroup Bulgaria? A glance at the roster of high-ranking officials would quickly reveal that the new organization relied exclusively on the expertise of former Communist cadres who had occupied various sensitive positions.[11] The president of Multigroup was Ilia Pavlov, a former wrestler. In the 1980s he was married to the daughter of the director of Military Counterintelligence, and thus easily gained access to networks comprised of secret service officials and other insiders operating within the fortresses of Communist power. His first foray into the business world was with the registration of the company Multiart in 1988, that is, only weeks after a limited array of private economic activities were finally allowed by the Communist authorities. Even though the company's legal documents declare that Multiart would trade in "antiques and art objects," it began to export the products of Kremikovtsi, Bulgaria's largest metallurgical plant. At some point in late 1988, at a time when Bulgarian citizens were barred from traveling to the West, Pavlov was allowed to move to Malta to do business. His travel documents were handled personally by Grigor Shopov, the head of State Security at the time.[12] It is in Malta that the smart wrestler made his first big "hit": he bought submarines from the Soviet Black Sea military fleet (Sovmorflot), then cut them to pieces and sold them as scrap metal to Turkish metallurgical plants. Since Soviet submarines were, to put it mildly, not exactly a product that could be freely purchased on the "world market," this operation suggests that Pavlov was extremely well connected to a network of arms dealers centered in Moscow and

---

10. Virginie Coulloudon, "Elite Groups in Russia," *Demokratizatsiya* 6, no. 3 (Summer 1998): 535–49.
11. The biographies of important actors on the post-Communist political scene are often ignored in studies of post-Communism. For a good argument against this tendency, see Rudolph L. Tokes, *Hungary's Negotiated Revolution* (Cambridge: Cambridge University Press, 1996).
12. See *Kapital*, February 7–13, 1994, 12–13.

spanning several nations. Apparently, Pavlov handled his assignment well; after 1989, he was sent back to Bulgaria to manage Multigroup's operations there.

The three vice presidents of the conglomerate were also intimately linked to strategic sectors: the secret service, organized labor, and the state-owned economy. One of them was a former head of the most powerful department in the former State Security, Department Six. The other was a former secretary of the largest trade union in Bulgaria, Podkrepa. The third was a former general director of Minstroi Holding, one of the largest state-owned industrial holdings.

Of the twenty general directors who headed "strategic departments" in the early 1990s, one was a former head of the personnel department of the Ministry of Internal Affairs (quite appropriately, he was put in charge of Multigroup's Department of Information and Analyses), three were former directors of state-owned enterprises (in the oil industry, industrial investment, and microprocessing), and eight were former deputy ministers who served in the ancien régime (in the ministries of energy, industry, agriculture, tourism, and foreign trade).

In the years after 1989 there was a steady flow of personnel from the state administration to well-paid positions in Multigroup. Here is an approximate list of important actors who "crossed over":

Ljubomir Filipov, former chairman of the Bulgarian National Bank; subsequently hired by Kredit Bank, the bank of Multigroup;

Veselin Blagoev, former chairman of the Privatization Agency; on the last day of his tenure, he sold to Multigroup 34 percent of the shares of a luxurious hotel in the mountains; on the next day he started managing the property as a representative of Multigroup;

Vassil Popov, former director of the National Sports Lottery (Toto); subsequently hired as Pavlov's "personal consultant" on gambling;

Trifon Tsvetkov, former head of the National Electric Company; subsequently employee of Multigroup;

Dimiter Sokolov, former chairman of the National Energy Committee; subsequently hired as a "consultant" by Multigroup;

Ivan Kolev, former deputy minister of trade in charge of commercial relations with Russia;

Spas Gelemezov, former director of Bulgartabak, the state-owned monopoly of tobacco trade; subsequently head of the tobacco department in Multigroup;

Krustyo Jankov, former chairman of the board of directors of the state-owned DZU, Bulgaria's largest electronic equipment producer; subsequently manager of Multigroup's privatization fund and in that capacity manager of the holding's shares in the same enterprise.

Once implanted on Bulgarian soil, the conglomerate began to grow rapidly; in 1993, only a year after its registration in Bulgaria, the volume of its business operations exceeded $1 billion, more than any other state or private business in Bulgaria with the exception of Petrol, the state-owned oil trading company. By the end of 1996 Multigroup controlled more than 120 Bulgarian companies.

Multigroup rarely sought the services of Western financial institutions and experts, never developed an interest in recruiting ambitious young Bulgarian MBAs, and shunned business contacts with reputable transnational companies. Instead, it played the role of a focal point around which former nomenklatura could pool their knowledge about the state-owned economy.[13]

By now, it is a commonplace—and deservedly so—that the hordes of former nomenklatura who burst onto the post-Communist economic scene as entrepreneurs were parasites who targeted state-owned enterprises. Multigroup was no exception: its major asset was its status as a preferred "business associate" of various state-owned enterprises. Hardly surprisingly—reflecting a trend that transpired all over Eastern Europe—the profits of the private conglomerate were invariably accompanied by the losses of its state-owned "partners."[14]

In what follows, I will explore in more detail three affairs in which Multigroup was involved, the "Topenergy affair," the "Himko-Kremikovtzi affair," and the "DZU affair."[15] These affairs transpired on different institutional levels, involved different strategies, and were made possible by the utilization of different kinds of resources. The Topenergy affair took place on the international level. It resulted in the imposition of a disadvantageous long-term contract on the Bulgarian state and was propelled by the mobilization of social capital embedded in transnational networks. The Himko-Kremikovtzi affair took place on the national level. It was facilitated by the restructuring of Bulgaria's financial markets and was energized by connections between Multigroup and high-ranking executive officials. The DZU affair unfolded on the company level. It was

---

13. Ivo Prokopiev, "Durzhavata Multigrup," *Kapital*, July 31–August 6, 1995, 23–25.

14. See, for example, Jadwiga Staniszkis, *The Dynamics of the Breakthrough in Eastern Europe* (Berkeley: University of California Press, 1991), and Joseph R. Blasi, Maya Kroumova, and Douglas Kruse, *Kremlin Capitalism* (Ithaca: Cornell University Press, 1997).

15. This is just a small sample of Multigroup's numerous successful business operations. Among the "affairs" *not* discussed here are the "Bulgartabak affair" (using a state-held patent to privately market tobacco products); the "DSK affair" (ensuring cheap credits to Multigroup-controlled banks); and the "Bartex affair" (illegal importing of sugar). The impact of these large-scale operations on the respective branches of the economy was no less momentous than the effects of the three affairs discussed in this chapter.

made possible by the compartmentalization of an existing state-owned enterprise and involved utilization of the local knowledge of individual managers. These stories also bring into a sharp relief recurrent patterns of dynamically changing interactions between "winners" and state agents. My inquiry into these interactions is informed by the following questions: How do winners resist attempts to change the status quo from which they benefit? What is the impact of this resistance? How do their tactics affect the institutional environment in early post-Communism? Through an empirical survey structured along these lines, I elucidate the interplay of structural factors, organizational dynamics, and emergent modes of agency in scenarios of winning and suggest how we should think of "success" as a factor that affects directly the revamping of the state structures in post-Communism.

Topenergy

It is impossible to understand fully the dynamic of Bulgarian domestic and foreign policy in the 1990s without acknowledging the significance of the simple fact that energy-poor Bulgaria has to import virtually all the gas it needs from Russia. The Topenergy affair illustrates how this dependence on a monopolistic supplier was deftly exploited by post-Communist entrepreneurs.

The gas that Bulgaria buys was monopolistically distributed on the domestic market by Bulgargaz, a state-owned company. In order to regulate their relations, in 1994 the governments of Bulgaria and Russia agreed to establish a joint venture. Russian oil giant Gazprom acquired 50 percent of the shares of Bulgargaz, and the remaining 50 percent was distributed among Bulgarian SOEs designated by the government.

On May 17, 1995, the Sofia District Court registered a new joint venture named Topenergy. Fifty percent of its shares were owned by Gazprom and 50 percent were owned by Bulgargaz. On the very same day, Nikita Shevarshidze, chairman of the Bulgarian Committee on Energy (an executive agency with the rank of a ministry) and a close friend of the "gas and energy experts" working for Multigroup, issued a special ordinance delegating to Topenergy the right to represent Bulgaria in negotiations with Russia. In addition, he ordered that Multigroup be allowed to purchase shares in Topenergy, even though the conglomerate, as a private company, was not eligible to participate in the distribution of ownership. When Shevarshidze's order was vacated by his colleagues in the Videnov government, he appointed Andrei Lukanov to Topenergy's board of directors. Lukanov, whose role in Bulgarian post-Communist politics was discussed in chapter 2, had resigned as prime minister and become Ilia Pavlov's most important business mentor. Once again, the government tried to block Multigroup's maneuvering: Lukanov's appointment was canceled, and Shevarshidze was fired. At this moment, Multigroup's strategy changed. Realizing that his "friends" in the government did not possess enough leverage to engineer Multigroup's entry into the gas business, Pavlov sought the support of Gazprom officials, some of whom he knew from his glory days in Malta. Only days after Lukanov's ouster, Gazprom announced that Lukanov would be appointed to Topenergy's board of directors, this time representing the *Russian* side. Thus a member of the Bulgarian parliament became an official representative of a Russian company in its negotiations with the Bulgarian government.[16]

Unable to cope with Gazprom's intransigence, the Videnov government finally relented. Toward the end of 1995, it was decided that, first, Topenergy would become the exclusive supplier of gas to Bulgargaz, and, second, that Multigroup-controlled companies would be allotted 16.5 percent of the membership of Topenergy. And as the participation of the Bulgarian state in the joint venture fell below 50 percent, Multigroup could ally itself with one of the biggest companies in the world and extract rents from one of the poorest nations in Europe.

Immediately thereafter, the price of gas deliveries started to climb, even though no upward trend was observed on the world market, and in the course of less than two years Bulgaria was buying the most expensive gas in Europe (the price went from $85 per 1,000 cubic meter in 1995 to $107 in 1996, a 20 percent increase in less than a year). For the sake of comparison, France, located at the other end of the continent, was paying Gazprom $90, and Turkey, which was located further down the North-South pipeline, was paying only $98. Had the Bulgarian government been able to arrange gas deliveries at the price offered to France—as later developments would show, not an unfeasible prospect—its gas bill would have been smaller by $100 million each year. (To put this sum in perspective, the World Bank's loans for infrastructural projects in Bulgaria totaled $125 million in 1995 and $121 in 1996.)[17] Pocketing this money was arguably the biggest success in Multigroup's short but rather dramatic history.

In a sense, the Topenergy affair is a textbook example of a rent-extracting scheme: a private group was able to charge public institutions an artificially boosted price. What is noticeable in this case, however, is that as the relationship between Multigroup and the Bulgarian state agencies evolved, the clashes surrounding Topenergy metamorphosed

---

16. For more details, see "Bulgarian Update," *East European Constitutional Review* 4, no. 3 (Summer 1995): 5–6. In the summer of 1996, Andrei Lukanov finally left Topenergy, and, as mentioned in chapter 2, three months later he was assassinated in Sofia.

17. See *Transition: The Newsletter about Reforming Economies* 8, no. 1 (February 1997): 3.

from backstage administrative maneuvering into a full-blown international affair with palpable geopolitical implications. Realizing that their connections in the Bulgarian government might be insufficient, Pavlov and his associates opted for a more ambitious strategy that eventually led to the entrapment of the state in a long-term relationship from which future governments found it costly to disengage.[18] A network of high-ranking officials from the formerly dominant superpower—contacts that Multigroup's president was apparently able to forge during his stint as a commercial "partner" of the Soviet Navy—was mobilized in order to structure the gas trade in Bulgaria in a way beneficial to Pavlov's conglomerate. To search for "imperial designs" behind Gazprom's behavior may be a sign of unwarranted paranoia.[19] The timing and nature of its interventions, however, allow us a glimpse at the diverse team of victorious entrepreneurs in post-Communism, a team whose ability to pressure the state into entering disadvantageous long-term contracts and, most important, ensuring the enforcement of such contracts, figures quite prominently.

The Himko-Kremikovtzi Affair

The Himko-Kremikovtsi affair signaled the emergence of Multigroup as a powerful collective player with whom everyone would have to reckon. Originally conceived in the secrecy of impenetrable executive offices, eventually it evolved into a drama featuring parliamentary investigations, Constitutional Court rulings, and assassination attempts. More than any other episode in Multigroup's turbulent history, the Himko affair is perceived in Bulgaria as an emblem of the flexibility, ingenuity, and ruthlessness involved in the seemingly chaotic restructuring of the former state economy.

---

18. It took an epic effort on the part of the next governments—headed by Stefan Sofiyanski and Ivan Kostov—to dislodge the network from its privileged position. Finally, after a full year of negotiations, this strategic task was accomplished and Multigroup was pushed aside. In April 1998 the Bulgarian-Russian agreement was renegotiated, Gazprom agreed to deliver gas directly to Bulgargaz at $82.50 per 1,000 cubic meter, and Topenergy became a property of Gazprom (see *Banker*, May 11, 1998). Although the determination of the Bulgarian government certainly contributed to the outcome, a major factor was the precarious position of Gazprom in Russia itself: besieged by domestic competitors, it could not afford to cause further complications with foreign governments just for the sake of pleasing a network of "ex-comrades." Thus an important tentacle of Multigroup's rent-extracting machine was amputated.

19. For an interesting analysis of how Gazprom is implicated in Russia's foreign and domestic policies, see Clifford G. Gaddy and Barry W. Ickes, *Russia's Virtual Economy* (Washington, D.C.: Brookings Institution, 2002).

Himko is a giant chemical plant located in Vratza, in northwestern Bulgaria. In the early 1990s it produced a variety of high-quality chemical products, enjoying a virtually unchallenged monopoly at home and a secure market abroad. Kremikovtsi, the other state-owned giant involved in this affair, is the largest industrial complex in Bulgaria, specializing in the production of steel and ferrous metals for domestic and foreign markets. By early 1994, both SOEs were falling behind in their payments to Bulgargaz, the state-owned monopoly that delivers gas to all industrial consumers in Bulgaria. In an attempt to enforce those payments, on April 14, 1994, the government of Prime Minister Ljuben Berov issued a special ordinance determining that all debts to Bulgargaz should be considered debts to the national treasury and should be collected by state officials. On May 16, the director of Himko notified his financial boss, the minister of finance, that he was ready to resume payments to Bulgargaz, provided that the schedule of payments was altered. The minister did not respond.[20] But the news that Himko had set aside the financial means necessary to cover its debts apparently did not go unnoticed. Two weeks later, on May 28, 1994, a meeting was held between Angel Popov, director of Bulgargaz, and representatives of Multigroup. After brief negotiations, and in an apparent violation of the ordinance of April 14, the private company was authorized to collect from Himko and Kremikovtzi debts owed to Bulgargaz, while Multigroup agreed to transfer a small amount of the collected debts to the national treasury and to undertake unspecified "construction work" on behalf of the state company. Several days later, with slight modifications, the contract signed by Popov and Multigroup was ratified by the Council of Ministers. Multigroup became the "owner" of the debts that two of the largest SOEs in Bulgaria owed Bulgargaz.[21]

At the time, this contract was a complete novelty in Bulgarian business practices. Trading and swaps of debts were neither legally regulated nor used in everyday economic activities. The innovative approach adopted by Multigroup attests to conglomerate managers' vision, legal expertise, and administrative competence to design and implement complex financial transactions.

As Himko and Kremikovtzi began to make regular payments to Multigroup, information about the deal was leaked to the press and instantly turned into a major issue. Under public pressure, the next government, headed by Zhan Videnov (installed in February 1995), vowed to take the necessary measures to void the contract. A month later, the cabinet

---

20. *Kapital*, July 31–August 6, 1995.
21. *Kapital*, January 9–15, 1995.

submitted to parliament a special amendment to the 1995 Budget Law, which retroactively declared that all debts owed to Bulgargaz were "state revenue" and could not be transferred to "third persons." At that point, a truly unusual development ensued: fifty-four deputies from different parliamentary caucuses signed a petition to the Constitutional Court, arguing that the new amendment violated the freedom of contract guaranteed by the constitution. The Bulgarian Constitution denies citizens, as well as civic and business organizations, standing to petition the Constitutional Court,[22] and the Himko case was the first incident in which members of parliament had appealed to this august body on behalf of a private entity. This alone testifies to the fact that Multigroup had a powerful political lobby. In a widely publicized decision, the court declared the amendment to the budget unconstitutional and pointed out that disputes between the government and Multigroup regarding the "cession" should be resolved by the ordinary courts.[23]

Thus the process of constitutional adjudication yielded mixed results. On the one hand, the government's attempt to have the deal canceled by means of retroactive legislation was blocked by the justices. On the other hand, the stage was set for a series of administrative and judicial battles in which the fate of the "cession" would be determined.

It was during this stage of the confrontation that skirmishes between Multigroup and various state structures erupted.

The directors of the two state-owned enterprises were pressured, through formal and informal channels, to proceed with the payments to Multigroup, despite occasional court injunctions barring them from doing so. Dimiter Kalistratov, director of Himko, announced that he would submit a new repayment schedule to Bulgargaz, a schedule much more advantageous than what Multigroup offered. The Multigroup-friendly officials at Bulgargaz, however, declined the offer. Kalistratov then declared that he would transfer the money Himko owed to the Ministry of Finance; he did so, and subsequently the funds were redirected to Multigroup's coffers. Meanwhile, he was the target of three assassination attempts. Finally, Kalistratov was fired, and on May 9, 1995, his successor, making oblique references to "insurmountable pressures," officially acknowledged Himko's debt to Multigroup and vowed to resume its regular payments to the conglomerate. Thus Multigroup continued to

---

22. According to Article 150.1 of the Bulgarian Constitution, the right to petition the court is granted to one-fifth of the deputies, the president, the Council of Ministers, the Supreme Court of Cassation, the Supreme Administrative Court, and the prosecutor general.

23. Constitutional Court Decision No. 22, 1996, published in *Reshenija I Opredelenija na Konstitutzionnija Sud, 1996* (Sofia: Akademichno izdatelstvo, 1997), 230–34.

collect huge payments from Himko. Needless to say, the construction work by means of which Multigroup was supposed to repay Bulgargaz was never undertaken.

As the conflict deepened, Kremikovtzi, the other debtor, continued to make regular payments to the conglomerate—although various ministers had given contrary orders. Attempts by government officials to monitor Kremikovtzi's finances were persistently resisted by the managers of the state-owned enterprise. As the battle moved to the courts, a new pattern of intimidation of judges and other court officials transpired. For almost a year, the entire Vratza Judicial District, where the case was tried, was forced to operate in a siegelike atmosphere. Local judges were repeatedly intimidated and threatened. After a series of decisions, appeals, and new rulings a district court finally ruled that Bulgargaz had transferred to Multigroup something it did not possess and that therefore the "cession" was void. The Supreme Court affirmed this decision.[24]

By that time, however, Multigroup had found a way to "transpose" the contested resources it had acquired into new fungible assets. It offered the debts collected by Bulgargaz as collateral for a loan from the State Savings Bank of more than seven hundred million leva. At the very moment when the government was disputing Multigroup's claims, another state institution recognized them as legitimate and was ready to accept them as collateral. Naturally, when the original deal between Multigroup and Bulgargaz was declared void, the State Savings Bank in effect lost the collateral. It is hard to say exactly how much Multigroup gained in the aftermath of the affair, but according to the best available estimates Multigroup pocketed in the neighborhood of $70 million.[25] Even though Multigroup was legally obliged to return most of what it had collected, the court's decision was never enforced.

Overall, the protracted battle produced results that were quite favorable to Multigroup. It engineered a massive redistribution of profits generated in the state-owned sector of the economy, collected millions of dollars from state-owned enterprises, and persuaded a number of strategically located officials to "defect" and participate in rent-seeking schemes. All throughout, Multigroup was able to block the efforts of government officials to put an end to its dubious activities. Pavlov and his associates successfully redirected the flow of resources from state-run institutions to a more open-ended cycle with several "privatized" outlets. Although Multigroup ultimately lost the legal battle, virtually all judicial and administrative institutions involved were so enfeebled

---

24. See "Krajat na odisejata Himko—Multigroup," *Sega*, no. 14, 1997.
25. For more details, see *Kapital*, January 9–15, 1997, 12.

that enforcement of the final judicial decision was rendered unlikely. Having milked Himko and Kremikovtzi, Multigroup made sure that the government's Pyrrhic legal victories would not lead to the restitution of hijacked resources.

The DZU Affair

Diskovi Zapametjavashti Ustroistva (Digital Information-Storing Instruments), commonly know as DZU, was one of the jewels of Bulgarian socialist industry. It was created in the 1980s with the purpose of boosting Bulgaria's reputation as powerhouse of computer technologies within COMECON (the Council for Mutual Economic Assistance), the Eastern bloc equivalent of the European Economic Community. For that purpose a top-secret decision of the Party-State Commission on Scientific and Technical Development, adopted October 30, 1986, specified the "leading role" of the Ministry of Interior in the whole project. The ministry was authorized to establish front firms in the West in order to acquire embargoed technologies. All business contacts were to be monitored by officers from the ministry, and bank accounts were to be handled by representatives of the same institution.[26] After 1989, DZU continued to enjoy a privileged position, and its requests for credits and additional investments were rarely turned down by local and national politicians.

The link between Multigroup and DZU was cemented in early 1995. At that time, Krustyo Jankov, former chairman of DZU's board of directors, was appointed Multigroup's vice chairman in charge of privatization deals, and Atanass Atanassov was reappointed director of DZU. Atanassov had occupied this position in the 1980s, when the strategic expansion abroad took place. Temporarily dismissed in the early 1990s, he became Multigroup's representative in Stara Zagora, the city where DZU is located. Considered by many to be the ultimate insider, Atanassov immediately set out to exploit the numerous opportunities that the new appointment opened to him and his new patrons. Almost simultaneously, a third member of the Multigroup conglomerate, Lilia Hristova, a deputy director of Multigroup, was appointed to represent the state on the five-member board of directors.

In mid-1995 DZU, which at that time had only one operative production line for compact discs, set up a joint venture with a Swiss company called Intercom. Although the provenance of that company is impossible to trace, one thing is publicly known: its representative in Bulgaria is Sasho Donchev, at the time one of Multigroup's vice presidents. This is a sure sign that the Swiss company is part of the Multigroup conglomerate.

---

26. See *Kapital*, February 2–9, 1995.

The purpose of the joint venture was to purchase new equipment for the production of compact discs. It was bought and installed on the premises of DZU. As soon as the equipment became operative, DZU sold all its shares to its partner. Thus Intercom-Multigroup became the sole owner(s) of the assembly line. The equipment remained on the premises of the SOE, it was operated by workers paid by the state, and all maintenance costs were absorbed by DZU. Obviously, Multigroup's representatives assumed that it was DZU's obligation to pay royalties to the musicians whose compact discs it issued. When this was not done, and as the DZU-produced CDs flooded the lucrative Russian market, Bulgaria appeared on the list of countries grossly violating international copyright laws.

The interesting part of the story begins when, in the aftermath of the 1997 general elections, newly appointed government officials tried to restore government control over the state-owned DZU. Envoys from the Ministry of Industry quickly discovered that the contract between DZU and Intercom could not be found and that the business transactions between the two "partners" were impossible to monitor. Bent upon resolving this matter, the government appointed a general from the Ministry of the Interior to the board of directors. He soon concluded, however, that the entire documentation related to DZU's partnerships and export activities was missing. Then an effort was made to establish more stringent control over the export of DZU-manufactured CDs to Russia and to enforce some of the provisions of the copyright law. At this juncture, Intercom/Multigroup arranged for airplanes owned by Russian oil giant Gazprom to ship the CDs directly from Stara Zagora, thus circumventing Bulgarian customs regulations. Within DZU itself, the maintenance of the CD assembly equipment became the sole purpose of Atanassov's team of managers, and as the high-tech business of Intercom thrived, DZU, once a mighty electronics manufacturer, was reduced to producing ovens, simple alarm systems, and lamps. In late 1997, Atanassov was finally dismissed—only to resume his career in Multigroup—but subsequent efforts to resuscitate the DZU were largely unsuccessful. Moreover, with the disappearance of the information about the Bulgarian electronics industry previously stored at DZU, a huge black hole was opened in the informational data base available to state officials. The prospects for a national strategy for the revival of this branch of the economy being worked out any time soon are dim.

The case of DZU suggests that the activities of winners might be directly related to what may be broadly defined as deindustrialization of SOEs in post-Communism. In the literature on post-Communist Eastern Europe this process is always attributed to exogenous factors, such as the vicissitudes of global industrial competition and the influx of cheap imports in the wake of economic liberalization.[27] In this case, however, deindustrialization was endogenously created by actors within the SOE itself by means of what one might call "compartmentalization." The lines between "high-tech" and "low-profit" types of production are drawn *within* the same industrial unit, with the predictable result that the state and its private partners enjoy quite different rates of profit. Deindustrialization through compartmentalization is propelled not by uncontrollable global processes but by localized techniques for redistributing profits.

Ultimately, Multigroup lost its hegemonic position. After the electoral victory of the anti-Communist opposition in 1997 the political fortunes of Multigroup took a downturn, and its formidable economic influence began to wane.[28] But these three affairs undoubtedly lead to the conclusion that the "entrepreneurs" running the conglomerate were the archetypical post-Communist winners. Their victories affected Bulgaria's geostrategic position, transformed entire sectors of the Bulgarian economy, and altered the patterns of management of the largest publicly owned enterprises. But there is more to the story of Multigroup than the familiar message that the nomenklatura of yesterday will be the economic Gullivers of today.

The Nature and Consequences of Vetoes and Redistributive Conflicts

Arguably my most important empirical finding is that we need to distinguish between elements of "collusion" and "antagonism" in the relationship between winners and various state agencies. It is undeniably true that relatively early in the process of economic restructuring Multigroup was involved in conversions of power—it mobilized nomenklatura-centered networks in order to gain strategic positions in various sectors of the economy. Lobbies operating *within* the administration were indisputably used when winners tried to gain access to state resources. Contacts with insiders constituted the cornerstone of future victories. The "collusion stage" is to a large extent characterized by the same impetus that propelled the

---

27. See Gernot Grabher, "Adaptation at the Cost of Adaptability?" in *Restructuring Networks in Post-Socialism*, ed. David Stark and Grabher (Oxford: Oxford University Pres, 1997), 107–33.

28. When the non-Communist Union of Democratic Forces (UDF) government was replaced by a government headed by Bulgaria's former king, Simeon Saxkoburggostski, in 2001, Multigroup attempted a—partially successful—comeback. It managed to place several sympathizers in key positions in the executive branch and the legislature. This partial revival was cut short, however, when Ilia Pavlov was assassinated in Sofia in early 2003—one of many unsolved politically important murders.

separation and the early conversions: the disappearance of—to use an expression coined by Guillermo O'Donnell—the "publicness" of state institutions (and primarily those entrusted with the management of state property) and their transformation into tools deployed for private uses.[29] Notably, however, at this stage the institutions themselves remained standing. The Multigroup saga suggests, however, that the situation of early winners remained precarious, and they soon faced the prospect of being dislodged from the lucrative niches where they operated. A succession of governments repeatedly tried to eliminate Multigroup from the gas trade, to cancel its contracts with large state-owned enterprises, and to restore central supervision over strategic "locales" dominated by the conglomerate. A second phase in the relationship between winners and state agencies ensued. This "antagonism" stage was marked by state agencies' efforts to reestablish control over resource-rich locales and flows of assets. From this point on, Multigroup's success hinged on its ability to guard its slice of the gas trade, to prevent the government from overseeing the financial operations of the largest state-owned industrial giants, and to stave off the efforts of the center to monitor the management of key industrial units. As the struggle to dislodge the conglomerate intensified, contested sites of rent extraction were plunged into darkness and turned into dangerous zones that governmental agents found increasingly hard to penetrate. It is important, therefore, to specify the analytically important aspects of Multigroup's veto power.

In his analysis of the role of powerful actors in political decision making, Giovanni Sartori asserts that empirical claims about the influence of "controlling groups" (such as the winners in post-Communism) should be grounded in a conceptual framework that illuminates the nature of power wielded by these groups.[30] There are two possible ways to conceptualize the "veto mechanisms" that allow winners to prevail, and both are related to conflicting interpretations of the notion of "veto points." According to one interpretation, cogently developed by Ellen M. Immergut, "veto points" are defined as "points of strategic uncertainty that arise from the logic of the decision-making process itself."[31] This understanding of veto

---

29. Guillermo O'Donnell, "On the State, Democratization, and Some Conceptual Problems," in *Counterpoints* (Notre Dame, Ind.: University of Notre Dame Press, 1999), 133–58.

30. Giovanni Sartori, *The Theory of Democracy Revisited*, vol. 1 (Chatham, N.J.: Chatham House, 1987).

31. Ellen M. Immergut, "The Rules of the Game," in *Structural Politics*, ed. Sven Steinmo, Kathleen Thelen, and Frank Longstreth (Cambridge: Cambridge University Press, 1992), 57–89. Along the same lines, see George Tsebelis, "Decision Making in Political Systems," *British Journal of Political Science* 25, no. 1 (Fall 1995): 289–325.

power presupposes the existence of procedures operating in a more or less coherent political environment. Accordingly, the emphasis is on how political actors are empowered and constrained by formal rules, their participation in electoral struggles, and their involvement in the dynamic process of institutionalized decision making. An alternative view of "veto points" is suggested by Minxin Pei in his comparative study of "complete" and "incomplete" forms of state socialism. "Veto power" is the ability of strategically located actors to create bottlenecks to the implementation of policies that they perceive as threatening, for example by withdrawing information and causing procedural delays.[32] Although political outcomes still reflect the preferences of identifiable organized actors, the tactics of these actors bear little resemblance to the imposition of "vetoes" in the context of a constitutionalized decision-making process. Rather, the emphasis here is on informal influence, subterranean sabotages, and the dynamics of policy implementation more generally. By dint of simplification, one may assert that scholars such as Helmann are more likely to cast the behavior of post-Communist winners in terms of Immergut's "veto points"; based on my research, I am persuaded that Pei's interpretation is more adequate in a post-Communist context.

This analytical perspective mandates an important adjustment of focus. It requires a shift away from the official political arena and toward a more elaborate analysis of the patterns of "local" interactions between successful post-Communist entrepreneurs and concrete state agencies. It also necessitates a novel interpretation of the connectedness of economic change and the reconfiguration of state structures in post-Communism. Hector Schamis has argued that "privatization is more about state building than about state shrinking and retreating," and my analysis of Multigroup's success confirms the cogency of this general insight.[33] Where I part ways with Schamis is on the question of whether the interplay of privatization and institutional change makes the state stronger or weaker. Schamis concludes that because "market reform does not necessarily dismantle rents; in fact it can generate new ones," this process necessarily entails "the reassertion of state power." In contrast, I have shown that the veto power exercised by nonstate actors may in fact *undermine* the logistical capacity of the state to dominate the organizational landscape. My analysis of the success of Multigroup suggests that the process of uncaging resources formerly held in the public domain may ultimately culminate in the fracturing of the state monopoly

---

32. Minxin Pei, "Microfoundations of State Socialism and Patterns of Economic Transformation," *Communist and Post-Communist Studies* 29, no. 2 (Spring 1996): 131–46.

33. Compare Hector Schamis, *Re-Forming the State* (Ann Arbor: University of Michigan Press, 2002), 6.

on political decision making. The link between privatization and state transformation does *not* necessarily run through the policy-making process, and emerging institutional configurations do *not* necessarily reflect the policy preferences of decision makers. It is the conflictual dynamic triggered by logistical rivalries on the microlevel rather than the macro incompatibility between "market mechanisms" and "bureaucratic regulation" that shapes patterns of fluctuation in administrative capacity in early post-Communism.

Let me now acknowledge the inherent limitations of the case study approach in the analysis of winners and state weakness. There are important questions related to the impact of "post-Communist success" on state capacity that I cannot answer. More systematic data is needed in order to formulate hypotheses regarding the factors that determine the relative strength of prostate and antistate coalitions. Perhaps even more important, I cannot determine under what conditions "winners" will gain a foothold in a fledgling market domain and thus gradually scale down their predatory forays into the state domain. When will winners feel the need for a stronger state and be willing to cooperate in its creation and maintenance? A case study is not a good empirical foundation for tackling these theoretical challenges.

Another caveat: the story of the rise and fall of a single corporate actor does not constitute a promising launching pad for those willing to venture generalizable statements about what one might call "patterns of diffusion of state decay." Certainly some state agencies are more likely to be targeted by predators than others, and it is plausible to assume that this pattern of decay will spread beyond the locale of immediate clashes between winners and state agencies. Further research may help us determine how and when that will happen, and in what direction decay is more likely to spread. However, my attempt at reconnaissance of this analytical terrain does lend credence to an important hypothesis. A look at the concrete state structures that sustained logistical damage as a result of being targeted by Multigroup—state monopolies supposedly defending the public interest (like Bulgargaz); large industrial units in the public sector (like DZU); bureaucratic agencies that monitor and coordinate the activities of state-owned enterprises (like the Ministry of Industry); key state institutions that solidify the infrastructure of market exchanges (like lower-level courts)—suggests that winners have an incentive to neutralize or render ineffective precisely those components of the state machinery that might be used in the pursuit of gradual, meticulously managed, rationally planned modes of "transition to a market economy." Much has been written about the issue of whether shock therapy and similar neoliberal blueprints for rapid marketization are "utopian"—and the scholarly consensus, perhaps for a good reason, tends to favor a positive answer to this question. What my analysis of the statist implications of winners' behavior hints at is that strategies for marketization that assume the existence of the administrative machinery necessary for careful, farsighted, and socially responsible gradual reforms might be equally far-fetched. Rather than a confrontation between "utopianism" and "realism," the overheated debates about the vices of shock therapy should perhaps be considered a clash of two ultimately quite similar modes of wishful thinking.[34]

Although the cases I examine here will not bring such intellectual exchanges to an end, they might at least make it clearer that the problems of early post-Communism cannot be explained in terms of the generic effects of capitalism and markets. The case of Multigroup highlights the most conspicuous difference between post-Communist and market-based societies. In a capitalist economic domain, Randall Collins has argued, success goes to those who use the state to force others to play by market rules while they themselves remain exempt from these rules.[35] Post-Communism is a habitat in which powerful networks seek to become exempted from the state itself. Insofar as the veto power of winners exacerbates the atrophy of state structures that might potentially be used to reverse early post-Communist successes, it creates the concrete institutional preconditions of such exemptions.

Economic Changes and State Restructuring

As Karen Barkey has pointed out in an influential book, to analyze state transformation is to dissect the dynamics of "the diversity of conflicts" that erupt if and when state structures are established or radically altered.[36] The Multigroup story elucidates one particular facet of the conflicts that left a lasting imprint on the edifice of the Bulgarian post-Communist state: the conflict unleashed by winners who were prone to find themselves in a precarious situation. What is particularly important to grasp is that the rivalry unleashed when collusion is eclipsed by hostility is structurally determined. The clash between state agencies and newly emerging nonstate actors stems from the very nature of redistributive struggles in post-Communism: what is subject to redistribution are resources hoarded in the public domain. As the prominent Bulgarian economist Roumen Avramov noted, this redistribution is "the truly relevant process changing

---

34. For a similar insight into the ongoing discussions of the course of economic changes in Russia in the 1990s, see M. Steven Fish, *Democracy Derailed in Russia* (New York: Cambridge University Press, 2005).
35. Randall Collins, *Conflict Sociology* (New York: Academic Press, 1975).
36. Karen Barkey, *Bandits and Bureaucrats* (Ithaca: Cornell University Press, 1994), 235.

the nature of economy and society."³⁷ The state sector of the economy, or the resource base targeted by powerful predators, is the *same* resource base from which post-Communist politicians derive their revenue—in fact, it is the *only* resource base deliberately nurtured and unexpectedly left unguarded by the defunct state-socialist regimes. As such, it is bound to be a domain of organizational outflanking and predatory campaigns. Why particular governments decide to dislodge temporarily entrenched nonstate actors is largely irrelevant for the purposes of my analysis—such steps may be undertaken by politicians wishing to streamline public resources and respond to constituency pressure or by state agents hired by rival networks bent on obtaining their cut of the spoils. But the crucial fact is that redistributive strategies in post-Communism inevitably pit winners against state agencies. Multigroup was compelled to resort to its veto power when the Bulgarian government attempted to renegotiate strategic gas deals, when governmental officials tried to monitor financial transactions, and when ministries got serious about exercising their ownership rights. And, logically, it emerged victorious when the government's negotiating power was reduced, administrative agencies were undermined, and generals from the Ministry of the Interior could not retrieve vital economic information. Once we construe "economic restructuring" as "redistribution of state resources," we are in a better position to understand "vetoes." These activities are intended not so much to block specific policies as to reduce the scope of effective policy implementation in general. The three cases give us an idea about the kinds of weapons available in the arsenal of winners: hijacking information, theft of important documents, assassination of or death threats against state officials, disruption of channels of communication. Precisely because winning is sustained by a peculiar amalgam of formal decisions and informal practices, to interpret the strategic opportunities opened to the nomenklatura exclusively in terms of "rent seeking" and "market distortions" would be somewhat misleading. Although the tightly knit group of cadres that coalesced around Multigroup's Ilia Pavlov tried to exploit relations with public officials, these parasitical activities were not "rent seeking."³⁸ The concept occludes important aspects of the strategies of winners and thus obscures the full ramifications of post-Communist success. To be sure, post-Communist winners enjoyed and still enjoy the support of political lobbies, but, as the case of

---

37. Roumen Avramov, "Macroeconomic Stabilization," in *Economic Transition in Bulgaria*, ed. Avramov and Ventzeslav Antonov (Sofia: AECD, 1994), 7–37.

38. For some critical comments regarding the indiscriminate use of the term "rent-seeking," see Jane Prokop, "Industrial Conglomerates, Risk Spreading, and the Transition in Russia," *Communist Economies and Economic Transformation* 7, no. 1 (Fall 1995): 35–50.

Multigroup amply demonstrates, the resort to "normal" interest-group politics is a sign of weakness rather than of strength. The favors of parliamentarians and courts are sought only when low-level, subterranean connections are disrupted. To deepen our analytical understanding of the role of winners, it is necessary to move beyond abstract designations such as "rent seeking"—designations coined with other economic systems and institutional orders in mind—and consider context-specific theoretical and empirical questions, questions that better capture the peculiarities of the post-Communist institutional landscape. How the winners' veto power affects state structures and administrative capacity is a question that opens such an alternative analytical path. It was not on the national political arena that Multigroup imposed its vetoes, but through the systematic incapacitation of state organs that interfere with local mechanisms for redistributing national wealth.

One corollary of the view of veto power adumbrated above is that the institutional consequences of winners' domination should be distinguished from, and perhaps accorded greater significance than, social consequences. Hellman is certainly right in maintaining that the protracted domination of early winners has a deleterious effect and precipitates a large-scale redistribution of resources that leaves most people much worse off. But the case of Multigroup also suggests that, prior to being a phenomenon whose macro effects could be understood in terms of social stratification, winning in post-Communism should be considered as a set of micro social actions that undermine the institutional framework of governance. It is precisely within the domain of political institutions that the behavior of winners reverberates with independent causal power. The analytically amplified understanding of the nature of "vetoes" presented in this chapter—an understanding that lies at the intersection of two broader theoretical themes, post-Communist success and the transformation of state structures—allows us to better comprehend the syndromes of state dysfunctionality that bedeviled Bulgaria after 1989. Multigroup's actions further aggravated the institutional problems created by the separation of party and state and the conversion of political power into economic influence. Once winners began to systematically target resource-rich locales (such as DZU), the "transaction costs of ruling" these locales increased exponentially—field-level officials became more difficult to monitor, information-gathering mechanisms grew harder to maintain, and regulations became harder to enforce.[39]

---

39. On "the transaction costs of ruling," see Margaret Levy, *Of Rule and Revenue* (Berkeley: University of California Press, 1988), chaps. 1 and 2.

The blunting of existing tools of governance cannot be easily offset by constructing new administrative units. It should not be assumed, once information is hijacked and channels of communication are disrupted, that insight, political will, and the resources of the state elites will lead to corresponding institutional creation. With the institution-building process stalled, the conditions "underlying effective state intervention" may not obtain.[40] And once winners are challenged to respond to public officials' attempts to reassert the state's institutional supremacy, they instantly resort to what Joel Migdal has called of "the politics of dirty tricks": persistent and at times violent intimidation of state agents, including physical assault and assassinations.[41] Winners' vetoes, then, weaken the state by making various segments of the public sector impervious to coordinated reforms, rapidly diminishing the operational capacity of the bureaucratic machinery, and infecting the social milieu with fear, rendering the quick regeneration of state structures unlikely.

The Multigroup story also suggests that the flip side of post-Communist success is the deinstitutionalization of the public domain. Ronald L. Jepperson defined "institutionalization" in the following way: "An institution is a social pattern that reveals a particular reproduction process. When departures from the pattern are counteracted in a regulated fashion, by repetitively activated, socially constructed, controls—that is, by some set of rewards and sanctions—we refer to a pattern as institutionalized."[42] Long-term winners' projects, such as the Himko and the DZU affairs, eventually seek to ensure the following outcome: departures from state-sanctioned patterns of behavior will not be "counteracted in a regulated fashion" and will be scrutinized only intermittently, if at all. In the course of the competitive struggle for control over resources, the reproduction of informal networks necessitates the incapacitation of formal state structures. That is why the attempt of winners to preserve their influence will have a deinstitutionalizing effect on the system of rule enforcement.

The crux of the Multigroup story, then, can be summarized in the following way: the amassing of private fortunes during early post-Communism was a process that constituted part of the broader dynamic reshaping the

---

40. Peter Evans and Dietrich Rueschemeyer, "The State and Economic Transformation," in *Bringing the State Back In*, ed. Evans, Rueschemeyer, and Theda Skocpol (Cambridge: Cambridge University Press, 1985), 44–77.

41. Joel Migdal, *Strong Societies and Weak States* (Princeton: Princeton University Press, 1988), 214–26.

42. See Ronald J. Jepperson, "Institutions, Institutional Effects, and Institutionalism," in *The New Institutionalism in Organizational Analysis*, ed. Walter W. Powell and Paul J. DiMaggio (Chicago: University of Chicago Press, 1991), 145.

infrastructure of governance. But it also suggests something else: the most important functional characteristic of post-Communist winners is that they are state *breakers,* not state *makers.* Admittedly, the intermittent clashes between powerful actors and assorted agencies hardly resembles the captivating scenarios conveying the drama of state breaking that feature ethnic rebels, secessionist movements, and civil wars. And yet the subaltern institutional rivalries, the low-visibility logistics of organizational outflanking that are the central theme of this chapter, have an impact on state institutions that is no less profound and debilitating. Unlike Tillian "rulers," Marxist "ruling classes," or Olsonian "redistributive coalitions," powerful elites in post-Communism do not need the state. This is the paramount element of historical specificity in the analysis of the post-Communist political condition. The winners in post-Communism are not forced to rely, directly or indirectly, on the extractive and redistributive capacities of the state because everything they need has already been extracted for them and stored in the loosely monitored "public domain." Hence the deliberate weakening and even demolition of state structures is a sine qua non for "winning." The demolition of the state does not come about as the realization of an insidious comprehensive plan; state structures are whittled away as winners strive to perpetuate their victories. That is why rethinking the patterns of relations between winners and states as it evolves in the course of redistributive struggles is a major challenge for analysts willing to probe the dilemmas of post-Communism.

What are the implications of these relations? In various writings, Mancur Olson objects to the widespread usage of the metaphor "slicing the pie" as a way of depicting the activities of "distributional coalitions." These activities, he argues, are much more destructive than the benign imagery suggests; we'd do better to think of these actors as "wrestlers struggling over the contents of a china shop."[43] Even Olson's updated and emphatically more sinister metaphor is inadequate in the context of early post-Communism. Mechanisms for reallocation of resources under these conditions trigger what I will call the Dorian Gray Effect. The story to which I refer is told by Oscar Wilde in his remarkable novel *The Picture of Dorian Gray.* Dorian Gray is a reckless and arrogant person who keeps a picture of himself in the attic of his house. As the years pass by, he slides ever deeper into the abyss of immorality and crime. Miraculously, however, his stunning looks seem impervious to change: not a single wrinkle or a shade of emotional turmoil mars a youthful face that preserves its irresistible appeal. At the same time, however, the face on the

---

43. See, for example, Mancur Olson, *The Rise and Decline of Nations* (New Haven: Yale University Press, 1982), and Olson, "A Theory of the Incentives Facing Political Organizations," *International Political Science Review* 7, no. 2 (1986): 169–83.

picture in the attic grows ever uglier and more repulsive, changing for the worse after every act of moral transgression perpetrated by Dorian. This strange synergy makes it impossible to consign the existence of Dorian and his picture to separate spheres of being. It is the picture that bears testimony to the true nature of Dorian's actions; it is Dorian's behavior that provides the key for comprehending the seemingly unfathomable forces that propel the degrading metamorphosis of the picture.

It seems to me that the Dorian Gray metaphor captures at least two aspects of post-Communist redistribution better than Olson's "wrestlers in a china shop." To begin with, the process is much quieter—the disconcerting sound of breaking china is not likely to be heard until much later, when the main protagonists have already vanished from the scene. From a societal point of view the re-allocation of resources takes place as silently as the magic emanations of Dorian's misdeeds are registered upon the painting. The well-financed lobbying campaigns that pit powerful organized groups against each other and trigger successive rounds of backstage and onstage maneuvering do not have a functional equivalent in early post-Communism. Even in cases when relations between winners and state agencies escalate to a phase of open hostilities, information about important events is scarce, and hardly anybody possesses the information necessary to connect the dots. The media campaigns, talk show duels, committee hearings, and official disclosures in which Olson's well-organized "wrestlers" are compelled to participate in were not embraced as tactical weapons by winners during the first decade of post-Communist transformations. Second, the process is much less visible; it does not take place in a shop or other public area. Occasional bloody skirmishes, which rarely lead to arrests, are all that the casual observer witnesses. Post-Communist redistribution is rarely "mediated" by the visible parts (government or parliament) of the institutional edifice; rather, it unfolds in the impenetrable universe of administrative agencies, ministerial departments, and customs offices.

The Dorian Gray Effect conveys the idea that analysts of post-Communist "economic success" have every reason to conclude, like Tom Stoppard's Gildenstern, that the phenomenon is indicative of something besides the redistribution of wealth. The flip side of the engrossing stories of this or that conglomerate's triumphs is the shrinking of the assets available for alleviating the numerous crises of the transition— as well as the institutional means that may be employed in pursuit of salutary state intervention. The effects of dominant modes of redistribution in post-Communist political capitalism necessarily entail the deepening of wrinkles and scars on the institutional "face" of the state. The health of networks, cronies, and winners accounts for the chronic malfunctioning of the instruments of governance. One hopes that, sooner or later, a post-Communist version of the process of Schumpeterian "creative destruction" will sweep predatory victors off the historical stage. A glance at the ubiquitous mechanisms that underpin the Dorian Gray Effect would suggest, however, that an alternative outcome is also possible: it is state structures that may be destroyed and thrown by the wayside, empty shells that may serve as a lasting reminder of the inglorious deeds of post-Communist winners.

5 Weak-State Constitutionalism

> What are the roots that clutch, what branches grow out of
> this stony rubbish?
>
> T. S. Eliot, *The Waste Land*

The collapse of one-party regimes in Eastern Europe marked the beginning of ambitious constitutional reforms whose ultimate objective was to lay the institutional basis for democratic governance and the rule of law. These reforms constitute the archetypical form of "state-building," a term defined by Francis Fukuyama as "the creation of new government institutions and the strengthening of existing ones."[1] Fukuyama's definition is not perfect, but it does rest on a commonsensical proposition whose soundness is hard to dispute, namely that inquiries into state-building should encompass both dimensions of institutional change, that is, the deliberate making of *new* institutions and the revamping of *inherited* state apparatuses. Any comprehensive narrative about the engineering of novel constitutional configurations should embrace the state-centered perspective on the metamorphoses of existing state structures as a necessary component. Once the exploration of constitution-making is wedded to analysis of the transformation of nonconstitutional administrative and bureaucratic structures, it becomes possible to adequately depict the contradictory dynamic and complex outcomes of large-scale institutional change during the crucial first decade of post-Communist transformations. Such conceptually sharp and theoretically engrossing depictions, in turn, allow us to distill from the post-Communist experience a set of general hypotheses about what is likely to happen when constitutional experiments mimicking Western models are launched in a historically structured non-Western setting.

---

1. Francis Fukuyama, *State-Building* (Ithaca: Cornell University Press, 2004), ix.

By superimposing a detailed account of Bulgarian constitutional experiments onto the preceding inquiry of institutional change, I hope to make a two-pronged contribution to the study of the multiplicity of processes that might be legitimately subsumed under the category "state-building" in a concrete historical context. First, I offer a novel interpretation of the complexity of outcomes observable in the aftermath of constitutional reforms. As will become clear in a moment, I contend that all of the following statements more or less adequately depict various aspects of Bulgarian post-Communist constitutionalism: as a result of the dynamic of state-building after 1989, political elites were reined in; as a result of the dynamic of state-building after 1989 political elites retained their ability to engage in unrestrained predatory action; institutional changes led to the solidification of the framework of governance—institutional changes led to the unraveling of the framework of governance; by the mid-1990s the political field was structured and stabilized; by the mid-1990s the political field was smashed. How such seemingly contradictory claims can be reconciled will become clear once we buttress them with a coherent conceptual analysis of emerging institutional configurations. Moreover, the two chapters that follow will examine the peculiar *patterns* of success and failure of constitutional initiatives. Some constitutional experiments in Bulgaria worked rather well, and others failed—a divergence of outcomes which is hard to explain by looking at the determining factors which scholars who analyze constitutional reforms habitually invoke. In sum, my exploration of the complexity of constitutional developments will pay heed to the empirical richness of observable outcomes without abandoning the ambition to situate such outcomes in a theoretically informed analytical framework.

The second contribution that the following chapters will make is to explain exactly how and why the *institutional context* shaped the course of constitutional experiments. The general proposition that "context matters" is fairly uncontroversial. But, as Kathryn Stoner-Weiss remarked, a similar consensus does not surround "more interesting questions" such as "how, why and what aspects of context are more important."[2] The state-centered approach articulated in the three previous chapters elucidates the dynamic characteristics of the institutional environment, particularly the palpable trend toward heightened dysfunctionality of state structures, decreased capacity of bureaucratic apparatuses, and ongoing plundering of the state domain, all of which constitute the relevant context in which freshly minted constitutional structures will have to survive . . .

---

2. Kathryn Stoner-Weiss, *Local Heroes* (Princeton: Princeton University Press, 1997), 3.

or die. A corollary of this is that factors such as culture, levels of socioeconomic development, the nature of political cleavages, and the strategic calculus of constitution makers had limited impact on the coalescence of institutional arrangements. The combined emphasis on complexity and context bespeaks a methodological choice in favor of inductive examination of observable empirical trends and actually emerging institutional configurations. This bias, however, should not be construed as a manifestation of the ill-conceived desire to engage in ideographical pursuits unencumbered by nomothetic ambitions. In fact, the exact opposite is true—as Paul Pierson points out, "it is probably only through careful tracing of particular historical processes that many of the key theoretical questions about institutional change could even be formulated."[3] It is precisely the accumulation of better-quality data in the quest for theoretically important questions about state-building in post-Communism that my integrative approach—an approach that encompasses the creation of the new and the metamorphosis of the existing—seeks to accomplish. What forms of predatory elite behavior are relevant under conditions of state-building—and how? What are the possible scenarios when the dynamic "creation from above" intersects with the dynamic of "revamping from below"? Which aspects of the Bulgarian experience may help us get a better grip on the problems likely to arise when state-building modeled after Western experiences with democracy and the rule of law is attempted in a non-Western milieu? These are the questions that inform my analysis of the Bulgarian case.

In this chapter I present a general overview of the attempt to construct a wholly new set of state structures in post-Communist Bulgaria. In chapter 6, I will focus on the significance of contextual factors for institutional experiments by examining patterns of success and failure of institution-building "from above"—specifically at the widely diverging trajectories of rather similar institutional experiments, the attempt to establish an autonomous constitutional court and to create an independent central bank.

The Study of Post-Communist Constitutionalism

The attempt to institutionalize new political systems in post-Communist Eastern Europe has attracted scholarly attention, and yet research programs that focus on this large-scale phenomenon have been somewhat *one-sided* and *underdeveloped*. They have been one-sided because one question has eclipsed all others: whether Western constitutional practices have been successfully transplanted on post-Communist soil. A historical

---

3. Paul Pierson, *Politics in Time* (Princeton: Princeton University Press, 2004), 140.

contrast will clarify this contention. In his commentary on the wave of constitution-making that swept across the world in the aftermath of World War II, Karl Loewenstein pointed out that technical legalistic analyses of constitutional provisions "overshadow what may be called the *ontology of constitutions*, that is, the investigation of what a written constitution really means within a specific national environment [and] how real it is for the common people."[4] In the mushrooming literature on post-Communism, the opposite tendency has prevailed. To be sure, constitutional norms have been subject to assiduous textual interpretation, constitutionally established regimes have been carefully classified, and the similarities and differences with Western models duly pointed out.[5] And yet, even the most technical studies of the constitutional aspects of political change in Eastern Europe inevitably return to "ontological" questions: Is the essence of Western constitutionalism adequately replicated in local contexts? Have the values of liberal democracy been sincerely embraced? Is the rule of law real?

Maybe it was this obsession with the authenticity of fledgling constitutional orders and the deep meaning of constitutional norms that prompted the prominent German social scientist Klaus von Beyme to quip that "political science has left constitutional engineering to lawyers."[6] What his complaint suggests is that research programs that focus on post-Communist constitutionalism have been *underdeveloped* because debates about legal and jurisdictional issues have overshadowed analytical accounts about how constitutional norms have shaped political practices and the institutional environment more generally. To be sure, certain aspects of constitutional reform have attracted the attention of political scientists. The events of 1989, for example, marked the reopening of a set of normative issues that fueled the prescription-oriented debates about the best institutional strategies for building democracy. Simmering controversies about the relative merits and disadvantages of presidentialism vs. parliamentarism, majoritarian vs. proportional representation (PR) electoral systems were rekindled after 1989.[7] Predictably, however, the bulk of analyses were

---

4. See Karl Loewenstein, "Reflections on the Value of Constitutions in Our Revolutionary Age," in *Constitutions and Constitutional Trends since World War II*, ed. Arnold J. Zurcher (New York: New York University Press, 1951), 191; emphasis added.

5. See, for example, Rett R. Ludwikowski, *Constitution-Making in the Region of Former Soviet Dominance* (Durham: Duke University Press, 1996).

6. Klaus von Beyme, "Institutional Engineering and Transition to Democracy," in *Democratic Consolidation in Eastern Europe*, ed. Jan Zielonka (Oxford: Oxford University Press, 2001), 3.

7. See Juan J. Linz, "Introduction: Some Thoughts on Presidentialism in Postcommunist Europe," in *Postcommunist Presidents*, ed. Ray Taras (Cambridge: Cambridge University Press, 1997), 1–14; Donald L. Horowitz, "Comparing Democratic Systems," in *The*

devoted to institutional choice: Why do elites choose to institutionalize one set of arrangements over available alternatives? Why do some countries have bicameral parliaments, whereas others choose single-chamber legislatures? What are the strategic considerations in the light of which one set of electoral rules would appear to relevant political agents to be superior to available alternatives?[8] And there has been a veritable cottage industry dedicated to the comparative study of post-Communist presidencies. What is the calculus behind the choice of a presidential over parliamentary constitutional system? Why do constitution makers choose to make a presidency strong . . . or weak? What are the likely implications of the installment of presidential regimes? These questions have been repeatedly addressed by astute observers of post-Communist politics.[9] It would perhaps be premature to assert that a consensus has begun to emerge with regard to all these issues.[10] But it cannot be gainsaid that scholarly exchanges about the post-Communist presidencies revolve around clearly defined hypotheses, and have been integrated in research programs. They are also vibrant and interesting.

Global Resurgence of Democracy, ed. Larry Diamond and Mark Plattner (Baltimore: Johns Hopkins University Press, 1996), 143–49; Stephen Holmes, "Back to the Drawing Board," *East European Constitutional Review* (Winter 1993): 24–28; Maurice Duverger, "The Political System of the European Union," *European Journal of Political Research* 31, no. 1 (Spring 1997): 137–40. On electoral systems, see Arend Lijphart, "Constitutional Choices for New Democracies," in *Global Resurgence*, 162–74, and Guy Lardeyret, "The Problem with PR," *Global Resurgence*, 175–80.

8. On the design of legislatures, see Jon Elster, "Transition, Constitution-Making and Separation in Czechoslovakia," *European Journal of Sociology* 36, no. 1 (1995): 105–34, and Petr Kopecky, "The Czech Republic," in *Democratic Consolidation in Eastern Europe*, 319–46. On the factors conditioning the choice of electoral systems, see Pauline Jones-Luong, "After the Break-Up," *Comparative Political Studies* 33, no. 5 (June 2000): 563–92.

9. See, for example, Ray Taras, ed., *Postcommunist Presidents* (New York: Cambridge University Press, 1997); Gerald Easter, "Preference for Presidentialism," *World Politics* 49, no. 2 (January 1997): 184–211; Timothy Frye, "A Politics of Institutional Choice," *Comparative Political Studies* 30, no. 5 (October 1997): 523–52; Jon Elster, "Miscalculations in the Design of the East European Presidencies," *East European Constitutional Review* 2, no. 4 (Winter 1994), and 3, no. 1 (Spring 1995): 95–98; Stephen Holmes, "Semipresidentialism and Its Problems," *East European Constitutional Review* 2, no. 4 (Winter 1994), and 3, no. 1 (Spring 1995): 123–26; and M. Steven Fish, "The Dynamics of Democratic Erosion," in *Postcommunism and the Theory of Democracy*, ed. Richard Anderson et al. (Princeton: Princeton University Press, 2001), 54–95.

10. There seems to be a consensus that the strength of the presidency is negatively correlated with economic progress and democratic consolidation. See, for example, Juan Linz and Alfred Stepan, *Problems of Democratic Transition and Consolidation* (Baltimore: Johns Hopkins University Press, 1996); for a general overview of this debate, see Joel Hellman, "Constitutions and Economic Reform in the Post-Communist Transitions," in *The Rule of Law and Economic Reform in Russia*, ed. Jeffrey Sachs and Katharina Pistor (Boulder: Westview Press, 1997), 55–78; and Fish, "Dynamics of Democratic Erosion," on institutional design and democratic consolidation.

In stark contrast, institutions other than the presidencies and periods other than those immediately preceding the choice of institutional configurations have received much less attention. To the extent that the overall evolution of newly established constitutional systems has been traced at all, this has been done primarily by scholars with legal backgrounds. A series of articles on "constitutional borrowing," for example, is much more likely to appear in a journal on constitutional law than in a comparative politics journal.[11] A book-length study of constitutional courts in Eastern Europe is much more likely to be authored by a professor of law than a professor of political science.[12] And chapters on constitutional change after 1989 are much more likely to be written by constitutional lawyers than by comparativists.[13] From this vantage point, von Beyme's complaint is certainly justified.

To the extent that political scientists have speculated about the fate of constitutional experiments, one particular hypothesis has been repeatedly conjured up, the hypothesis that the fate of institutional experiments is determined by the degree of compatibility between imported Western institutions and local cultural traditions. In an important article, entitled "The Primacy of Culture," Francis Fukuyama asserted that "the chief issue is quickly becoming one of culture" and that in the absence of a "deeper" cultural change, "social engineering on the level of institutions [will] hit a massive brick wall."[14] Along the same lines, Armin Hoeland, in a contribution to *European Legal Cultures* on post-Communist constitutional reforms, maintained that the import of Western constitutional models, far from contributing to democratization, will "create new opportunities for old failures."[15] And Harry Eckstein opined that constraining political action through constitutional means is "the most intractable problem in engineering social transformations" in nondemocratic cultures.[16] In the absence of the requisite cultural preconditions, institutional imports are likely to degenerate into "political mutations" or "rickety institutions which continue

---

11. See the special issue on "constitutional borrowing" of the *International Journal of Comparative Law* 1, no. 2 (April 2003).

12. See also Herman Schwartz, *The Struggle for Constitutional Justice in Postcommunist Europe* (Chicago: University of Chicago Press, 2002), and Wojciech Sadurski, *Rights before Courts* (Heidelberg: Springer, 2005).

13. See, for example, the country reports in Zielonka, *Democratic Consolidation in Eastern Europe*.

14. Francis Fukuyama, "The Primacy of Culture," in *Global Resurgence*, 322.

15. See Armin Hoeland, "Imposition without Adaptation?" in *European Legal Cultures*, ed. Volkmar Gessner, Hoeland, and Csaba Varga (Dartmouth, England: Aldershot, 1996), 484.

16. Harry Eckstein, "Lessons for the 'Third Wave' from the First," in *Can Democracy Take Root in Postcommunist Russia?* ed. Eckstein et al. (Lanham, Md.: Rowman and Littlefield, 1998), 273.

to exist, but are weak, deformed and cannot fulfill the proper function which they were originally assigned."[17] This preconceived notion may be why most accounts of constitutional reforms in Eastern Europe are permeated by a mood imbued with democratic gloom and constitutional angst. As Martin Krygier has noted, during the 1990s participants in the passionate debates about the future of Eastern Europe found it particularly hard to resist "the seductive, often apparently irresistible charms of pessimism."[18] When looked at through such analytical lenses, Bulgaria appeared particularly prone to suffer constitutional setbacks. Claus Offe summed up the conventional wisdom about that country when he bemoaned that "Bulgarians are not alone today in seeming far removed from the consciousness of ... a commitment ... to a new political beginning. Instead, the political majority culture of an 'authoritarian egalitarianism' that seems to prevail ... stands in the way both of a market economy and of democracy as uncontested goals for the process of reform."[19] The "charms of pessimism," then, have emanated from a rational hypothesis: the more immersed a society is in the values and cultural traditions of the past/East, the less likely it is to make the transition to the future/West. This line of reasoning would accordingly generate the hypothesis that constitutional experiments in Bulgaria would fail.

Was this prediction vindicated by subsequent developments? Did constitutional reforms in Bulgaria achieve their objectives ... or not? This stark question is important and should receive an adequate answer. The adequacy of the answer, however, can be ensured only if the analytical weaknesses that debilitate current research programs on post-Communist constitutionalism are overcome. The *one-sidedness* of such programs, or their obsession with "the ontology of constitutionalism," can be remedied by means of a more thorough and detailed empirical analysis. In other words, there is a dearth of knowledge about what exactly happened in countries such as Bulgaria. I offer a "thick description" of constitutional developments to give my analysis a firmer empirical grounding. All too often, the attempt to reduce the inquiry into constitutional reform to stylized accounts of how particular societies have or have not embraced Western models has led scholars astray; this problem can only be mitigated if the process whereby institutional novelties are transplanted onto local soil is scrutinized more assiduously than is usually the case.[20]

---

17. See Robert Sharlet, "Legal Transplants and Political Mutations," *East European Constitutional Review* 7, no. 4 (Fall 1998): 59–68.

18. Martin Krygier, "Traps for Young Players in Times of Transition," *East European Constitutional Review* 8, no. 4 (Fall 1999): 67.

19. Claus Offe, *Varieties of Transition* (Cambridge: MIT Press, 1996), 40.

20. On the pitfalls of a deductive analysis of post-Communist politics, see Michael Bernhard, "Institutional Choices after Communism," *East European Politics and Societies* 14, no. 2 (March 2000): 316–47.

The *underdevelopment* of research programs on post-Communist constitutional reforms, or the neglect of issues *not* related to the choice of institutional arrangements and the design of presidencies, can be redressed by exploring the diachronic aspect of institutional reforms, that is, how they unfolded over time. Of course, an overview of the basic principles and norms of the Bulgarian Constitution is indispensable, but my focus in on the constitutional practices and the evolution of the major constitutional structures from 1989 to 1997. As Alison Stranger has pointed out, during the first decade of state-building "from above" in Eastern Europe, scarce attention was paid to "the comparative study ... of what connections might exist between the constitutional revision process and subsequent political developments."[21] It is precisely the time dimension of constitutional experiments—how newly created structures evolved after the moment of choice—that is at the foreground of my inquiry.

Finally, an adequate answer to the question about the results of constitutional reforms should go beyond the somewhat simplistic success/failure dichotomy. Such an answer should expand our conceptual repertoire and enable us to assess the interrelatedness of the two different dimensions of state-building. It should enable us to gauge the functionality of institutional configurations that congealed when a set of deliberately created political institutions was superimposed on a preexisting grid of state structures. More broadly, an analytically sharpened survey of constitutional developments in a rapidly changing institutional environment should highlight both the transformative impact of human agency and the structural limits of attempts to radically revamp historically formed institutional environments through deliberate action. The major conceptual innovation I propose in this chapter, the notion of *weak-state constitutionalism*, lies at the intersection of such general themes pertaining to human agency, structural context, and institutional change, and demonstrates how these themes may be interwoven in a comprehensive account of state transformation in post-Communism.

Constitutional Choices

As the euphoria of the momentous events of 1989 began to recede, the task of laying the constitutional basis of the democratic order became the inescapable horizon of political thought and action in Eastern Europe. Right from the beginning political elites, Communist and

---

21. Compare Alison Stranger, "Leninist Legacies and Legacies of State Socialism in Postcommunist Central Europe's Constitutional Development," in *Capitalism and Democracy in Central and Eastern Europe*, ed. Stephen E. Hanson and Grzegorz Ekiert (Cambridge: Cambridge University Press, 2003), 182. The term "constitutional revision" used by Stranger is identical to the generic term "constitution-making," which I prefer.

non-Communist alike, had to tackle an imposing dilemma: Should they proceed at an accelerated speed with the adoption of a new constitution? Or should they postpone this immense endeavor until the seismic perturbations of the transition had calmed enough to allow for a shared vision of a good constitutional polity to emerge? The former strategy risked the final product of their collective effort looking more like the hastily scribbled notes of a passionate amateur than a brilliant masterpiece. Temporizing, on the other hand, could inadvertently usher in a protracted period of endless tinkering with an all-but-defunct institutional framework and eventually foreclose the constitutional option altogether. Bulgarian political elites, almost unanimously and without hesitation, committed themselves to creating a new constitution. Bulgaria, then, may serve as a case study of the benefits and disadvantages of the quick-fix type of constitution-making; only twenty months after the palace coup that deposed Zhivkov (November 10, 1989), a new basic law went into effect (July 13, 1991).

Consensus on a decision to hold general elections for a Great National Assembly (empowered to adopt a new constitution) was achieved during the roundtable held between Communist officials and representatives of the democratic opposition in January–April 1990.[22] At this early stage, Bulgaria's experiments with institution building were of a limited nature. Attaining a measure of trust and opening up heretofore blocked channels of communication between old and new elites was clearly a priority that overshadowed concerns about the enshrining of particular institutional models in a permanent legal framework. Even though the roundtable precipitated the passage of important amendments to the Communist constitution, the widely shared perception was that none of the existing political institutions was legitimate enough to be entrusted with the task of constitution-making and all reforms ought to be suspended until a popularly elected assembly was instituted.

The first multiparty elections, held in June 1990, were won by the former Communists, who controlled 217 votes in the 400-member Great National Assembly. The other seats were distributed among the major opposition parties, the Union of the Democratic Forces (UDF), with 144 deputies; the party of ethnic Turks, the Movement for Rights and Freedoms (MRF), with 23; and the Bulgarian Agrarian National Union (BANU), with 16. It should be stressed that despite this outcome the newly elected assembly clearly possessed what Elster calls "upstream legitimacy" or legitimacy from having come into being in a legitimate

---

22. On the roundtable, see an excellent study by Rumyana Kolarova and Dimiter Dimitrov, "The Roundtable Talks in Bulgaria," in *The Roundtable Talks and the Breakdown of Communism*, ed. Jon Elster (Chicago: University of Chicago Press, 1996), 178–213.

way.[23] But in due course it became clear that this legitimacy was vulnerable to the corrosive impact of a very specific factor: while working out the final text of the constitution, the assembly also busied itself with the passage of ordinary legislation, that is, with the governance of the country. As time progressed and the country began to slide into the depths of economic and social crisis, the legitimacy of the constitution-making process was questioned. The public proved susceptible to the view that if a group of politicians are incapable of solving the problems of "normal politics," there is no reason to expect they will fare better when confronted with the challenges of "constitutional politics." In the short run this functional duality—constitution-making paralleled by ordinary legislative activities—turned out to be a perilous threat to the legitimacy of the new constitution. That it was adopted by an assembly dominated by unrepentant ex-Communists did not help either.

The festering problems of the Great National Assembly were further exacerbated when it became clear that work on the constitutional text was consigned to the periphery of the parliamentarians' variegated interests. Rather than perfecting the métier of institutional engineering, the parliamentary majority seemed bent on indulging in the simple pleasures of incumbency. The sluggish work of the assembly provoked a group of thirty-nine members of parliament from the opposition to boycott parliament and launch a hunger strike, demanding an explicit deadline for the adoption of the constitution.[24] This rebellious act succeeded in spurring BSP elites into action, but at a high price. It aggravated tensions within the UDF, which soon split into three factions. The most radical faction remained implacably hostile to the new constitution and refused to sign it, whereas the two moderate factions continued their work alongside the former Communists. The constitution was not endorsed by a popular vote, although interesting stories unfolded regarding its ratification. First, a referendum was scheduled to forestall the allegations of monarchists that any constitution that did not heed popular opinion on the issue of the monarchy would be illegitimate. (Despite the visibility enjoyed by some monarchists, the overwhelming majority of Bulgarian citizens remained firmly committed to the idea of republican rule.) Then, for reasons that remain obscure to this day, the referendum was called off.

---

23. See Jon Elster, "Constitutionalism in Eastern Europe," *Public Administration* 71 (1993): 178. In the immediate aftermath of the June elections some opposition leaders questioned the electoral results; after a series of intense debates, however, the UDF took the official position that the outcome of the elections should be recognized. For more on UDF's dilemmas in 1990, see Nasja Kralevska, *Bez zaglavie* (Untitled) (Sofia: Rabotilnitza za knizhnina Vassil Stanilov, 2006).

24. On the hunger strike, see Iren Ribareva and Vjara Nikolova, eds., *Protestut na 39te* (The Protest of "the 39") (Sofia: 2000).

When in July 1991 the constitution was finally adopted with the requisite two-thirds majority of the Great National Assembly, President Zhelyu Zhelev refused to sign it. It was promulgated and subsequently published in the *State Gazette* with the signature of the chairman of the Great National Assembly. (Since Zhelev's signature was not necessary, his act had a purely symbolic significance.)

The new constitution forcefully corroborates the hypothesis that fundamental laws adopted by parliaments that possess *pouvoir constituant* usually ensure a strong role for the legislature in the freshly minted system of governance.[25] Article 1 of the Bulgarian Constitution proclaims that Bulgaria is a "republic with a parliamentary form of government." Despite the fact that parliament has to share the distinction of "representing the people" with a popularly elected president, its supremacy is guaranteed by the basic law. Policymaking falls squarely within the domain of parliament and the government: the president does not have the power to appoint ministers, cannot introduce draft legislation, and has a very weak veto (the veto may be overridden by an absolute majority vote in parliament). At the same time, the president does possess some power potential: the authority to make strategic appointments (ambassadors, four of the twelve Constitutional Court justices, several members of the board of directors of the National Bank, high-ranking military officers, and so on); guaranteed access to the national electronic media; and regular contacts with foreign dignitaries and opinion makers. The president cannot be dismissed by parliament (although, under Article 103, he may be impeached by the Constitutional Court pursuant to a motion filed with the court by no less than two-thirds of all deputies), and parliament can be dismissed by the president only if it fails in three successive attempts to install a government (Article 99). The constitution also established the office of vice president—arguably the only remnant of the past that somehow survived the constitution-making process. This position was first introduced in April 1990, that is, when the old constitution was amended by the last all-Communist parliament after the agreements made at the roundtable. At present, Bulgaria is the only East European country with a vice president, and it is plausible to assume that this position was not abolished by the new Bulgarian Constitution simply because it was already "there."

Bulgaria also has a Constitutional Court that consists of twelve members, with the president, the Great National Assembly, and the assembly of all judges sitting in the Supreme Court of Cassation (the highest appeals court) and the Supreme Administrative Court each appointing one-third of the justices (Article 147). The Constitutional Court has the power

---

25. See Elster, *Constitutionalism in Eastern Europe*, 192.

to invalidate laws that contradict the constitution (Articles 151 and 149); the fate of this institution is discussed in more detail in chapter 6.

In addition to establishing the fundamental political institutions, the new constitution contained numerous provisions related to the rights of Bulgarian citizens. Commenting on the options of constitution makers who have to deal with this issue, Otto Kirchheimer once observed that "founding fathers" may resort to one of two strategies: either "make concessions" and "reach a compromise" that leads to an unambiguous regulation or simply amalgamate the wishes of all politicians and create "a unique linking and acknowledgment of the most varied value systems."[26] The Bulgarian constitution makers took the second path—and with an astonishing zeal at that. The constitution guaranteed to all Bulgarian citizens a variety of rights and entitlements. In addition to all "classical" political rights, Bulgarian citizens are entitled to state assistance in the upbringing of their children (Article 47.1), the right to work (Article 48.1), healthy and nonhazardous working conditions, guaranteed minimal pay, rest and leave of absence (Article 48.5), the right to strike (Article 50), social security and welfare aid (Article 51.1), unemployment benefits (Article 51.2), free medical care (Article 52), education (Article 53), the right to avail themselves to national and universal cultural values and develop their own culture in accordance with their ethnic self-identification (Article 54), and the right to a healthy and favorable environment (Article 55).

In the early 1990s, Bulgaria's choice of a quick-fix solution to its constitutional problems was greeted with skepticism by academics that at times bordered on ridicule.[27] What skeptics failed to appreciate, however, was that the very process of constitution-making injected a welcome amount of stability and predictability into a turbulent and volatile environment. Cooperative work on a constitution that will fix the rules of elite competition and determine in a credible way the spoils to be savored by the winners and the guarantees to be enjoyed by the losers can serve as what Guiseppe Di Palma has felicitously called "a shortcut to habituation,"; in other words, it may stimulate "democratic" behavior in a conflict-ridden milieu and engender a minimum of respect among previously antagonistic elites.[28] By institutionalizing a comprehensive set of incentives for elite behavior, the framers brought to a civilized

---

26. Otto Kirchheimer, "Weimar—and What Then?" in *Politics, Law, and Social Change* (New York: Columbia University Press, 1969), 53–54.

27. See, for example, Jon Elster, "Ways of Constitution-Making," in *Democracy's Victory and Crisis*, ed. Axel Hadenius (Cambridge: Cambridge University Press, 1997), 123–42; Holmes, "Back to the Drawing Board," 24–28; Offe, *Varieties of Transition*.

28. Guiseppe Di Palma, *To Craft Democracies* (Berkeley: University of California Press, 1990), 87.

close burgeoning controversies over alternative constitutional models, controversies that are insoluble. As perspicacious analysts have pointed out, "Arguments for or against a presidential or parliamentary system are inconclusive, while the need for some kind of stable constitutional order is urgent."[29] The perception that there are rules and procedures to be followed preceded the realization that the presidency is too weak or the Constitutional Court too strong.

Thus the solution came fairly quickly; it remained to be seen what it might fix.

Constitutional Practices

Of course, the passage of a constitution should not be confused with the rise of constitutionalism. The mere existence of a legal document called a constitution does not necessarily mean that politics will be conducted in a constitutional manner. Importing Western models may, ideally, mark the beginning of a qualitatively new stage in a country's political history. Equally plausibly, it may turn out to be an inconsequential episode of mimicry that brings out the widening gap between the global core and its peripheries. How, then, can we distinguish between constitutional polities and political regimes that simply have constitutions—and how should the political system that came into being in the 1990s in Bulgaria be classified? The analytical framework offered by Joseph Raz is a solid starting point for such an endeavor.[30] Raz discusses two kinds of constitutionalism, "thin" and "thick." "Thin" constitutionalism refers solely to the existence of a law that establishes and regulates the main organs of government and the general principles under which a country is governed. "Thick" constitutionalism, by contrast, is a more comprehensive concept defined by a combination of seven features: (1) a *canonical formulation of the basic law*, meaning this law is enshrined in one or several written documents; (2) the basic law is *constitutive* of the central political and legal structures; (3) it is a *superior law*; (4) the constitution has an *entrenched character* and cannot be amended by simple majorities; (5) it is *stable*; (6) it is also a *justiciable law*, with legal procedures through which the superiority of the fundamental law is enforced; (7) the constitution expresses *a common ideology*, reflecting the shared beliefs of the population about the way in which their society should be governed.

As we already saw, Bulgaria possesses the first attribute of "thick constitutionalism," a *canonical formulation of the basic law*. This law is *constitutive*.

29. Jan Zielonka, "New Institutions in the Old Eastern Bloc," in *Global Resurgence of Democracy*, 224.
30. Joseph Raz, "On the Authority and Interpretation of Constitutions," in *Constitutionalism*, ed. Larry Alexander (Cambridge: Cambridge University Press, 1998), 152–93.

It shapes the structure and powers of the different branches of government and thus creates the framework within which "normal" politics is carried out. "Perverse institutionalization," or the delimitation of special domains dominated by unaccountable elites and impervious to constitutional accountability, did not take place in post-Communist Bulgaria.[31] There have been no attempts to either suspend the constitution or resort to emergency measures that would allow temporarily empowered executive agents to change unilaterally the constitutional framework. Bulgarian political practices bear little resemblance, for example, to what Max Weber calls "pseudo-constitutionalism"—a regime in which the balance of power is tipped in favor of undemocratic forces, "emergency powers" are constantly invoked to justify encroachments on basic rights, and the functioning of representative institutions is repeatedly obstructed.[32] Of course, the growth of constitutional mores does not preclude the eruption of occasional skirmishes between the various branches. At least so far, however, Bulgaria has been spared one specific type of political turmoil—institutional chaos. Although the expression "war of institutions" seems to have become permanently in vogue in the country and figures prominently in the rhetoric of politicians and commentators, as a description of the mode of contention between various political authorities it is untenable. In fact, disputes over jurisdiction, "expansionist" institutional strategies, and truculent "usurpations" of authority are rare occurrences. What is subject to vehement criticism is the ineffective policies of respective institutions and not their authority to enact these policies. And sometimes the "war" is in fact nothing more than the principle of separation of powers in action, for example when the Constitutional Court declares legislation unconstitutional or parliament overturns presidential vetoes.

The fact that conflicts between the branches have been regularly resolved through constitutional procedures lends credence to the argument that the Bulgarian Constitution is *superior law* in the sense of its standing above the will of temporary majorities. On several occasions the leaders of the BSP unleashed egregious attempts to tip the institutional balance in their favor, but so far these campaigns have been successfully stalled by the judiciary. For example, in 1995 the BSP-dominated parliament sought to curtail the prerogative of the president to appoint ambassadors by incorporating into its standing orders a text stating that all candidates

---

31. On "perverse institutionalization," see J. Samuel Valenzuela, "Democratic Consolidation in Post-Transitional Setting," in *Issues in Democratic Consolidation*, ed. Scott Mainwaring, Guillermo O'Donnell, and Valenzuela (Notre Dame: University of Notre Dame Press, 1992), 52–67.

32. Max Weber, *The Russian Revolutions* (Ithaca: Cornell University Press, 1995).

for an ambassadorship should be subject to "hearings" and "approval" by the parliamentary Committee on Foreign Relations; on an appeal filed by the president, the Constitutional Court declared this norm void.[33] In a similar fashion, in 1996 parliament declared that the president can only appoint the chairpersons of the Supreme Court of Cassation and the Supreme Administrative Court if the respective decree is countersigned by the minister of justice, that is, the presidential prerogative in this domain was subjected to a ministerial veto. Promptly, the Court invalidated this provision as well.[34] The availability and enforcement of such constitutional remedies suggests that it is unjustified to apply to constitutional practices in Bulgaria Otto Kirchheimer's powerful metaphor of "the Rechtsstaat as a magic wall." According to the prominent German legal scholar, the core feature of systems hidden behind this wall is the lack of enforcement of basic rules:

> Whether available procedures are put in motion and whether legal rulings once obtained will be enforced or complied with has to be investigated.... Without making such an effort, a rule of law, resting only on the rhetorical availability of legal remedies, somehow resembles a modern house whose glass wall, the major attraction for all visitors, already stands, but whose wooden utility walls no one has bothered so far to build.[35]

Borrowing from Kirchheimer, one could say that there is ample prima facie evidence that "the wooden utility walls" of the Bulgarian Rechtsstaat have been built.

As a system of fundamental rules put beyond the reach of temporary majorities, the constitution has proved to be remarkably *stable* and *entrenched*. Even though attempts to amend it began soon after its adoption, during the first dozen years of Bulgarian post-Communist constitutionalism such initiatives failed. In 1994, for example, when Prime Minister Berov resigned, none of the three parliamentary factions controlled enough votes to elect a new government, and the danger that the deputies would fail to elect a successor on three successive votes loomed large. President Zhelev promptly announced that if that happened he would follow the constitution, which mandated the dismissal of parliament and authorized the president to schedule new elections

---

33. Decision 4/95, published in *Reshenija i opredelenija na Konstitutsionnija Sud na Republica Bulgaria 1995* (Decisions and Resolutions of the Constitutional Court of the Republic of Bulgaria) (Sofia: Akademichno izdatelstvo, 1996), 49.
34. Decision 13/96, published in *State Gazette*, No. 66/1996.
35. Otto Kirchheimer, "The *Rechtsstaat* as a Magic Wall," in *Politics, Law, and Social Change*, 430.

and appoint a caretaker government. At that point, party leaders realized that the constitution does not contain any provisions regarding parliamentary control during the interim period. In addition to the obvious risks stemming from unbridled executive action, some deputies were fearful that for several weeks they would be deprived of their parliamentary immunity and hence exposed to possible investigation in corruption cases. Hasty arrangements were made during the last days of the parliament, and a proposed amendment establishing some form of parliamentary control and declaring that all deputies would retain their immunity was passed on a first reading (constitutional amendments are passed by a three-fourths majority of all deputies on three readings held on three different days, Article 155). Subsequently, however, the plan began to unravel, and no further readings were held prior to the dissolution of parliament.

Finally, during the second half of his presidency, President Zhelev repeatedly expressed the view that Bulgaria should become a "presidential republic" and that the constitutionally delineated domain of presidential prerogatives should be expanded. This rhetoric did not crystallize into concrete proposals, and to the present time the concept of a "presidential republic," while still floating in the air, remains murky.[36]

Since the adoption of the constitution, political majorities of various persuasions have found themselves constrained in a "vertical sense" by constitutional norms beyond their reach.[37] If and when amendments are in fact considered—for example, in the context of Bulgaria's accession to full EU membership—they are deliberated on and passed—or rejected—in strict conformity with the procedural rules envisaged by the constitutional text itself. It is also noteworthy that, in accordance with the normative prescriptions of liberal constitutional theorists, the role of parliament in the process of amending constitutions has been central and uncontested.[38]

That Bulgaria meets Raz's criterion about the constitution as a *justiciable law* is an argument which I will defend in chapter 6.

With regard to Raz's last feature of "thick constitutionalism," namely that the constitution expresses a *common ideology*, such an ideology is

---

36. The constitution was amended for the first time in 2003 in order to synchronize some of its provisions with the requirements of the European Union; see *Durzhaven Vestnik* no. 85 (September 26, 2003).

37. On constitutional rules as "vertical constraints," see Jon Elster, Claus Offe, and Ulrich Preuss, *Institutional Design in Post-Communist Societies* (Cambridge: Cambridge University Press, 1998), 30–31.

38. On why parliament should play a central role in this process, see Stephen Holmes and Cass R. Sunstein, "The Politics of Constitutional Revision in Eastern Europe," in *Responding to Imperfection*, ed. Sanford Levinson (Princeton: Princeton University Press, 1995), 275.

relatively difficult to operationalize and detect. It would be presumptuous to maintain that the majority of Bulgarian politicians have "internalized" the lofty values of Western civilization; meanwhile, it is undeniable that in their maneuvering and infighting these politicians do not veer away from the constitutional text and deploy political rhetoric that reaffirms rather than denigrates the constitutive function of the basic law. Throughout the 1990s Bulgaria was a country in which there were no political prisoners, no arbitrary arrests, freedom of speech was respected, freedom of association vigorously exercised, independent journalists worked largely free of political intimidation, and freedom of religion was guaranteed.[39] On the local political scene, there were no political entrepreneurs who were able, Weimar style, to rally massive support behind anticonstitutional causes. To what extent the citizens of the fledgling Bulgarian democracy are committed to their constitution is a matter of speculation; what is clear is that both political leaders and the citizenry seem to share the perception that ambitious projects involving the suspension or radical revamping of the constitution would generate only marginal benefits that would not outweigh the incalculable social costs.

Perhaps the claim that constitutional norms actually shape political behavior might be best defended by means of detailed survey of the way the political crisis of December 1996–January 1997, the most acute political crisis that Bulgarian democracy had to face in the 1990s, was resolved.

On December 21, 1996, after almost two years in office, the government of BSP chairman Zhan Videnov resigned. By all accounts, this was the most corrupt, inefficient, and inept government in the post-1989 period not only in Bulgaria but possibly in the entire region. The country's grain was shipped abroad by BSP-affiliated "trading companies," which pocketed hefty profits while the country was thrown into the vertigo of a disastrous grain shortage. The savings of millions of citizens simply evaporated when BSP-appointed "bank managers" siphoned off bank deposits into private accounts in foreign banks and then promptly disappeared abroad. Inflation reached 320 percent in 1996, the GNP shrank by 9 percent, and nothing could stop the free fall of the national currency.

Against the backdrop of these catastrophic failures, Videnov's resignation was widely perceived as an implicit admission of guilt and a token

---

39. This is not to say, of course, that there are not instances of human rights violations—for example, violations of prisoners' rights—but they do not occur in proportions and with a frequency that would substantiate the claim that Bulgarian political practices are "exceptionally bad" and therefore stand apart from more "normal" forms of human rights violations observable in other countries. See Venelin I. Ganev, "Prisoners' Rights, Public Services, and Institutional Collapse in Bulgaria," *East European Constitutional Review* 4, no. 4 (Fall 1995): 76.

of BSP's willingness to take a new direction. Very soon, however, these hopes began to dissipate. The BSP confidently blamed all disasters on the opposition (the UDF which had been out of power since October 1992) and reiterated its determination to continue its rule. This arrogant behavior on the part of politically bankrupt party leaders was the straw that broke the back of popular patience. Mighty waves of protest spread throughout the country. After years of lethargic muddling through Bulgaria found itself in a potentially explosive situation.

With Videnov's resignation the country entered a period of governmental crisis. The constitution (Article 99) established the following procedure for solving this type of crisis: on consultations with all parliamentary groups, the president bestows the mandate to form a government on a prime minister designate, nominated by the largest parliamentary party (in this case, the BSP). Should the prime minister designate fail to complete this task within seven days, the mandate is passed to a prime minister designate nominated by the second-largest party (in this case, the UDF). Should the new prime minister designate fail to accomplish the mission within seven days, the task of forming a cabinet is entrusted to a prime minister designate nominated by one of the smaller parliamentary parties, which were the People's Union (a center-right alliance), the MRF, representing the Turkish minority), and the Bulgarian Business Bloc (a populist party). If an agreement is not finalized within seven days, the president appoints a caretaker government, dismisses the National Assembly, and schedules new elections. Given the configuration of forces in this particular situation, and specifically the determination of the opposition not to form a government that would have to abide by the whims of a BSP-controlled parliament, two outcomes were possible: either a new BSP government, or new general elections. Consequently, the major demand of the hundreds of thousands of men and women who took part in the daily anti-BSP rallies was that the ruling party give up its mandate to form a government and agree to new elections.

With the intensification of popular protest, two lines of conflict became increasingly visible. The first divide pitted the BSP against everyone else. Most of the leaders of the BSP, including the infamous Videnov himself, claimed that since their party had a majority in parliament (125 of the 240 seats) it should be allowed to proceed with the formation of a new government. This contention was countered by the forceful claim that should the BSP install a new government, popular discontent would become unmanageable. In institutional terms, this conflict placed the BSP-controlled parliament and cabinet against the presidency of Zhelyu Zhelev. Zhelev occupied his position until his term expired on January 21, 1997. Petar Stoyanov, who dealt a crushing defeat to his BSP opponent Ivan Marazov in the November 1996 presidential elections, occupied it thereafter. On January 8, 1997, the BSP nominated Interior Minister Nikolay Dobrev as prime minister designate and demanded that he be given a mandate to form a government. Outgoing president Zhelev declined to issue the requisite decree, arguing that since Stoyanov would have to work with the new government, he should possess the prerogative to confer a mandate. Immediately on assuming office, Stoyanov, an ardent opponent of the BSP, pledged to fulfill his duty and give a mandate to Dobrev, even though he was personally convinced that scheduling new elections was the only viable alternative to total political collapse. On January 29, Dobrev was presented with a presidential decree that authorized him to form a new government. At this point, all institutional hurdles to the formation of a new BSP government were cleared; in anticipation of Dobrev's decision, the interaction between the major political institutions (president, parliament, and government) came to a halt.

In this context, the second line of conflict, the friction between hard-liners and moderates within the BSP, acquired special significance. There were signs that while the majority of BSP leaders were adamantly opposed to any compromise and were prepared to resort to bloody reprisals to quell popular protest, an influential minority, led by Dobrev himself, was leaning toward a peaceful solution, which inevitably would amount to a refusal to form a government. On several occasions the collective leadership of the BSP urged Dobrev to present his cabinet's lineup to parliament, but he procrastinated, obviously wary of the inevitable consequences. The conundrum with which conciliatory-inclined politicians had to grapple was how to resolve both conflicts simultaneously without relying on the regular channels of institutional interaction (which were blocked by intransigent BSP hard-liners), and how to throw a veil of legitimacy over an outcome that radicals within the BSP were likely to declare nonbinding.

As it turned out, the framers of the Bulgarian Constitution had engineered an alternative institutional site, which was brilliantly deployed by President Stoyanov and Prime Minister–designate Dobrev to diffuse the impending crisis. Article 100.3 of the constitution provides that the president presides over a Consultative National Security Council, an entity lacking clearly defined prerogatives and constitutional status. On February 4, 1997, with Dobrev's mandate to form a government about to expire at midnight, the president summoned the Council and invited all leading politicians in the country (including Videnov and several of his ministers) to take part in it. After deliberations, which lasted several hours and over Videnov's obdurate protestations, the Council issued a resolution announcing that the BSP would decline to form a government, that none of the other parliamentary factions would use their mandate for that purpose, and that new general elections would be held in April.

In the past, the Council had been used as a forum where political leaders would exchange views in an attempt to alleviate looming strife, but it had never served as a decision-making body empowered to issue resolutions affecting the functioning of other political institutions. In this case, however, the Council's resolution triggered the dissolution of parliament and the formation of a caretaker government appointed by the president. With the benefit of hindsight one may assert that this tour de force was a brilliant success: further public protests were canceled, the caretaker government turned out to be functional and efficient, and the hard-liners suffered a defeat in the intraparty settling of scores within the BSP.

As designed in the Constitution, the procedure for installing a new government—granting a mandate to a single individual who has to comply within a preset deadline (seven days)—bore no signs of precocious originality but accomplished at least two objectives coveted by traditional institutional craftsmen. First, it precluded the possibility of a protracted gridlock: parliamentary forces are pressured either to install a new government or accept the dissolution of the National Assembly. The other beneficial impact is more intangible and elusive, and yet not without importance. By entrusting the momentous decision to a single individual (as opposed to a collective entity like a parliamentary faction or a party's governing body) the framers of the Bulgarian institution sought to counter the strategic calculations inherent in group decision making with the prudent and conscientious considerations of an individual who will be destined to face the consequences of his actions. At least in the case of Dobrev, this insight in political psychology worked quite well: as he pointed out during his press conference on the evening of February 4, his conduct was motivated primarily by his personal determination not to stain his hands with blood. Certainly, no institutional arrangement will pacify an unscrupulous would-be dictator. Nevertheless, forcing the option of stepping down or resorting to massive use of violence against unarmed civilians does seem to create an incentive to negotiate among politicians at least marginally disturbed by the prospect of bloodshed.

The constitution also "engineered" an alternative institutional setting where an authoritative decision may be reached when the continuous flow of "normal" decision making is interrupted. It is to be noted that the Council did *not* act as an "emergency committee" that arrogates to itself "extraordinary powers."[40] Rather, its intervention was construed

---

40. On the question of emergency powers and post-Communist constitutionalism, see Venelin I. Ganev, "Emergency Powers in the New East-European Constitutions," *American Journal of Comparative Law* 45, no. 3 (Summer 1997).

by all participants, including the BSP, as a legitimate mode of operation of a constitutionally established body whose function is not inimical to, but rather conducive to, the continuation of normal political processes. It should also be underlined that the decision reached by various political actors was *not* a "pact" in the sense defined by O'Donnell and Schmitter, namely "an explicit, but not always publicly explicated or justified agreement among a select set of actors which seeks to define (or better, to re-define) rules governing the exercise of power."[41] The resolution of the Council was presented to the public as a fully transparent act of a state institution that resolved a particular conflict *without* redefining any rules pertaining to the exercise of power. The institutional potential inherent in the constitution was utilized with a view to furthering the democratic process.

Finally, existing political institutions proved capable of sustaining a balance between adversarial and consensual elements in the decision-making process. Without a doubt, the resolution of the Council reflects the preferences of the non-Communist opposition and does attest in many respects to the political defeat of the BSP. And yet virtually all rivals made it clear that a decision endorsed by the BSP carries much greater political weight and legitimacy. There was a sustained effort on the part of President Stoyanov to cajole Dobrev and to obtain his signature under the resolution of the Council; and when the prime minister designate finally lent his support to this strategy, virtually all leaders of the opposition praised him as a man of integrity and a responsible politician. Thus the defeat of the BSP was perceived as a victory of collective reason, a victory in which the trustworthy leaders of the BSP partook. Conversely, the conspicuous failure of the hard-liners within the BSP was perceived as a triumph of the spirit of constitutionalism over a reactionary clique bent on subverting the principles that underpin the constitutional process.

During the dizzying days of January 1997 the novel edifice of Bulgarian constitutionalism trembled mightily but did not yield. Mass protest spurred by a devastating socioeconomic crisis was absorbed by the fledgling system without any negative consequences for the institutional frameworks and without transgressions on entrenched constitutional principles. The hundreds of thousands of citizens who were willing to protest to get rid of a thoroughly discredited government used their constitutional rights to do so. And politicians who were willing to resolve all conflicts in a peaceful manner had the requisite institutional means at their disposal. What started out as a cacophony of despair ended like a carefully orchestrated symphony of hope.

---

41. See Guillermo O'Donnell and Philippe Schmitter, *Transitions from Authoritarian Rule* (Baltimore: Johns Hopkins University Press, 1986), 37.

Whether or not these events bespeak a true commitment to a common democratic ideology might be a matter of debate; what cannot be questioned is that both civic activists and political leaders demonstrated their desire and ability to use—rather than suppress, circumvent, or disavow—constitutional norms and procedures in the midst of dramatic political conflict. More broadly, the foregoing analysis shows that "institutional engineering" has made a difference in Bulgaria. The overused distinction between "Central Europe," a cultural terrain hospitable to Western ideas and practices, and "the Balkans," a space of eternal backwardness where Western institutional transplants are destined to perish, is unsustainable.[42] The constitutional experiment in Bulgaria did generate changes that were important . . . and positive. As a response to the palpable threat of chaos and arbitrary rule, institutional engineering was successful to the extent that it bolstered rule-governed elite behavior and predictable patterns of institutional interaction. As a specifically democratic endeavor, the effort to cement the institutional basis of communal life promoted respect for rights and the legitimacy of political pluralism. Finally, the functioning of major political institutions made possible the defusing of disruptive conflicts between irreconcilable worldviews, and thus contributed to the "normalization" of highly charged controversies.

The Two Dimensions of State-Building Revisited

What is the best way to characterize the outcome of state-building in post-Communist Bulgaria? Was the large-scale constitutional experiment successful or not? The answer to this question should combine common sense with analytical insight. Common sense demands that general assessments of the outcome of Bulgarian constitutional reform should be grounded in a realistic understanding of what might have happened differently and what alternative scenarios were actually feasible. Analytical insight is necessary in order to approach this outcome in a theoretically rigorous way and to illustrate how and why the conceptualization of this outcome might advance our knowledge about state-building in post-Communism.

Any student of constitutional reform in post-Communist Bulgaria will be compelled to reaffirm two commonsensical propositions. The first is that, on the whole, the constitutional experiment worked rather well—much better, in fact, than anyone had anticipated. Even the most fastidious observer would have a hard time detecting in the Bulgarian

---

42. Compare Milada Vachudova and Timothy Snyder, "Are Transitions Transitory?" *East European Politics and Societies* 11, no. 1 (1997): 1–35.

constitutional system of the 1990s the sickening vices and syndromes itemized in the vast literature on failed democratizations, illiberal authoritarianisms, and repressive populist regimes. Unless the Bulgarian case is measured against normative standards that would make even the most mature actually existing constitutional system appear radically defective, the conclusion that, for the most part, the importation of constitutional structures from the West produced viable local transplants cannot be seriously disputed.

The second commonsensical proposition, however, should push our analyses in a radically different direction. This commonsensical proposition was cogently summarized by Michael L. Wyzan, who accorded to Bulgaria the dubious distinction of being "the only European former Soviet satellite where both the right and the left proved unable to get a hand on the situation."[43] This sentiment was echoed by the *New York Times*, which, in October 1996, characterized Bulgaria as "the worst managed state in Europe."[44] And indeed, by the end of 1996, Bulgaria had become the poorest country on the continent, with an average monthly salary of $12 and an average monthly pension of $4—considerably less than in war-torn Bosnia.[45] There is no reason to doubt, therefore, that the view that state-building in Bulgaria, whatever its achievements, was accompanied by dramatic fiascoes and spectacular failures—by a chronic inability "to get a handle on the situation"—would be endorsed by knowledgeable observers as well the great majority of Bulgarian citizens.

The main analytical insight that might help us integrate these somewhat contradictory commonsensical propositions into a coherent account I would characterize as follows: the case of Bulgaria demonstrates the interrelatedness but also the relative institutional autonomy of the two dimensions of state-building identified by Fukuyama, the creation of new state structures "from above" and reconfiguration of older state structures. And the best way to describe this outcome would be by means of a new concept, *weak-state constitutionalism*. Weak-state constitutionalism is an institutional configuration characterized by a relatively high degree of functionality of constitutional structures and a much lower degree of functionality of existing tools of governance. Although the notion of weak-state constitutionalism is obviously influenced by Fukuyama's dictum, it departs from his original conceptualization in one crucial respect: his view that the successful creation of new institutions

---

43. Michael L Wyzan, "Bulgarian Economic Policy and Performance," in *Bulgaria in Transition*, ed. John D. Bell (Boulder: Westview Press, 1998), 92–132.

44. Jane Perlez, "Looted by Its Own Officials, Bulgaria Faces the Day of Economic Reckoning," *New York Times*, October 28, 1996, A4.

45. For more data, see *Democratsija*, January 31, 1997.

Table 1. Different Outcomes of State-Building

	Existing Institutions	
New institutions	Strengthened	Weakened
Functional	Consolidation of constitutional democracy	Weak-state constitutionalism
Dysfunctional	Preservation of a neoauthoritarian or neopartimonial status quo	Prolonged crisis of stateness

is necessarily accompanied by "the strengthening" of existing ones. In fact, the two dimensions of state-building might be subservient to what, borrowing loosely from Diego Gambetta, might be called "concatenation of dynamics," or transformative impulses that independently push various ingredients of the state edifice in difference directions.[46] More specifically, what Bulgaria's weak-state constitutionalism demonstrates is that new institutions may be successfully built at the same time as already existing institutions are radically weakened. The general contention that state-building may produce different outcomes depending on whether the dynamics that propel institutional developments in the two dimensions of this large-scale process converge or diverge may be graphically illustrated (see table 1).

Construed as an effort to structure the *behavior of political elites*, constitutional engineering in Bulgaria created powerful incentives for maintaining nonviolent forms of elite rivalry. Rather quickly, the motley crew of Bulgarian party leaders metamorphosed into a Schumpeterian political class that, for all its penchant for "transgressions," is well aware of the "rules of the game."[47] Although the constitution did succeed in fending off what—to refer to a memorable distinction belabored by Alexis de Tocqueville—might be called the "striking crimes" that authoritarian leaders may perpetrate, it proved to be no cure for the multitude of "smaller vices" that quickly became a permanent fixture of post-Communist politics: rent seeking, arrogance, corruption,

---

46. The notion of "concatenation of dynamics" is loosely structured after Diego Gambetta's "concatenations of mechanisms"; see Gambetta, "Concatenations of Mechanisms," in *Social Mechanisms*, ed. Peter Hedstrom and Richard Swedberg (Cambridge: Cambridge University Press, 1998), 102–24.

47. "The democratic method is that institutional arrangement for arriving at political decisions in which individuals acquire the power to decide by means of a competitive struggle for the people's vote." Joseph A. Schumpeter, *Capitalism, Socialism, and Democracy* (New York: Harper Colophon Books, 1975 [1942]), 269.

and rapacious profiteering.[48] What the Bulgarian experience shows us is that it is possible to make a first step from authoritarian repression to elite cooperation, and even the second step toward democratic consolidation; but that there is no institutional logic or historically preordained script that guarantees that the next desirable steps—to positive-sum bargaining and efficient policymaking—will necessarily follow soon thereafter.

Conceived as a *strategy for regulating interactions between institutions*, constitutional engineering in Bulgaria accomplished the venerable task of imposing order wrested from arbitrariness and confusion. However, as parliamentarians learned that their laws might be struck down by the Constitutional Court, and as executive officers realized that their discretion is limited by general laws, the new constitutional system's functional capacity for governance diminished markedly. To invoke another useful distinction relevant to the political analysis of constitutions, although the constraining aspect of constitutionalism has been robustly on display in Bulgarian political practices, the enabling elements inherent in the constitutional edifice have remained inoperative.[49] The constitutional domain was structured in accordance with fundamental norms that were not transgressed—but the domain did not spontaneously generate the positive action characteristic of good governance.

Finally, institutional engineering successfully recast the *relations between state and society*. In contrast to what was going on before 1989, the demos asserted its central role in the political process. At the same time, the newfangled representative system was characterized exclusively by—to paraphrase Shugart and Carey—"negative efficiency," or the ability of the electorate to get rid of incumbents.[50] *Positive efficiency*, or voters' capacity to manage the political process in such a way as to make it beneficial to important social constituencies, has been conspicuously absent.

As a master plan for reforming the political institutions of a former dictatorship Bulgarian constitutionalism was a stunning success. The institutions built "from above" did allay nagging preoccupation with the possible recrudescence of abusive state practices. As a stratagem for replacing an unresponsive system of government with a set of efficient

48. On "striking crimes" and "smaller vices," see Alexis de Tocqueville, *Recollections* (New Brunswick, N.J.: Transaction, 1992), 5.
49. In the distinction between "inhibitive" and "enabling" elements of institution building, see Stephen Holmes, "Constitutionalism," in *The Encyclopedia of Democracy*, ed. Seymour M. Lipset (Washington, D.C.: Congressional Quarterly, 1995), 1:302.
50. See their description of the positive aspects of "efficiency": Matthew Shugart and John M. Carey, *Presidents and Assemblies* (Cambridge: Cambridge University Press, 1992), 7.

institutional tools employed in the pursuit of good policies, the same experiment resulted in a miserable failure. A self-sustaining constitutional order was able to coexist with a radically malfunctioning infrastructure of governance.

It is the weakness of subconstitutional structures of governance, then, that constitutes the relevant *context* in which the constitutional experiment unfolded. In the aftermath of 1989, the interrelated processes of the separation of party and state and conversions of political power into economic influence, and the multiplications of the Dorian Gray Effect triggered the disintegration of bureaucratic structures. This development stripped state institutions of their penetrative ability and thus rendered potentially salutary action virtually impossible. Agents acting on a constitutional level could wage their garden-variety wars over policies, in strict compliance with the constitution, and when the controversies were finally cleared politicians would invariably discover that they were bereft of qualified bureaucratic manpower and did not command sufficient logistical resources to deliver on their promises. With the fragments of surviving Communist institutions unusable and the newly inaugurated agencies still underbuilt, the effort to solidify the institutional basis of positive state intervention was bound to be futile.

The outcome of constitutional reforms, then, cannot be adequately depicted and analyzed unless we rely on a *dynamic interpretation of context*, an interpretation that conjures up not static measurable variables, but ongoing developments and evolving relations. The state-centered perspective provides such an analytical vantage point. It is the logistical conflicts attendant on the prolonged separation of party and state that made up the background against which constitution makers tried to lay the organizational basis of a new form of governance. It is the dynamic of conversions that constituted the matrix of interactions on which novel institutions were superimposed. It is the self-interested behavior of predators pursuing success that determined the immediate fate of freshly erected constitutional structures. The vicious circle in which institutional engineering was locked might be depicted in the following manner: whereas a corrupt state can only be monitored by powerful social actors, under post-Communism these actors were likely to be involved in kickbacks with the state. Designed to establish democratic institutions, constitutional engineering may become fully successful only when it energizes society at large, a formidable task with no quick solution.

Weak-state constitutionalism is also a heuristic device that may help us transcend the limitations of the false/authentic dichotomy that is habitually used to assess constitutional experiments in non-Western environments. How strong have the Western institutional "roots that clutch" grown in non-Western environments? The Bulgarian case cannot be construed as a story of how rules adopted with pomp are irrelevant in practice—or how informal rules triumph over formal norms. An alternative way to depict the contradictions and disbalances of the Bulgarian constitutional system in the 1990s is through the prism of Walter Bagehot's shrewd constitutional insights. According to this connoisseur of political complexity, constitutions have two parts: "First, those [parts] which excite and preserve the reverence of the population—the *dignified* parts. . . . And next, the *efficient* parts—those by which it, in fact, works and rules."[51] Bagehot was deeply worried that one of the ingredients of the English constitution may develop disproportionately and thus marginalize the other ingredient, a phenomenon that might be called *unbalanced constitutionalism*. Specifically, he has wary of "those practical men who reject the dignified parts" and seek to reduce "the old and complicated" artifices that constitute the dignified parts—and it is, of course, the British monarchy that he had in mind—to "the modern and simple" mechanisms of "getting things done." Only when the two components are harmoniously developed, Bagehot argued, can a constitution "work better than any instrument of government that has yet been tried."[52]

With some simplification, I would assert that the problem in Bulgaria was an unbalanced constitutionalism of a different sort, namely one characterized by well-developed *dignified* parts, with underdeveloped and malfunctioning *efficient* parts. The dignified parts—the constitution as a symbol of normative aspirations, political ideals, and moral principles—are neither superfluous nor decaying. But it is the mechanisms for "getting things done" that are out of order. What Bulgaria's weak-state constitutionalism brings into sharp relief is the duality of the constitution as an instrument of governance, a duality cogently conveyed by the metaphor "fundamental law." On the one hand, it is a *law*, an assemblage of rules and principles to be honored in the political process. On the other hand, it is a *fundament* on which the edifice of effective government is to be built. It is precisely this second aspect of constitutionalism that has remained stunted in post-Communist Bulgaria.

In the chapter that follows, I will continue my exploration of the concatenation of dynamics that characterized state-building in post-Communist Bulgaria. More specifically, I will demonstrate that the attempts to attach novel institutions to the body politic may clash with favored predatory elite

---

51. Walter Bagehot, *The English Constitution* (Ithaca: Cornell University Press, 1963), 61; emphasis in original.
52. Ibid., 65.

strategies and local reconfigurations of power. What are the mechanisms of "rejection" that bring about the demise of undesirable "transplants"? What are the implications of the observation that the dysfunctionality of existing state structures is the most relevant feature of the setting in which new institutions are being engineered into existence? These are the lines of inquiry that I will pursue as I explain why, amidst the "stony rubbish" of a crisis-ridden Balkan country, certain Western transplants survived while others perished.

6 The Shrewdness of the Tamed

> The moment of survival is the moment of power.
> ELIAS CANETTI, *Crowds and Power*

One of the central challenges confronting democratic constitution-makers in the modern world is how to institutionalize a system of checks and balances to constrain the exercise of political power. With this particular objective in mind, the framers of Bulgaria's postauthoritarian constitutional order created two autonomous bodies charged with the task of imposing limits on the behavior of democratically elected elites: a constitutional court and a central bank. These two experiments, however, produced strikingly dissimilar outcomes. By 1997, the Constitutional Court had established itself as an authoritative and influential player on the national political scene; in stark contrast, the attempt to engineer into existence an independent central bank was an unmitigated failure. The effort to install from above the institutional scaffolding of limited government yielded decidedly mixed results.

Perhaps a casual onlooker would find this empirical puzzle worth probing: Why did the life trajectories of such comparable institutions diverge so widely? But an informed observer would surely see that behind it lies a set of analytical issues that are arguably even more absorbing. What are the factors that determine the degree of incompatibility between newly introduced "parchment institutions" and local sociohistorical settings?[1] Why is it that in one and the same context attempts to restrain political elite action may produce radically different outcomes? What do these outcomes tell us about the transformation of state structures and the perplexities of state restructuring in Eastern Europe more generally? These are the issues I explore in this chapter.

---

1. On "parchment institutions," see John M. Carey, "Parchment, Equilibria, and Institutions," *Comparative Political Studies* 33, nos. 6–7 (August–September 2000): 735.

The analysis that follows draws on the state-transformation themes adumbrated in chapter 5: it presents a thicker, facts-centered narrative about the course of institutional experiments, pays special attention to the diachronic aspect of constitutional change, recognizes the complexity of the observable institutional configurations, and aims to dissect the interrelatedness of the two distinct dimensions of state-building (construction of new institutions and the metamorphoses of existing ones). In addition, I wish to take the analysis in novel, somewhat different directions. First, I will look at the institutional level *lower* than the general constitutional order. The narrative "thickens" not as a result of a more detailed description of the aggregate results of institutional engineering but because it goes beyond the point of view of the analyst who is interested in the overall picture. Indeed, if our analysis is confined to the constitutional process broadly defined, then intriguing puzzles related to important state structures—such as the striking contrast between the Court's success and the Bank's debacle—will be systematically overlooked. To the extent that they are heeded at all, the overarching concern would likely be the relative importance of an autonomous court or an independent bank for the process of democratic governance, and the implications of the success of the former and the failure of the latter for the "coding" of Bulgaria as a "consolidated" or an "unconsolidated" democracy. The diverging outcomes of these two institutional experiments would be registered and integrated into the analysis, but there would be no compelling reason to treat such outcomes as a fertile topic that might lead us to important insights about how local contexts affect constitutional constructs. Looking at individual trees in addition to a survey of the forest, then, might be a helpful heuristic strategy for expanding current research agendas on state-building.

The diachronic dimension of constitutional experiments is at the foreground of my analysis. But my inquiry into the fates of the Constitutional Court and the Bulgarian National Bank will rely unabashedly on otherwise suspect categories such as "success" and "failure." As mentioned, as general depictions of multilayered institutional engineering, such dichotomous categories may be simplistic. As a verdict about specific institutional innovations, however, they may be quite adequate—and stimulating. I will use the notion of "successful institution-building" in the sense specified by Timothy Frye, according to whom a new institution might be held to have been "successfully" established if fairly soon after its creation it begins to elicit the compliance of the relevant political actors, and if it survives intact the inevitable skirmishes with opponents for whom its continuing existence is a source of considerable inconvenience.² In the case of the Court and the Bank, then, success would mean that these state structures shape elite behavior and, through their ongoing operation, nurture an environment in which the basic legitimacy of countermajoritarian institutions is not questioned.

Obviously, to link the outcome of such experiments to elite behavior means to reopen the question of strategic agents' calculus in the period *following* the making of original constitutional choices. How self-serving actors will react to institutions that have *already* been formally established is not a question that has received enough attention. To the extent that context-specific structures of incentives constitute an important aspect of the milieu in which institutional experiments are destined to run their course, we need to know how such incentives shape self-interested elite behavior, as the true relevance of newly erected institutional hurdles emerges. The study of the rise and fall of political institutions moves beyond the snapshots of strategic situations preceding the adoption of new constitutions and toward a dynamic understanding of the ways in which powerful elites' reactions to opportunities and constraints propel the reconfiguration of state structures.

The most enticing promise that a thicker, diachronically oriented narrative about the success and failure of concrete institutional experiments holds is that it will help us comprehend the nature of what might be labeled "mechanisms of rejection," and add to our knowledge more observations and propositions about state-building in non-Western contexts. As Kathleen Thelen has pointed out, arguments about "the 'crystallization' of particular institutional configurations obscure more than they reveal unless they are explicitly linked to complementary arguments about the mechanisms" that brought these crystallizations about.³ The study of political institutions such as the Court and the Bank may help us understand the mechanisms at work behind the uneven institutional landscape in early post-Communism. From a methodological point of view, such research makes it feasible to treat as *constant* certain factors habitually invoked to explain the development of constitutional reforms—for example, culture, national historical tradition, and geographical proximity to the West. As these factors are discarded as an explanation of the diverging trajectories of similar "parchment institutions," the impact of

---

2. Timothy Frye, *Brokers and Bureaucrats* (Ann Arbor: University of Michigan Press, 2000), 43–44. In Frye's study, the specific forms of compliance under investigation are the use of standard contracts and the rate of contract reporting.

3. Kathleen Thelen, "Historical Institutionalism in Comparative Politics," *Annual Review of Political Science* 2 (1999): 391.

other contextual factors may be more fruitfully scrutinized. Such a comparative exploration may help us overcome the analytical limitations of general statements regarding the "recalcitrance" of local contexts and "the incompatibility" between Western models and non-Western habitats, and allow us to hypothesize about identifiable actors, interactions, and circumstances that stifle institutional transplants.

To put it somewhat flamboyantly, from a methodological point of view this chapter might be considered as an experiment with a particular method of inquiry which, in homage to Plutarch's chef d'oeuvre, I would like to call "parallel lives of political institutions."[4] The famous Greek duly acknowledged that he was not going to record and compare every detail relevant to the political careers of his sets of two protagonists. His inquiry rested on the following analytical premise: "An expression or a jest sometimes informs us better of [heroes'] characters and inclinations than the most famous sieges, the greatest armaments, or the bloodiest battles."[5] The comparative analysis of the evolution/devolution of two freshly erected state structures builds on this cogent intuition. Sometimes analytical vignettes about pairs of seemingly obscure but interlinked institutional developments may shed as much light on the complexities of historically specific political contexts as more stylized narratives about economic reform and democratic consolidation in a larger set of countries—this is the Plutarchian insight that inspires my parallel study of comparable political experiments. My purpose is not to present an exhaustive account of experiences with judicial review and central banking in post-Communist Bulgaria but to demonstrate how the "lives" of the two institutions provide the analytical background for understanding the impact of contextual conditions on institutional change and the precise nature of the indigenous political forces that render the products of state-building "from above" dysfunctional. In other words, the genre of parallel lives of political institutions allows us to create an analytical space where several themes may be examined in an empirically grounded manner: How can the assumption of self-interested elite action help us understand not only institutional choice but also the compliance or sabotage that follow this choice? How do various arenas of state-building overlap with one another? What are the analytical—and sometimes ironic—ramifications of state weakness? The inquiry into the peculiar pattern of success and failure of institutional reform in Bulgaria will serve as an analytical microscope that helps us

---

4. That my approach bears some resemblance to Plutarch's was first brought to my attention by Roumen Avramov, to whom I would like to express my deep gratitude.

5. Plutarch, "Alexander," in *Lives*, ed. Roman T. Bond (New York: Tudor Publishing, 1935), 534.

comprehend such issues and ultimately answer the question of how and why certain features of post-Communist context attain particular saliency for post-Communist constitutional state-building.

The Two Institutions

The first question that should be addressed is whether the Court and the Bank are comparable institutions. If the nature of the two institution-building projects is radically different, then variation in outcome will be very easy to explain and there will be no heuristic benefit from the comparison. What we will be confronted with will be two largely unrelated stories with different endings, and the only conclusion that could be plausibly drawn will be that the "transplantation" of one of the institutions turned out to be "easier" than that of the other, an observation that is empirically quite true and analytically uninspiring. But if the projects are similar, then the variation of outcomes becomes more intriguing: it suggests that behind the observable patterns of success and failure there may be factors at work that are not reducible to the inherent difficultness of institution-building experiments. An inquiry into the parallel lives of political institutions will then make it possible to formulate broader conclusions about the dynamic and prospects of "engineering from above."

There are two differences between the Court and the Bank that should be emphasized. One of them seems to suggest that the establishment of an independent bank would be easier than that of a constitutional court, whereas the other one makes it reasonable to assume that the opposite might be true. The first difference is that the Court is a completely new institution, whereas the Bulgarian National Bank was founded 120 years ago and thus was not entirely alien to the Bulgarian national political tradition.[6] Of course, under socialism the bank was far from being "independent" of the party and state. It operated as a branch of the finance ministry and diligently provided money for the projects of the ruling elite.[7] But it bears emphasizing that the BNB *did* exist before 1989: it possessed a building and equipment, it was staffed by "bankers" who at least had a theoretical familiarity, if not practical experience, with the notion of independent central banking. In contrast, Bulgaria had never had a constitutional court. In 1991 the institution was created from scratch, and it had to be staffed by jurists who had no professional knowledge of, or experience with, judicial review.

---

6. See *120 Years Bulgarian National Bank, 1879–1999*, ed. Roumen Avramov (Sofia: Bulgarian National Bank, 1999).
7. For a cogent and succinct analysis of the status of central banks under the one-party *old* regimes, see Dwight Semler, "Introduction," *East European Constitutional Review* 3, nos. 3–4 (Summer–Fall 1994): 48–52.

The other difference is related to the formal status of the institutions. The legal standing of the Court was arranged in the 1991 Constitution (Chapter VIII). The autonomy of the Bank was ensured by means of ordinary legislation, namely the Law on the Bulgarian National Bank, adopted in 1991 by the same parliament that subsequently passed the Bulgarian Constitution. This institutional arrangement implies that the degree of constitutional entrenchment of the Court is higher than that of the Bank, and that therefore the justices are less vulnerable to political interference than the central bankers. Does the difference in legal status reflect a strategic intent to render bankers easier to manipulate? The answer to this reasonable question is no. In fact, a more adequate explanation would be that the discrepancy stems from the very logic of "imitation" that was one of the motors of the constitution-making process. Three Western constitutions in particular served as models for Bulgarian elites: the German, the Spanish, and the French. All three constitutions contain provisions regarding the prerogatives of an independent body entrusted with the task of judicial review, but none of them mentions an independent central bank. Even though the independence of the BNB was not formally elevated to the status of a constitutional matter, there were clear signs that party elites were committed to the principle of bank autonomy. Virtually all experts writing on the subject in the early 1990s greeted the passage of the law as the veritable beginning of independent central banking in Bulgaria.

Based on the analysis of the differences between the two institution-building projects, it would be hard to assess a priori each autonomous body's chances of survival. Legally, the Court looked stronger—it could only be assailed by constitutional amendments to curtail its authority, and passing amendments to the constitution is extremely difficult. In contrast, it is relatively easy to change ordinary legislation such as the Law on the Bulgarian National Bank. From a historical perspective, the Bank's chances of survival looked better—it was more rooted in the infrastructure of governance. It would be reasonable to assert, then, that there is no compelling reason to perceive the Court and the Bank as two institutional experiments destined to unfold in dramatically different ways.

This proposition is lent further credence by the fact that the Court and the Bank shared three kinds of fundamental characteristics: *institutional*, *functional*, and *political*. The institutional principles according to which the Court and the BNB were structured were remarkably similar: security of tenure and diffusion of the power to appoint. According to the constitution, the justices cannot be removed during their nine-year terms. The Law on the BNB established a similar five-year tenure for the chairman and the board of directors of the Bank; although the term is shorter than that of a justice, it is longer than a parliamentary term (four years). Furthermore, no political body holds a monopoly on appointments to either institution. Four of the twelve justices are appointed by the president, four are elected by parliament, and four are selected at a joint meeting of the justices of the Supreme Court of Cassation and the Supreme Administrative Court (Article 147 of the Bulgarian Constitution). In a similar fashion, the chairman of the board of directors of the BNB and his three deputies are elected by parliament, while the remaining five members of the board are appointed by the president pursuant to the nomination of the chairman (Article 12 of the Law on the BNB).

Second, the two institutions have a very similar *political function*: to restrain political majorities. In fact, in the recent literature on institutional reforms in fledgling democracies, the Court and the Bank are mentioned in the same breath. In a wide-ranging study of processes of democratization, Lawrence Whitehead observed that "the rationale behind the shift to central bank independence" is analogous to the raison d'être of an "institutionally secure and autonomous judiciary": increasing the degree of accountability in the constitutional system.[8] Along the same lines, Jon Elster, another prominent student of democratization, has argued that independent courts and banks are institutional devices grounded in the same principle. Commenting on the effort to integrate such autonomous bodies into the institutional configuration of fledgling East European democracies, he pointed out that both institutions are intended to "act as salutary chains on the tendency of democratic majorities to act under the sway of passions or a short-term interest."[9] Given the similarity of functional objectives, it is reasonable to expect that they will face the same generic problem: frustrated parliamentary majorities.

Finally, the two institutions were conceived and established in the same political "climate of opinion." As Kim Lane Scheppele has cogently argued, this "climate" was characterized by what she called "aspirational" and "aversive" tendencies. The "aspirational" component of the constitution-making process stemmed from the forward-looking desire to establish a democratic polity based on the rule of law. The "aversive" component was rooted in the backward-looking determination not to repeat the errors of the past. Remarkably, both tendencies converged on the idea that the delegation of some power to political bodies not subject to immediate democratic control is one of the legitimate objectives of liberal constitutionalism.[10] This convergence accounts for the fact

---

8. Laurence Whitehead, *Democratization* (Oxford: Oxford University Press, 2002), 145.

9. See Jon Elster, "Constitutional Courts and Central Banks," *East European Constitutional Review* 3, nos. 3–4 (Summer–Fall 1994): 66.

10. Kim Lane Scheppele, "Aspirational and Aversive Constitutionalism," *International Journal of Constitutional Law* 1, no. 2 (2003): 299–300.

that during the protracted constitutional deliberations in the Bulgarian legislative assembly the idea that the country should have an independent Court and Bank engendered little dissent and never gave rise to the bitter controversies that surrounded, for example, the presidency or the permissible scope of political pluralism.[11] The ease with which the constitutional provisions regarding the Court and the Law on the BNB were passed strongly suggests that these related acts of institutional engineering reflected a Rawlsian "overlapping consensus" about this particular facet of the constitutional framework.

Despite the differences, the two institutional experiments are analogous, first, because their institutional arrangement is comparable; second, because their function is identical—imposing constraints on elite behavior; and third, because the political considerations that motivated their creators were similar. The following analytical premise therefore seems warranted: subsequent divergences that marked the evolution of the Court and Bank *cannot* be traced back to the way in which these two institutions were originally set up. These divergences can only be accounted for if we explore the way in which the new institutions fit into the concrete sociopolitical context.

The Court

The argument that the Court was an absolute novelty in post-Communist Bulgaria can be understood in three different, though not unrelated, ways. First, the notion that policies should be enacted and implemented in accordance with general rules and principles enforced by courts appeared to be alien to Bulgaria's *patrimonial political culture*, which bestowed legitimacy on the view that reliance on personal networks and kin-based connections was the accepted way of getting things done in politics.[12] Second, an institutional configuration in which a high court is assigned a prominent role had never been a part of the national *political tradition*, which knew no precedents of judges restricting the activities of legislators and executive officials. Finally, the very concept of judicial review was at odds with the professional sensitivities and habits of mind of the Bulgarian judiciary, who have been thoroughly integrated into a continental jurisprudential tradition that—to use Alec Stone's apt characterization—was grounded in the principle that "to recognize

---

11. For more details about the deliberations of the Bulgarian Great National Assembly, see Venelin I. Ganev, "Emergency Powers in the New East-European Constitutions," *American Journal of Comparative Law* 45, no. 3 (Summer 1997): 585–612.

12. On the importance of patrimonial legacies on post-Communist Bulgaria, see Herbert Kitschelt et al., *Post-Communist Party Systems* (Cambridge: Cambridge University Press, 1999), chap. 1.

judge-made law is to diagnose pathology, and judicial review is all but unthinkable."[13] The Court was established only months after the adoption of a new constitution in 1991, and at that time a knowledgeable observer of Bulgarian politics would have confidently predicted that the Court would become nothing more than an institutional ornament loosely connected to a hastily assembled institutional edifice. In fact, the very attempt to launch such an institutional experiment was greeted with skepticism that at times bordered on ridicule.[14]

With the benefit of hindsight, we can assert today that such predictions were misguided and thoroughly disproved by subsequent developments. As it turned out, the experiment was much more successful than originally anticipated. The new countermajoritarian institution effectively reined political majorities that were at times truculent. The Court's first clash with politicians pitted it against the loose anti-Communist coalition that briefly ruled the country in 1992. Some of the lustration-type laws passed at that time imposed restrictions on the rights of former high-ranking Communist officials. One legislative act, the amendments to the Banks and Credits Law, established a five-year ban on appointments of a restricted number of former party functionaries (members of the Central Committee of the Bulgarian Communist Party and secret service agents) on the boards of directors of Bulgarian banks. A second act, an amendment to the Pensions Law, declared that the time that high-level officials spent on the payroll of the Communist Party and its satellite organizations would not count as "employment" for the purposes of the pension law (and hence their pensions, which are calculated on the basis of "years of employment," ought to be substantially reduced). The Court struck down both laws as unconstitutional.[15]

But by far the most important political battles the Court fought were with the former Communists, who quickly recovered their politically dominant position in early 1993. In some respects, the years 1993–96 were a period of what Steven Fish calls "democratic erosion" in Bulgaria—as

---

13. Alec Stone, *The Birth of Judicial Politics in France* (New York: Oxford University Press, 1992), 23. Of course, the emphasis on judicial deference to political will was fully congruent with Leninist legal theories and practices that thrived in Bulgaria during the Communist era.

14. See, for example, Jon Elster, "Ways of Constitution Making," in *Democracy's Victory and Crisis*, ed. Axel Hadenius (Cambridge: Cambridge University Press, 1997), 123–42; Stephen Holmes, "Back to the Drawing Board," *East European Constitutional Review* 3, no. 1 (Winter 1993): 24–28; Offe, *Varieties of Transition*.

15. On the Banks and Credits Law, see Decision 8/1992; on the Pensions Law, see Decision 1/1992, both published in *Reshenija i opredelenija na Konstistutzionnija Sud, 1991–1992* (Decisions and Rulings of the Constitutional Court) (Sofia: Akademichno izdatelstvo, 1993).

the lowering of is Freedom House "democracy index" indicates.[16] During their ill-conceived campaign to remonopolize all political power during these years, the former Communists resorted to a variety of "techniques" to "cleanse" the independent judiciary. The Law on Judicial Power, passed in 1994, marked the climax of this effort and brought to fruition the ex-Communists' endeavor to settle accounts with their perceived opponents on the bench. The major objective of the law was to introduce retroactively new eligibility requirements for the country's top judges (needless to say, these requirements were crafted in such a way as to eliminate all judges appointed after 1989) and to dismiss immediately all those who did not qualify. The Constitutional Court declared all provisions establishing the retroactive force of the new law unconstitutional and struck down a text allowing parliament to dismiss judges "if their behavior undermines the prestige of judicial power." Then, the BSP decided to wield "the power of the purse": in 1996 the budget was amended and financing for the judicial system slashed. This amendment was protested by the president and invalidated by the Court.[17] Thus the BSP's campaign came to a naught, and the integrity of the judicial system was maintained.[18]

During the same period—from 1993 to 1996—the justices also proved capable of protecting citizens against the predatory forays of revenue-maximizing politicians. The Court invalidated a law that allowed state-owned enterprises not to pay their debts to private companies, thwarted the government's attempt to raise taxes by decree, and declared unconstitutional tax legislation that placed too much discretion in the hands of tax officials without specifying the relevant criteria for assessing the liability of each taxpayer.[19]

Perhaps nothing illustrates the influence of the Court better than the so-called Pirinski case, which was decided in 1996. At that time, the ruling Bulgarian Socialist Party had accumulated as much power as any party in a pluralist system can: it controlled the legislature, the executive branch, local government, and the national electronic media. Georgi Pirinski was the foreign minister in the Socialist government, and in September 1996

16. On the concept of "democratic erosion" and the fluctuation of Bulgaria's Freedom House index, see M. Steven Fish, "The Dynamics of Democratic Erosion," in *Postcommunism and the Theory of Democracy*, ed. Richard Anderson et al. (Princeton: Princeton University Press, 2001), 54–95.

17. Decision 17/96, published in *Durzhaven Vestnik* 3 (November 1996): 5–8.

18. For a detailed discussion of these developments, see Venelin I. Ganev, "Judicial Independence and Post-Totalitarian Politics," *Parker School of Law Journal of East-European Law* 3 (1996): 224–28.

19. On the unconstitutionality of debt cancellation, see Decision 22/1996; on the unconstitutionality of taxes imposed by decree, see Decision 3/1996; on the unconstitutionality of vague tax legislation, see Decision 9/1996. All decisions are included in *Reshenija i oprededelnija na Konstitutzionnija Sud, 1996* (Sofia: Akademichno izdateltsvo, 1997).

he was nominated as his party's candidate in the upcoming presidential elections. At that moment, legal experts pointed out that Pirinski might not meet one of the constitution's eligibility requirements requiring the president be a "Bulgarian citizen by birth" (Article 93). The problem was that Pirinski was born in New York, and it was unclear whether he obtained his Bulgarian citizenship by birth or by naturalization. The Court was asked to step in and clarify this matter. Without referring to Pirinski by name, the Court offered a rigorous legal interpretation of the relevant texts of the constitution that, in effect, rendered him ineligible to be president. A torrent of vicious attacks was unleashed against the Court, but to no avail. Invoking the Court's ruling, the Central Electoral Commission refused to register Pirinski as a presidential candidate, and a unanimous Supreme Court turned down his appeal against the decision of the commission. Thus the justices effectively disqualified the candidate of the most powerful party and—what is even more important—the legitimacy of its decision was recognized by state officials and institutions with which the Court itself did not have a direct link.

Visibly irritated by the Court's independent stance, several BSP leaders contemplated normative changes that might have made this institution more subservient to the will of political majorities. But this faction was led by an erratic lawyer, Velko Vulkanov, who was rather adept at delivering fiery diatribes against the Court but lacked organizational abilities.[20] The anti-Court lobby was numerous and vocal, but it never acquired the critical mass needed to press forward with its reformist agenda. The BSP-inspired attempt to subdue the Court eventually fizzled out.

By the mid-1990s, the Court had asserted itself as the sole institution possessing the authority to interpret the constitution. It issued dozens of decisions that decisively shaped constitutional practices in post-Communist Bulgaria. Even though the Court never displayed the missionary zeal that emanated from certain decisions of the Hungarian Constitutional Court, it managed, acting as a "moderator, rather than an active participant," to defend its turf amid the general political turbulence that frequently rocked the national political scene.[21] Less than half a decade after its establishment, the Court was generally recognized as an arbiter in all disputes related to separation of powers. Its assistance in clarifying the ambiguities of various texts was regularly sought by politicians. Bulgaria's most powerful parties, which otherwise share little in common, are unanimous in

---

20. For Vulkanov's views, see his autobiography, *Na kolene pred istinata* (Sofia: Bulvest 2000 [1996]).

21. On the Hungarian Constitutional Court, see Andras Sajo, "Reading the Invisible Constitution," *Oxford Journal of Legal Studies* 15, no. 3 (1995): 253–67. On the Bulgarian Court as a "moderator," see Rumyana Kolarova, "Bulgaria," *East European Constitutional Review* 2, no. 2 (Spring 1993): 48–51.

their view that conflicts between major institutions should be definitively resolved by the twelve justices. And its rulings were met with acquiescence: deputies, executive officials, judges in ordinary courts, and local political activists, while frequently criticizing the Court's interventions in the political process, complied with its decisions. In short, the Bulgarian Constitutional Court successfully fulfilled its major functions: to interpret the constitution, resolve conflicts between the political branches, and impose limits on majority rule.

The Bank

As mentioned above, the status of the Bank, unlike that of the Court, was not "constitutionalized": it was regulated by means of ordinary legislation. However, there is ample evidence that the belief that management of the country's financial system should be entrusted to an independent institution was embraced by all influential participants in Bulgaria's constitution-making process. Their views converged on the idea that the Bulgarian National Bank should be able to resist actions of the executive that could jeopardize the internal and external value of the national currency.[22] This consensus ensured the relatively quick and unproblematic adoption of the Law on the Bulgarian National Bank, which was passed in late 1991 and was supported by all parliamentary groups.[23] Even a cursory reading of the law will demonstrate that the legislators appeared to be quite serious in their determination to ensure the autonomy of the new institution and intended it to be independent of the government. Arguably, the most revealing article in this respect is Article 47: "In performing its functions, the BNB shall be independent from instructions issued by the Council of Ministers and other state bodies." In addition, the BNB possessed a number of important prerogatives, most significantly the power to determine its own credit policy and maintain the hard-currency reserve.[24] Direct securitized lending to the government was explicitly prohibited, and *only* the central government was allowed to borrow from the BNB. Other institutions such as individual ministries, municipal councils, and nonfinancial organizations (such as SOEs) were denied access to the BNB.[25] The impression

---

22. See John A. Bristow, *The Bulgarian Economy in Transition* (Cheltenham, England: Edward Elgar, 1996), 135–38.

23. See *Durzhaven vestnik*, 12 December 1991. The full text of the law may also be found in *Bankovo pravo: Sbornik normativni aktove* (Sofia: Soloton, 1996), 1–22.

24. For more details, see Mariela Nenova, "Finansovata politika v Bulgaria v uslovijata na prehoda kum pazarna ikonomika," Occasional Papers (Sofia: Bulgarian National Bank, June 1996).

25. See Lubomir Hristov, "A Role for an Independent Central Bank in Transition?" in *The Bulgarian Economy*, ed. Derek Jones and Jeffrey Miller (Aldershot, England: Ashgate, 1997), 138.

that new political elites were firmly committed to the new experiment was strengthened when parliament almost unanimously elected Todor Vulchev, a respected and politically unaffiliated financier, as the BNB's first chairman. At the end of 1991, virtually all commentators, local as well as international, agreed that "the Law provides a solid legal basis for an independent BNB; it is consistent with virtually all important dimensions of central banking independence."[26] This fact was also registered by experts who rely on formal criteria to construct an aggregate measurement of bank independence—according to Cukierman, Webb, and Nayapti, BNB's independence index was higher than that of the U.S. Federal Reserve System and the Bank of England.[27] It appeared that, just like the Court, the Bank was perceived as a crucial component of the Western political model that reform-minded elites attempted to transplant on Bulgarian soil.

Predictably, when the euphoria of the constitution-making moment began to subside, the attempts of some of the newly appointed members of the board of directors to conduct the Bank's affairs in an independent manner began to incur the ire of elected politicians. In that regard, the situation of the Bank was no different from the situation of the Court: devised as countermajoritarian institutions, both were bound to clash with irascible majorities. What was different, however, was that the campaign against the Bank was more tenacious, logistically better organized, and carried out with firmer resolve. The initial skirmishes between the BSP-dominated parliamentary majority and the leaders of the Bank culminated in an ugly confrontation in mid-1993. Formally, the case was presented to the public as a legally intricate controversy, but in essence what transpired was a thinly veiled attempt to remove Emil Hursev, a deputy chairman who was in the middle of his five-year term and a vocal defender of the BNB's independence. From a legal point of view, the problem was that the chairman and deputy governors were elected several months before the adoption of the law, which allowed several deputies to argue that parliament needed to reappoint them in accordance with the provisions of the new legislative act. Finally, the issue was brought before parliament, and the deputies voted to reinstate Vulchev and two of his deputies. A vote on the other deputy, the troublemaker

26. See ibid., 139; see also Bristow, *Bulgarian Economy in Transition*, 136.
27. See Alex Cukierman, Steven Webb, and Bilin Neyapti, "Measuring the Independence of Central Banks and the Effect of Policy Outcomes," *World Bank Economic Review* 6, no. 1 (1992): 353–69. Their measurement is based on consideration of four clusters of issues: (1) the appointment, dismissal, and term of office of the chief executive officer of the bank; (2) the type of procedure established for resolution of conflicts between the executive branch and the bank in the budget process; (3) the objectives of the central bank; (4) limitations on the ability of the central bank to lend to the public sector. See also Hristov, "Role for an Independent Central Bank in Transition?" 136.

Hursev, was never taken, and he was de facto removed from power, despite the fact that the law provided that members of the board cannot be dismissed without a cause. At that point, it became painfully clear that "the shield of personal independence provided by the Law on the BNB proved too weak to protect them."[28]

Notably, the onslaught against the Bank was led by an identifiable group of BSP politicians who proved capable of systematic and coordinated action. Krassimir Premyanov is emblematic in this respect. This influential leader of the BSP served as chairman of the BSP's parliamentary faction in 1994–97 and led the attack against the central financial institutions.[29] He insisted that all nominees for members of the board of directors of the BNB should sign "a declaration of loyalty" to the BSP.[30] In addition to masterminding the backstage maneuvering that precipitated Hursev's removal he was instrumental in installing Bistra Dimitrova, a former employee of Multigroup as director of Bulgaria's second-largest state-owned bank, the State Savings Bank. What is particularly important to grasp is that Premyanov was only one of several powerful actors—including the leaders of thriving semilegal and quasi-criminal "economic holdings"—who pooled their efforts in order to pursue this common project, the annihilation of the Bank as an autonomous institution. The project was endowed with various resources, and, once launched, these resources—including ruthless intimidation and threats against both opponents and "unruly" members of Premyanov's own party—were widely used.[31] By all accounts, Premyanov and his lobby represented the most powerful predatory elites in parliament—once he spearheaded the assault against the independence of the autonomous banking institution, its fate was sealed.

For a proper understanding of the political dynamic that ultimately emasculated the Bank the question *what* is it that the anti-Bank coalition wanted is at least as important as the question *how* it went about achieving its goal. As could be expected, pressure was put on the Bank to finance the BSP-backed government's expenditures. In the aftermath of Hursev's dismissal, and with Vulchev apparently scared into submission, limits on lending to the government were routinely disregarded. On several occasions in 1993–96, up to 50 percent of the deficit was covered by the Bank, in open violation of its constitutional obligations. Direct budget subsidies

---

28. Hristov, "Role for an Independent Central Bank in Transition?" 145.
29. For Premyanov's career in the party, see *Kapital*, January 27, 1997, 9.
30. See "BSP izbra bankera na mutrite," *Kapital*, July 1, 1996, 18.
31. See, for example, "Prosto Premyanov," *Kapital*, October 25, 1996, 14; "Premyanov se olja," *Kapital*, November 2, 1996, 23–24; "Premyanov se olja II," *Kapital*, November 10, 1996, 18–19.

to the state-owned industrial sector were replaced by new credit injections administered by the Bank. But the principal demands that the Bank was compelled to meet were related not to governmental policies but to the refinancing of other banks (both state-owned and private). Again in violation of the law, the Bank was ordered to increase the credit ceilings of various banks, so that, as they were getting money from the Bank to cover losses incurred as a result of unrestrained lending, they were given the opportunity to give out even more credits.[32] For example, in 1994 the BNB was pressured to purchase 80 percent of the bad-debt loans of Economic Bank, which the government had used to subsidize the energy sector.[33] In 1995, the BNB acquired the debts of Agrobiznes Bank, a private institution that had incurred enormous losses.[34] Overall, during the period 1993–96 the volume of refinancing, that is, money given by the Bank to the government and commercial banks, quadrupled. Thus, rather than holding in check profligate politicians, "the BNB always acted as a lender of last resort, providing refinancing to badly performing banks."[35]

Giving out lavish credits was not the only way to subsidize powerful groups affiliated with the BSP. All kinds of pretexts—legal and illegal—were invoked to facilitate the transfer of resources from the coffers of the BNB. A good example was the "purchase" of a building from Orion, the small group of ruthless entrepreneurs close to BSP Chairman Zhan Videnov. The Bank paid Orion approximately $800,000 for a building that Orion did not own, and then did nothing to recover the money.[36] The Bank's resources were thus distributed in accordance with the official and unofficial guidance of powerful politicians and their protégés.[37]

As the high-ranking officials running the Bank were pressured to forego various political and institutional principles for the sake of partisan efficiency, institutional watchdogs that could expose the Bank's activities were dismantled. In 1995, the Agency for Economic Coordination and Development, the sole governmental critic of the Bank's

---

32. See Hristov, "Role for an Independent Central Bank," 147.
33. Roumen Avramov and Kamen Guenov, "The Rebirth of Capitalism in Bulgaria," *Bank Review* 4, no. 4 (April 1994): 20.
34. See the decision of the BNB board of directors published in *Bankov pregled* 11 (1995): 47.
35. Assenka Yonkova, Svetlana Alexandrova, and Latchezar Bogdanov, *Development of the Banking Sector in Bulgaria* (Sofia: Institute of Market Economics, 2000), 16; http://ime-bg.org/bg/top_left.html.
36. See *Sega*, November 26, 1998, 12–13.
37. See Roumen Avramov and Jerome Sgard, "Bulgaria: From Enterprise Indiscipline to Financial Crisis," Document de travail No. 96 (Paris: Centre d'études prospectives et d'informations internationales, 1996).

policies, was integrated into the Ministry of Finance and its leading economists were dismissed.[38] In the rare cases in which the board of directors tried to enforce some banking system rules, its directives were disregarded. Whenever the cooperation of the executive branch was needed in the course of audits and other forms of monitoring, logistical assistance was deliberately refused. Attempts by the BNB leadership to forge cooperative relations with key officials in the bureaucracy—which, as John B. Goodman has argued, is crucial for the maintenance of bank independence—were sabotaged by politicians.[39] For example, the leaders of the BNB repeatedly complained that they were denied the assistance they needed to monitor the banking system, and as a result "the foreign currency operations of commercial banks were largely unsupervised."[40]

After the return of the BSP to power, central bank independence became an empty, meaningless slogan that had nothing to do with political and financial practices in the fledgling Bulgarian democracy. It was finally abolished in 1996, when the BSP-dominated parliament amended the Law on BNB in order to make possible the dismissal of the chairmen and deputies without cause before the end of their term.[41] A new chairman was appointed, who was close both to the BSP and to Multigroup. On this date, the Bank became completely subservient to the BSP, both in its formal policies of supporting the government and its informal decisions regarding distributions of financial resources.

The result was not hard to predict: unmitigated financial disaster. Several months later, the banking system disintegrated, as almost all banks were either closed or put in a receivership, the national currency collapsed, and the savings of millions of citizens were wiped out. In February 1997, the BSP finally gave up its power and agreed to new elections, in which the opposition won an absolute parliamentary majority. One of the first acts of the new parliament was to create a currency board. The Currency Board is an autonomous unit within the Bank. Its function is to convert all domestic currency offered to it into a chosen convertible currency—in the Bulgarian case, the deutsche mark—at an exchange rate set by law at 1 deutsche mark = 1,000 leva. The volume of domestic currency in circulation can be increased only if the foreign exchange reserves of the Bank increase. In other words, the Bank does not possess any significant policy

---

38. Krassen Stanchev, *The Bulgarian National Bank and the Political Process* (Sofia: Institute for Market Economics, 1999), 1; http://ime-bg.org/bg/top_left.html.

39. John B. Goodman, "The Politics of Central Bank Independence," *Comparative Politics* 23, no. 3 (April 1991): 335.

40. See Nenova, "Finansovata politika v Bulgaria," 2.

41. The amendments were published in *Durzhaven vestnik*, April 7, 1996, 4–7.

instruments.⁴² In terms of "democratic self-binding," there is something ambiguous about the Currency Board. On the one hand, it ties the hands of politicians—there is nothing they can do to shape financial policies. On the other hand, it reduces the role of the Bank and deprives it of the prerogative to make important decisions, for example to fix the exchange rate. But there is no doubt, insofar as the effort to "engineer" an independent bank is concerned, the establishment of a currency board should be construed as an open admission of defeat. The BNB proved utterly incapable of restraining Bulgarian political elites. This Western transplant was prevented from taking root in the local political soil, and it quickly degenerated into one of many failed institutional constructions littering a depressing political landscape.

Parallels and Divergences

After a decade of reforms and institution building, Bulgaria emerged as a democratic polity with a strong Constitutional Court and robust judicial review on the one hand, and a defeated independent central bank and a ruined banking system on the other. The complexity of this picture may be easily obfuscated if the success of the Court is neglected and the collapse of the Bank is attributed to the invisible workings of a "Balkan political culture," or if the failure to establish an autonomous bank is disregarded and the rise of the Court is attributed to an abstractly defined "progress toward democracy." If the Court succeeded because the values it embodied were akin to the values of "local political culture," then why did not the same values inhibit elites from undermining bank independence? And if the fate of the Bank is yet another proof that the hubris inherent in ambitious attempts to mimic Western models is ultimately self-defeating, then why did the Court take root? The simultaneity and contradictory nature of these parallel lives must be recognized lest the chance to learn something from the Bulgarian case is lost. This complex story is very difficult to subsume under any of the general propositions that figure prominently in the literature on constitutional engineering. That is why we need an interpretation that explains these differing rates of success against a broader analytical framework structured around the theme of state-building.

---

42. For more on the currency board in a post-Communist setting, see Siim Kallas, "A Currency Board within a Central Bank," *East European Constitutional Review* 3, nos. 3–4 (Summer–Fall 1994): 53–56. On the Bulgarian Currency Board and the economic context in which it was created, see Georgy Ganev and Michael L. Wyzan, "Bulgaria: Macroeconomic and Political-Economic Implications of Stabilization under a Currency Board Arrangement," in *The Political Economy of Reform Failure*, ed. Mats Lundahl and Michael L. Wyzan (London: Routledge, 2005), 170–96.

Any explanation of the puzzle elucidated in this chapter on the parallel lives of political institutions should draw on and further develop the main idea presented in the previous chapter, namely that a dysfunctional infrastructure of governance constitutes the context in which novel state structures, including countermajoritarian devices, are introduced. The Court and the Bank were erected in an institutional environment in which specific syndromes of the dysfunctionality of state structures were readily observable. It is the underlying dynamic that generated such syndromes that ultimately determined the fate of the two experiments.

More specifically, there are two aspects of state weakness as a context that are relevant to the parallel lives of the two institutions: the fragmentation of monitoring mechanisms and administrative apparatuses, and the transformation of the public domain into a largely unguarded arena repeatedly raided by powerful predators. These concrete forms of state weakness had differing impacts on the Court and the Bank, and that is why one of the institutions survived and the other did not.

Monitoring and Administrative Capacity

In a system in which the costs of monitoring are considerable and the capacity of administrative structures is low, institutions whose success is contingent on the cooperation of functioning bureaucratic apparatuses have less of a chance of survival than those that may operate as discrete units. In the aftermath of the separation, conversion, and activation of the nomenklatura connections, levels of monitorability decreased rapidly in the early 1990s. The Court's effectiveness did not depend on elaborate data-gathering and enforcement procedures—the willingness of a small number of political actors to abide by its rulings was all that mattered. Why politically savvy animals like Premyanov, Lukanov, and the Orion circle chose to recognize rather than destroy the authority of the Bulgarian justices certainly has something to do with the fact that the justices were interfering with formal policymaking, whereas the main opportunities for personal enrichment and predatory expansion lay elsewhere. The opposite is true for the Bank, which could only carry out its functions if it was more or less tightly "hooked" to a system of supporting organizations (such as the Ministry of Finance and the network of commercial banks). Hence the opaqueness of the infrastructure of governance was not a principal hindrance to the Court but had a debilitating effect on the Bank.

The Public Domain as an Object of Extraction

Arguably, the most intriguing conclusion to which the state-centered perspective developed in earlier chapters leads us is that as the state was being "engineered from above," it was also constantly targeted as *an object of extraction*. This perspective makes it easier to understand why preying on the state is the dominant predatory project in the aftermath of the collapse of one-party Communist regimes. The attempt to import Western institutions and, specifically, to impose limits on elite behavior map onto this preexisting predatory project. At least in the short run, the fate of specific institutions depends on how they interfere with the extraction from the state. The crux of the matter may be conveyed in a formulaic fashion: given the incentive structure of the elites involved, if an institution in any way interferes with the process of extraction from the state, it is likely to encounter the resistance of most powerful cohorts, and its survival chances will be limited. If an institution is located "apart" from the channels of extraction, its enemies will be less formidable and, accordingly, its prospects will be less bleak.

From this context-sensitive vantage point it is quite clear that the BNB was certainly a bastion that had to be captured if the process of siphoning off resources from the state was to proceed at full speed. Literally, it was the most important cache that predators could tap into. It would have been costly for these predators to tolerate a bank leadership resistant to giving out lavish credits. Not surprisingly, the leaders of this faction of nomenklatura in the BSP were poised to use all forms of pressure to make the BNB available for extraction. The Court, in contrast, survived because it only had jurisdiction over issues that were not of primary concern to predators—like formal policymaking, demarcation of official spheres of influence, and protecting citizens. Bulgaria's post-Communist predators were only marginally interesting in legislating, disposing of their political rivals, or appropriating the resources held by the citizenry. Hence the unexpected effectiveness of the Court as a deterrent to majoritarian abuses of power.

It is perhaps worth accentuating that knowledge about how imported institutions will map onto preexisting predatory projects cannot be derived in an a priori fashion. It is plausible to assume that in a different historical situation it would be an institution like the Court, rather than the Bank, that would be targeted by predators. But it would be safe to say that general statements of the kind "national elites resisted the establishment of a Western-type, rule-of-law system" are uninformative, if not necessarily untrue. What they gloss over is the specific *types* of constraints predators rebuff and the *local logic* that makes such a course of action attractive to them. Behind every gutted institutional transplant there lies an identifiable mechanism of rejection—a series of steps taken over time in pursuit of comprehensible and context-specific elite projects. Put differently, in the eyes of powerful constituencies, countermajoritarian institutions are not the embodiment of a normative entity with which they have to reckon, but are an array of specific impediments. And, as Giuseppe Di Palma cogently remarked, "It is to this pool of specifics, and not to an abstraction, that political actors in a transition react ... in a variety of ways."[43] How this "pool of specifics" is perceived in early post-Communism—the reasons why powerful elites turn against specific imported constitutional devices designed to limit their behavior—is an important issue that the state-centered perspective illuminates. More generally, it was the dynamic stemming from the reconfiguration of the state domain that determined the relative political weight of institutional imports—or, to use Montesquieu's memorable phrase, that determined the extent to which they possessed "the ballast to resist other powers."[44] In the context of post-Communist state dysfunctionality, even though both the Court and the Bank had similar "ballast," the Bank had to fight more ferocious battles and resist greater powers.

Institutional Experiments and Other Games in Town

An alternative way of looking at the puzzle revealed by the parallel lives of the two political institutions is shown by using a popular metaphor. Summarizing their decades-long research on the structural characteristics and institutional dynamics of contemporary political regimes, Juan Linz and Alfred Stepan opined that "consolidated democracy is a political situation in which democracy has become 'the only game in town.'"[45] But what "other games in town" might attract the attention of powerful players in the aftermath of an authoritarian implosion? At first glance, the answer is self-evident: the term purports to encompass, in Geoffrey Pridham's words, the "non-democratic system alternatives" that threaten to derail the tentative and reversible process of democratization.[46] In other words, these other games in town may be driven by an explicitly antidemocratic animus and trigger covert or overt attempts to sabotage the democratic project. But—and this is the crux of my analysis—the democratic endeavor might unfold simultaneously with elite projects that do not seek to sidetrack democracy but nevertheless impede the consolidation of the

---

43. Giuseppe Di Palma, *To Craft Democracies* (Berkeley: University of California Press, 1990), 15.
44. Montesquieu, *The Spirit of the Laws* (Cambridge: Cambridge University Press, 1989), 63.
45. See also Juan J. Linz and Alfred Stepan, *Problems of Democratic Transition and Consolidation* (Baltimore: Johns Hopkins University Press, 1996), 5. The authors point out that they have borrowed the expression "democracy as the only game in town" from Di Palma, *To Craft Democracies*.
46. See Geoffrey Pridham, "The International Context of Democratic Consolidation," in *The Politics of Democratic Consolidation*, ed. Richard Gunther, Nikiforos Diamandouros, and Hans-Jürgen Puhle (Baltimore: Johns Hopkins University Press, 1995), 168.

institutional framework of democratic governance. With this abundant empirical diversity, the overarching analytical question is: What should be the proper countertheme in the analysis of democratic consolidation in the East European context? In contrast to other cases of postauthoritarian development (e.g., Spain and Greece), the proper counterpoint to the democratic theme is not the persistence of authoritarianism but the transformation of state structures and the enduring loss of state capacity. The diachronic dimension of constitutional experiments highlights the way in which the mechanisms of rejection that erode the integrity of the democratic framework gain momentum from this key other "game in town." It is in this sense that I hold the separation of party and state, conversions of power, and the Dorian Gray Effect to be not simply factors that shape the post-Communist context but *the* context in which a new set of political institutions will have to take root.

What we learn from the parallel lives of the Constitutional Court and the Bulgarian National Bank, then, is that the fate of institutional imports mimicking Western practices might be ultimately determined by how the constitutional project was superimposed on a set of other projects that were rapidly subverting the capacity of the state. This general insight may lead us to the formulation of testable hypotheses about what the institutional targets of predatory elites in post-Communism might be. If my contention that the relative importance of an institution depends on how it interferes with the extraction from the state holds true, then we should expect that an institution such as the Bank, which stood in the way of extraction, was a constant target for political interventions. In contrast, other institutions, such as the Court, that are detached from the flow of extracted resources, were relatively neglected by politicians.

Another possible pairing, amenable to another set of "parallel lives," would be the Privatization Agency and the army. Ever since its establishment in October 1992, and despite repeated vows to keep it above the political fray, the Privatization Agency has been subject to numerous attacks, with its personnel changed every time a new parliamentary majority took over; and the appetites of all politicians to place their confidants in it have proved impossible to contain.[47] In contrast, the army has been neglected by virtually all political elites. To be sure, the resources under the jurisdiction of the army have been targeted by crafty entrepreneurs, and during the first half dozen years of post-Communist transformations the BSP used this institution to provide relatively well-paid positions for its aging contingent of loyalists.[48] But its enormous potential

47. Zoya Mladenova and James Angressano, "Privatization in Bulgaria," *East European Quarterly* 30 (January 1997): 495–516.
48. See, for example, "Dalaveri v armijata," *Banker*, January 27, 1999, 14. See also details in the "Bulgarian Updates" for 1995, published in each issue of *East European Constitutional Review*.

as an instrument of mass coercion has never been exploited by post-Communist elites, and the BSP did not even attempt to establish firmer control over the army or use it for political purposes.[49]

Thus the question of why the Court survived while the Bank crashed cannot be satisfactorily answered if it is delinked from an up-close examination of the ways in which the interrelatedness of the two dimensions of state-building—imposing new structures over dynamically changing existing structures—plays itself out in a post-Communist context. The neo-Plutarchian approach demonstrates that this interrelatedness is not devoid of paradoxes and ironies. It is to G. John Ikenberry that we owe a heightened understanding of what he called "the irony of state strength": "a strong state" may be bound by prior commitments that render it incapable of controlling political outcomes in situations that require manipulative and flexible approaches.[50] My analysis throws light on another irony—the irony of state weakness. A vulnerable state that is targeted for extraction may prove to be "the distraction" that turns the attention of powerful predators away from the emaciated and defenseless citizenry and a fledgling judiciary. Given the nature of the dominant predatory project in post-Communism and the matrix of extractive activities, exotic institutional imports, such as the Constitutional Court, stand a better chance of survival than more traditional institutions such as the Bank. The incredible empowerment of those who were busy transforming existing institutions—and who were engaged in what, borrowing from Charles Tilly, we might describe as "the preliminary, unofficial, illegal, informal, immoral and private aspects of state-making"—constrained and also created opportunities for institutional engineers who wanted to remodel Bulgaria's constitutional edifice.[51]

A close-up look at the complex dynamic of state-building reflected in the parallel lives of political institutions might also persuade us to think about the diachronic dimension of constitutional experiments in terms of specific forms of "political learning" that inform the behavior of key elite coalitions—or in terms of what an admirer of Shakespeare's Katherine and Petruchio might call "the shrewdness of the tamed." Nancy Bermeo defines "political learning" as "the process through which people modify

---

49. This allowed constitutionally weak presidents to develop good rapport with the top brass and expand their influence as "commanders-in-chief"; see Venelin I. Ganev, "Semi-presidentialism in Bulgaria," in *Semi-Presidential Regimes in Europe*, ed. Robert Elgie (Oxford: Oxford University Press, 1999).

50. See G. John Ikenberry, "The Irony of State Strength," *International Organization* 40, no. 1 (Winter 1986): 105–37.

51. See Charles Tilly, "Reflections on the History of European State-Making," in *The Formation of National States in Europe*, ed. Tilly (Princeton: Princeton University Press, 1975), 8.

their political beliefs and tactics as a result of severe crisis, frustrations and dramatic changes in environment," and demonstrated how this process shapes democratic transitions.[52] Rulers and agents of civil society may learn some good things: how to resolve conflicts in a peaceful manner, respect basic rules, follow procedures, and maintain stability. But they may also learn some bad things. Politicians diversify their skills. The knowledge that political elites have gained in post-Communism may be summarized as follows: they have learned to participate in a series of structured interactions that proceed in the absence of conspicuous attempts to restrict constitutional rights and procedures, to adjust their behavior in accordance with legal requirements in a social milieu marked by the radical deficiency of available mechanisms for enforcing political accountability, and to combine low-intensity policymaking with connivance at high-intensity looting of state property. Constitutional constraints work: majorities act in a circumscribed manner, attempts to forcefully subdue civil society are inconsequential, and no entrenched faction stands a chance of annihilating its political and institutional opponents. However, that does not necessarily ensure the accomplishment of that most pressing of political tasks, the designing of a workable modern polis.

The learning that accompanied the transplanting of new structures on preexisting, state-focused predatory projects and propelled the mechanisms of rejection ultimately generated an outcome that might be called "displacement of arbitrariness." Benjamin Constant once remarked that arbitrary power displays the wonderful capacity to "multiply itself" in order to "seize" new objects.[53] This comment suggests that the analysis of arbitrariness in post-Communism should not be reduced to the unveiling of masked continuities with the Communist era, but should ask how unmonitored power goes about the process of "multiplication" and should describe its "new objects." The parallel lives of the Court and the Bank attest to the fact that the multiplying tentacles of arbitrary power no longer are wrapped around the minds and bodies of citizens but are now used to siphon off the resources of the state. Arbitrary appropriations do not threaten the citizens directly and immediately: they take place in the administratively defined "space" encompassing the management of state-owned enterprises, banks, and other agencies that possess residual rights over state property—in other words, a space that is the final destination of resources funneled through the Bank but that rarely intersects

---

52. Nancy Bermeo, "Democracy and the Lessons of Dictatorship," *Comparative Politics* 24, no. 3 (April 1993): 274.
53. Benjamin Constant, "The Liberty of the Ancients Compared to That of the Moderns," in *Constant* (Cambridge: Cambridge University Press, 1988), 324.

with the proper domain of judicial review. The most revealing manifestation of arbitrary power in early post-Communism is the seizure of the material and organizational resources accumulated by the state.[54]

Ultimately, contexts do not repulse imported institutions; political agents do. Beneath the debris of failed institutional experiments one may hear the ticking of specific mechanisms of rejection activated by knowledgeable actors involved in fathomable games in town. These mechanisms, however, do not follow the abstract logics of self-interest or culturally embedded historical tradition, but are grounded in historically specific state-building episodes. That is why Elias Canetti's wise observation that "the moment of survival is the moment of power" probably does not reveal the whole truth about political experiments. It might be precisely the weak, the marginal, and the irrelevant that would be spared. But to understand whether that might be the case, we have to stop forcing the story of post-Communism into the conceptual frame of a bildungsroman about the organic growth of state structures in a developing democracy. Given the peculiarity of the subject matter, a collection of short stories about ironic turns of events and the peculiar ways in which seemingly obscure incidents illustrate enduring dilemmas might be a more compelling genre.

---

54. See Venelin I. Ganev, "Bulgaria's Symphony of Hope," *Journal of Democracy* 8, no. 4 (October 1997): 135–38.

7 Post-Communism as an Episode of State Transformation

> In the best ordered of lives, there always comes a moment when structures collapse.... The realization that life is absurd cannot be an end, but only a beginning.
>
> ALBERT CAMUS, "On Jean-Paul Sartre's *La Nausée*," 1938

In an incisive short essay, John Dunn observes that there are two ways to investigate "a state in crisis." The first is detached and dispassionate, aspiring to grasp the facts, develop theories, and offer explanations. The second is permeated by ethical concerns and practical considerations that ultimately seek "to guide judgment and perhaps even to prompt action."[1] In this book I have attempted a balancing act that endeavors to reconcile the two approaches. Insofar as what I offer is an inquiry into the malfunctioning of the infrastructure of governance, my analysis is centered on to developments that render aspects of reality unacceptable from a normative point of view. The semantic overtones of the terms that I routinely use to designate the subject matter of this book—"weakness," "loss of logistical capacity," "institutional decomposition," "fracturing of administrative apparatuses"—seem to bespeak the frustrations of observers whose expectations about "good governance" after the implosion of authoritarian state socialism were shattered along with the unaccountably brittle state structures. But even though nontheoretical worries simmer behind the concerns that propelled this book, my inquiry into the fluctuation of post-Communist stateness deliberately eschews the accusatory slant and hortatory exultations implicit in such questions as "Who is to blame?" and "What is to be done?"[2]

---

1. See John Dunn, Preface to *Contemporary Crisis of the Nation State?* ed. Dunn (Oxford: Blackwell, 1995), 1.
2. An amalgamation of one's personal concerns and the broader theoretical objectives of scholarly analyses is indispensable for good work in comparative politics: this I take

In this final chapter, I spell out the implications of my case study of Bulgaria for the theoretical and comparative analysis of post-Communism. I hope that what will emerge is not only a sharper picture of the problems with which Bulgaria and other East European societies have had to grapple but also a clearer, if admittedly unsettling, vision of the formidable difficulties that obstruct any effort to create efficient instruments of democratic governance in the modern world.

In order to understand the reconfiguration of state structures in early post-Communism, we need to complement the state-centered approach with an analytical perspective that draws on major insights from the scholarly literature on the historical sociology of state formation. In a deservedly admired 1997 book, Thomas Ertman urges scholars exploring the transformations and transmogrifications of state structures in the post-Communist world to turn for intellectual sustenance to the rich literature on state making in early modern Europe. "The European state-building experience," Ertman argues, constitutes "the only case of sustained political development comparable in scale and scope to the one unleashed by the recent wave of state formation." That is why it may cast light on the key challenge facing post-Communist polities: "How is it possible, under conditions of rapid social and economic change, to construct stable and legitimate governments and honest and effective systems of public administration and finance, all while maintaining an often fragile national unity?"[3]

The engrossing investigative themes developed in the numerous studies of the politico-administrative institutions of postfeudal Europe are largely absent from scholarly works on post-Communism. Researchers who analyzed the permutations of state machineries in the former second world rarely if ever drew inspiration from the historical sociology of early modern governance. Observers who wished to understand the factors that militate against the creation of stable and legitimate government seemed oblivious of the past "European state-building experience." In short, the dialogue between those who study post-Communism and those who explore previous waves of state formation has failed to materialize.

In this final chapter, I wish to draw upon my state-centered study of Bulgaria to relaunch this dialogue. I have already demonstrated how the socialist state domain was reconfigured as a result of ongoing conflicts over the distribution of logistical resources, entrepreneurial conversions

---

to be the gist of Peter Evans's contribution to the symposium on "The Role of Theory in Comparative Politics," *World Politics* 48, no. 1 (October 1995): 2–10.

3. Thomas Ertman, *Birth of the Leviathan* (Cambridge: Cambridge University Press, 1997), 1.

of power, strategic exercise of specific types of veto power, and attempts to build new institutions "from above." Now I will use historical parallels to highlight the peculiar dynamic and directionality of these developments and link them to this most important attribute of the post-Communist political condition, the infrastructural weakness of post-Communist states. This comparative strategy will demonstrate both why Bulgaria should be considered an "episode which [has] relevance to theoretical debates"[4] and why any future inquiry into the fluctuations of post-Communist stateness should begin with attempts to conceptualize post-Communism as a historically specific period of state transformation.

The conceptualization I defend here rests on an analytical perspective that, honoring the foremost student of European state formation, Charles Tilly, I shall call "the reversed Tillyan perspective." It builds on two main presuppositions: that the crisis of state capacity was a consequence of the structural legacy of state socialism, and that this legacy should be examined through the optic of the historical sociology of statemaking. In other words, I compare what transpired during the first decade of post-Communist transformations in Bulgaria to previous waves of state formation in order to grasp the dynamic that reshaped the institutions of governance after the implosion of the ancien régime. The reversed Tillyan perspective seeks to combine conceptual rigor with heightened sensitivity to the historical specificity of early post-Communism. The analysis presented in the previous chapter demonstrates that this specificity is constituted by extant structural characteristics that impart an identifiable directionality to the processes affecting state structures, by a particular set of incentives that shape the predatory behavior of state agents, and by patterns of elite and mass positioning vis-à-vis the public domain. My case study of Bulgaria suggests that the analytical terrain that students of state-building in post-Communism must traverse should be structured around three broader questions.

First, what are the distinct features of the socioeconomic context and how do they impinge on the process of state-building? I take as a baseline of my analysis the proposition that "one cannot do historical sociology in a historical vacuum."[5] In other words, any comprehensive analysis of the reconfiguration of stateness should begin with a careful, theoretically informed examination of the sociohistorical context. The evidence from the Bulgarian case elucidates precisely the salient features of the context that should attract the attention of analysts willing to avoid the pitfalls of "vacuum theorizing." More concretely, it

---

4. John A. Hall and G. John Ikenberry, *The State* (Minneapolis: University of Minnesota Press, 1989), 15.
5. Philip Abrams, *Historical Sociology* (Somerset: Open Publishing, 1982), 18.

lends credence to the proposition that this context is primarily made up of the multilayered legacies of state socialism, specifically the state-owned economy and the merger of party and state. These legacies constrain certain modes of action while facilitating others. How this particular interrelatedness of empowerment and restraint affects the infrastructural capacity of the state is the key contextual question that historical-sociological inquiry into post-Communist state-building will have to answer. The reference to "legacies" should not be construed as a plea for studying continuities and *longues durées*. "The great virtue" of comparative historical perspectives, Samuel Beer has reminded us, is that they "show discontinuities we never suspected."[6] The analysis of theoretically important consequences of state socialism, then, may help us make sense of sudden reversals, institutional disjunctures, and the liquefication of seemingly solid structures. The loss of infrastructural capacity would then appear as a phenomenon occurring in a particular setting whose main facets must be interpreted from a comparative historical perspective.

Second, what are the strategic alternatives available to predatory elites? Modes of elite action have rightfully been put at the foreground of various analyses of post-Communism. Yet this line of inquiry has remained somewhat underdeveloped, concentrated exclusively either on formally instituted policies or on informally practiced "corruption."[7] Scarce attention has been paid to the structure of the concrete incentives that shape elite action. As Kiren Aziz Chaudhry has convincingly demonstrated, it is the survey of those incentives that may help us understand why in some cases coalitions of powerful actors will favor the maintenance of robust state apparatuses, while in other cases they would not.[8] A historically constituted opportunity structure shapes strategic behavior, which in turn determines whether efforts to reproduce patterns of domination will result in the creation of "strong states"—and national markets—or precipitate the fracturing of preexisting institutions. A descriptive labeling of post-Communist political elites as "predatory" or "corrupt" will not advance the heuristic potential of an explanatory framework. As Julia Adams points out, the notion of "predation," to be useful, must be suffused with "historically and systematically specific meaning."[9] A solid account of the predatory

---

6. Samuel Beer, "Political Science and History," in *Essays in Theory and History*, ed. Melvin Richter (Cambridge: Harvard University Press, 1970), 63.

7. For a good collection of essays on the subject, see Stephen Kotkin and Andras Sajo, eds., *Political Corruption* (Budapest: Central European University Press, 2002).

8. Kiren Aziz Chaudhry, *The Price of Wealth* (Ithaca: Cornell University Press, 1997).

9. Julia Adams, "Culture in Rational-Choice Theories of State Formation," in *State/Culture*, ed. George Steinmetz (Ithaca: Cornell University Press, 1999), 116.

practices of state agents and their institutional consequences should therefore figure prominently in analytical narratives about state-building in post-Communism—and it is the state-centered perspective on state restructuring in early post-Communism that provides such an account. Of course, the focus on patterns of elite action is something different from the analysis of elites' intentions and/or grand designs. Theda Skocpol, among others, has argued that truly historical sociological studies "attend to the interplay of meaningful actions and structural contexts, in order to make sense of the unfolding of unintended as well as intended outcomes in individual lives and social transformations."[10] My case study of Bulgaria demonstrates that what matters is not the intention of state agents but the peculiar ways in which post-Communist predatory practices intrude on what Gabriel Ardant called "the practical, concrete, and technical conditions" that affect the infrastructural capacity of modern states.[11]

Third, what are the implications of the various ways in which elites and masses position themselves vis-à-vis the public domain for the consolidation of state structures? Historical sociologists such as Stein Rokkan have persuasively argued that an essential aspect of state-building is the institutionalization of societal relations between ruling elites and populations.[12] The creation of state structures is not exclusively an elite-driven endeavor, and it inevitably involves interactions between power holders and numerous groups within society. Topics such as the exact nature of elite-mass cleavages and whether and how such cleavages are bridged should be incorporated in research agendas on state transformation. Predatory elite action is not simply unleashed on subordinate "masses"; it also gives rise to various modes of societal engagements involving large constituencies that eventually may crystallize in a reproducible framework of governance. The ways in which these larger constituencies become involved in ongoing attempts to negotiate elite-mass cleavages is an important determinant of state capacity and the organizational coherence of administrative apparatuses. An adequate interpretation of this interactive component of state-building in post-Communism will illuminate the nature of the social factors that contribute to—or militate against—the consolidation of state structures. Without even attempting to exhaust the complex question of popular reactions to

---

10. Theda Skocpol, "Sociology's Historical Imagination," in *Vision and Method in Historical Sociology*, ed. Skocpol (Cambridge: Harvard University Press, 1984), 1.

11. Gabriel Ardant, "Financial Policy and Economic Infrastructure of Modern States and Nations," in *The Formation of National States in Western Europe*, ed. Charles Tilly (Princeton: Princeton University Press, 1975), 164.

12. Stein Rokkan, *State Formation, Nation-Building and Mass Politics in Europe* (Oxford: Oxford University Press, 1999).

political change in Eastern Europe in the 1990s (a topic on which Bela Greskovits is the foremost authority), I will weave my findings about Bulgaria into a broader claim about the institutional consequences of the particular way in which larger constituencies are involved in predatory elite projects in post-Communism.[13]

The state-centered interpretation of the Bulgarian case thus brings together the hitherto parallel literatures on the historical sociology of state making, and on post-Communism. At the center of the intersecting field of inquiry stands a conceptualization of post-Communism as an episode of state transformation characterized by historically specific socioeconomic structures, patterns of elite agency that are both shaped by and in turn remold these structures, and modes of social engagement—involving predatory elites and the citizenry at large—that affect the level of institutionalization of governance.

The Reversed Tillyan Perspective

Why and how robust state structures emerge in history is not among the questions to which the scholarly community offers clear and unambiguous answers. There is, however, one particular account of this historical process that, in my opinion, is more powerful and insightful than anything else written on the subject: Charles Tilly's analysis of state formation in Western Europe. My argument about the causes of devolution of state capacity in post-Communism is structured around analytical scaffolding largely borrowed from Tilly's work. I hope to demonstrate that Tilly's explorations of the rise of modern states—explorations that "set the agenda for this kind of study of Western European history"—revolves around a coherent set of analytical themes.[14] Next, I will try to weave these themes into an analytical matrix and apply this matrix to post-Communism in order to highlight the factors at work in the weakening of the post-Communist state. More specifically, I will rely on my state-centered analysis of the Bulgarian case in order to depict in an analytical fashion the legacy of Communism and then explain why this legacy facilitated the rise of a new elite predatory project, which I will call "extraction from the state." From a historical-sociological perspective, the most conspicuous feature of this project is that it is inimical to the creation and maintenance of effective and strong state structures. The process of "elite selection" in the peculiar institutional setting left behind by collapsed Communist regimes favors logistically well-endowed groups—such as Orion and

---

13. Bela Greskovits, *The Political Economy of Protest and Patience* (Budapest: Central European University Press, 1998).
14. Samuel Clark, *State and Status* (Cardiff: University of Wales Press, 1995), 6.

Multigroup—that have no incentive to develop administrative-bureaucratic instruments of governance. This elite predatory project is not likely to encounter effective social opposition and may inflict enormous damage to state structures unless countered by democratically elected elites who have a vested interest in strengthening public institutions.

A good way to commence an in-depth survey of Tilly's ideas would be with his respectful criticisms of the ideas of Barrington Moore Jr., Stein Rokkan, and Lewis Mumford, criticisms that reveal a source of dissatisfaction with the literature on the emergence of state structures.[15] In a nutshell, he insists that more general analysis of societal change and the evolution of socioeconomic structures should be paralleled by a close-up look at the development of the mechanisms and institutions of governance.[16] Tilly argues, for example, that Moore has undoubtedly made a great contribution to the study of class coalitions, but "said little about the actual mechanisms that transferred a certain form of class power into a specific mode of government." Rokkan sensitized his readers to the variability of European political systems, but "his project left a muddled idea of the actual social processes connecting changes [in the relations among rulers, neighboring powers, dominant classes, and religious institutions] with alternative state trajectories." Mumford illuminated the significance of power and production as major factors in the growth of modern states but rather mechanically treated "forms of rule as outgrowths of prevailing technology."[17] For Tilly, then, the proper understanding of historical processes affecting state structures involves an account of elite strategies in a concrete historical environment, an analysis of the interplay between those strategies and specific social and economic structures, and an inquiry into the emergence of a coherent institutional framework of governance.

In his mature writings on state formation Tilly emphasizes that state structures should be considered neither as the natural offshoot of preordained evolutionary historical processes nor as epiphenomenal to the interplay of broadly defined "social forces."[18] His discussion of the

---

15. See Barrington Moore Jr., *Social Origins of Dictatorship and Democracy* (Boston: Beacon Press, 1966); Stein Rokkan, "Dimensions of State Formation and Nation Building," in *Formation of National States in Western Europe*, 562–600; Lewis Mumford, *The Myth of the Machine* (New York: Harcourt, Brace, 1970).

16. For a similar point about Tilly's approach to the study of social strife and modes of class contention, see Lynn Hunt, "Charles Tilly's Collective Action," in *Vision and Method in Historical Sociology*, ed. Skocpol, 250.

17. Charles Tilly, *Coercion, Capital and European States, AD 990–1992* (Cambridge: Blackwell, 1992), 12, 13, 14.

18. See Charles Tilly, "War Making and State Making as Organized Crime," in *Bringing the State Back In*, ed. Theda Skocpol, Peter Evans, and Dietrich Rueschemeyer (Cambridge: Cambridge University Press, 1985), 169–91, and Tilly, *Coercion*.

conditions that facilitate the rise of modern state forms revolves around a three-pronged argument designed to fit the peculiarities of West European development. State structures are shaped by what might be called the dominant elite project (in Tilly's interpretation, this project is war making), which unfolds within specific socioeconomic structures (Tilly focuses primarily on the various structures to be found in medieval Europe) that begins to crystallize in reproducible organizational forms (in Tilly's account, quasi-administrative agencies providing the resources necessary for war making). I think this argument is applicable to other historical settings, and to post-Communism in particular. To "transpose" this analytical scheme, it is imperative to understand the nature of the respective dominant elite project, to explore how it is embedded in socioeconomic structures, and to examine its organizational-infrastructural impact.

It is well known that Tilly integrates these distinct analytical concerns into a powerful account of the historical significance of war making.[19] It is also noteworthy that this astute observer—who rarely leaves the analytical stones along his path unturned—does not spend too much time explaining *why* war making became the dominant elite project in early modern Europe. To the question "Why did wars occur at all?" he provides the following succinct—and in my view convincing—answer: "The central, tragic fact is simple: coercion *works*, those who apply substantial force to their fellows get compliance and from that compliance draw the multiple advantages of money, goods, deference, access to pleasures denied to less powerful people."[20] Scholars bent on comprehending the dominant elite project in a certain age need not resort to obtuse theorizing—a careful examination of the historical record and sound intuition about the nature of politics during that age will suffice. At the same time, however, why in a concrete institutional setting certain types of elite projects are "rewarded" and how these projects affect state structures invites serious theoretical, conceptual, and comparative work.

In his analysis of the linkages between war making and state making, Tilly discards any simplistic notions of intentionality. On the one hand, he asserts that what powerful actors do matters a great deal, and in that respect his account undeniably belongs to a category that Rogers M. Smith has called "agency-sympathetic," that is, accounts confirming that "our commonsensical feelings of genuine agency are

---

19. See Tilly, *Coercion*, and also Brian Downing, *The Military Revolution and Political Change* (Princeton: Princeton University Press, 1992), and William McNeil, *The Pursuit of Power* (Chicago: University of Chicago Press, 1982).

20. Tilly, *Coercion*, 70; emphasis in original.

right."[21] On the other hand, he emphatically rejects the notion that rulers consciously created state institutions that would "optimize" their war efforts. "Rarely did Europe's princes," Tilly asserts, "have in mind a precise model of the sort of state they were producing, and even more rarely did they act efficiently to produce such a model state.... No one designed the principal components of national states."[22] But in the absence of deliberate design, how is the dominant elite project linked to the rise of state structures?

It is in this context that the problem of extraction becomes relevant. Drawing on intellectual precursors such as Vilfredo Pareto, Tilly defines extraction as "acquiring the means for carrying out [the rulers'] activities."[23] Notably, he uses that concept to elucidate not the timeless plot of how the strong exploit the weak but the concrete social dynamics that engender tangible institutional consequences. In particular, he demonstrates that the extraction of resources from potentially rebellious populations is closely linked to the enhanced "stateness" of modern political regimes and the rise of "statism" as a quasi ideology of governance.[24] The key question, then, is where are the resources that dominant elites strive to acquire "located" and what does it take to "extract" them? The term "location," of course, is not used in a geographical sense but to denote specific nodes in the web of institutions, practices, and conventions allocating control over resources in societies.

Accounts of context-specific modes of extraction play a dual function in Tilly's argument. On the one hand, he highlights the variety of social relations that elites need to enter into in order to procure the resources they need. On the other, he argues that these varying modes of engagement propel the rise of different types of quasi-administrative agencies that may then be used for governance.

Tilly demonstrates convincingly that different types of state structures may be traced back to the prevalence of various forms of "extraction" in specific areas. The "coercive-intensive path" to state formation occurred where the bulk of resources were held by countless peasants and artisans, which impelled rulers to squeeze the means for war from their

21. Rogers M. Smith, "Science, Non-Science, and Politics," in *The Historic Turn in the Human Sciences*, ed. Terence McDonald (Ann Arbor: University of Michigan Press, 1996), 124.
22. Tilly, *Coercion*, 25–26.
23. Tilly, "War Making," 181. See also Vilfredo Pareto, *Sociological Writings* (Totowa, N.J.: Rowman and Littlefield, 1966), particularly the numerous passages on "spoliation."
24. On "statism," construed as "a claim for increased power in the hands of the state machinery," see Immanuel Wallerstein, *The Modern World System*, vol. 1: *Capitalist Agriculture and the Origins of the European World Economy in the Sixteenth Century* (San Diego: Academic Press, 1974).

own populations. This is the most clear-cut case of coercive spoliation, which targeted primarily agricultural surplus. A relatively milder strategy for extracting resources was the "capital-intensive mode," in which rulers relied on "compacts with capitalists—whose interests they served with care—to rent out or purchase military forces." This mode spread in commercially more developed parts of Europe. Finally, there was the hybrid "capitalized coercion mode" that involved elements of both the "coercion-intensive" and the "capital-intensive" modes (historically "this form proved to be more effective in war and therefore provided a compelling model" that all European states soon followed).[25]

The other Tillyan insight that is relevant in this context is that the organizational infrastructures created by rulers will be larger if the cost of extraction is higher—in other words, he explains the rise and strengthening of bureaucracy and various state institutions in terms of a pressing need to extract. The scope and coherence of the set of administrative agencies established as the dominant elite project gained momentum is thus correlated with the "ease" with which extraction is carried out.

This broader view of state-building as a socioeconomic process is supplemented in Tilly's analytical scheme by what might be called an "institutionalist" perspective revolving around the following question: Under what conditions might the dominant elite project be constrained by various rules and regulations? Tilly demonstrates that predatory elite behavior inevitably encounters vehement resistance. And the "taming" of elite projects is what eventually leads to the metamorphosis of organizations originally created to assist rapacious elites into instruments of governance routinely used to satisfy popular demands. Developing an argument that incurred the wrath of orthodox "structuralists" such as Theda Skocpol, Tilly asserts that the values, perceptions, and participation of "the masses" matter: the active involvement of unruly populations in the dominant elite project precipitates "the internal forging of mutual constraints between rulers and ruled" within the polity and puts pressure on power holders "to concede protection [to the weak] and constraints on their own action."[26] This interpretation of the general directionality of elite-mass interactions attendant to processes of extraction is corroborated by the findings of historical sociologists who have studied non-European regions, for example, Barrington Moore's analysis of the "recognized procedures" whereby landlords in Tokugawa Japan "could make their will known and the peasants

---

25. Tilly, *Coercion*, 30.
26. Tilly, "War Making," 170, 186. For Skocpol's criticisms of Tilly, see her *States and Social Revolutions* (Cambridge: Cambridge University Press, 1979), 16.

[could] indicate just how far they are willing to obey."[27] In other words, it is through popular mobilization and participation that domains subservient to "checks and balances" are demarcated. That in a European context taxation became such a domain is due to the fact that it inevitably galvanized all social groups and provoked massive involvement in the political process.

In the absence of such "internal forging of constraints," state structures are bound to remain enmeshed in unrestrained predatory projects. Bertrand Badie's disquieting but insightful analysis of sub-Saharan states confirms Tilly's intuition: "The modest, often insignificant role played by taxation in financing [these] states tends to deprive the populace of a means to exert pressure on and exercise control over the government."[28] Thus in many states in contemporary Africa rulers are not forced to negotiate their projects with the population because they get the resources they need to maintain their coercive apparatuses from abroad. As a result, their predatory behavior is not subject to rules and regulations.

Tilly's argument, then, may be summarized as follows. Robust state structures emerged at a particular juncture in Western Europe because the elite project that dominated the historical scene—war making—required a constant supply of resources that elites did not directly control. Since these resources were held by other social groups, they had to be extracted, which in turn made it imperative for ruling elites to invest time, effort, and money in the creation and maintenance of a viable set of organizations involved in extraction. The extraction itself was an interactive process that was gradually institutionalized, thus leading to the emergence of rules and regulations that ensured to the weak at least some measure of protection against rapacious forays. The convergence of interests and attitudes made possible the rise of a structured, rule-governed, institutionalized domain of effective governance.

It is my contention that the explanatory framework developed by Tilly "travels" quite well: it is a heuristic tool that may be used to dissect processes and developments that differ markedly from the West European experiences that constitute the subject matter of his work. For example, Karen Barkey focuses on "the same variables that have been used to understand variation in Western Europe" in order to highlight the peculiarities of a non-European context of state-formation: the Ottoman route to centralization.[29] In what follows, I employ Tilly's paradigm in order to explain the devolution of state power in Bulgaria and post-Communism more generally.

27. Moore, *Social Origins of Dictatorship and Democracy*, 266.
28. Bertrand Badie, *The Imported State* (Stanford: Stanford University Press, 2000), 14.
29. Karen Barkey, *Bandits and Bureaucrats* (Ithaca: Cornell University Press, 1994), 9.

It would not be an exaggeration to assert that, in this particular historical context, the themes that I delineated above converge on the following question: What are the analytical ramifications of the fact that the transformation of state structures in post-Communism takes place simultaneously with the disintegration of a state-owned economy? As the most important aspect of the structural legacy of state socialism, the state-owned economy is important to the study of state transformation in three distinct ways. First, this structural legacy makes inevitable the rise of a qualitatively new dominant elite project, most aptly described as "extraction from the state." Powerful elites involved in this project prey on the wealth accumulated in the state domain. Second, since these elites are fully capable of manipulating flows of resources *within* the existing institutional edifice of the state, they have no incentive to develop strong state structures. Undermining key institutions from inside is necessary for the success of their project. Finally, this form of predatory behavior does not pit elites against large groups of title holders, which in turn means that (at least in the short to the medium run) the dominant elite project is not likely to encounter popular resistance and therefore to reckon with formal and informal constraints. These three empirically grounded analytical propositions make up the matrix that I call "the reversed Tillyan perspective." While Tilly tells the story of how predatory elites created robust state structures in the face of popular resistance, the post-Communist drama is about how predatory elites weaken state structures despite the persistence of popular demands for more and better governance.

The extraction from the state is a series of interactions whereby resources accumulated in the public domain are effectively removed from there. After forty years of Communist rule marked by relentless coercive appropriations, the party-state was in control of the entire wealth of the nation. Precisely these resources—amassed by the state—are targeted by political elites in post-Communism. These elites stand to reap enormous benefits if they succeed in gaining access to and appropriating strategic "locales" where state assets are stored. Tilly points out that "forms of extraction" that make state-building possible range from "outright plunder to regular tribute to bureaucratized taxation."[30] Similarly, the concrete manifestations of "the extraction from the state" may take a variety of forms. Sometimes what transpires is sudden, large-scale transactions whereby assets stored in the public domain are siphoned off through an intractable maze of offshore companies—which is what happened with the financial empire of Orion. At other times, what takes place is

---

30. Tilly, "War Making," 181.

continuing "refinancing" of private entities by state-owned agencies, as in the case of Multigroup—a practice that eventually comes to a halt when the former use their connections to get their debts cancelled, while the latter go bankrupt.[31] Frequently the extraction from the state involves institutionalized rent seeking, whereby elite-sponsored private entities effectively entrap governments in long-term asymmetrical relationships. The repertoire of post-Communist predators also includes corrupt accounting procedures that make possible the "privatization of profits generated in the public sector" and "nationalization of losses incurred in the private sector."[32] In certain strategic locales, entire sectors of the bureaucracy become "privatized" and begin to channel public assets for the benefit of nomenklatura networks—a mode of redistribution of the national wealth intimately linked to the large-scale processes of separation of party and state and to the "conversion of power."

The Bulgarian case suggests that the habitually used expression "collapse" is somewhat inaccurate: state structures have not disappeared but mediate the predatory projects of "cronies" connected through networks. In other words, they reproduce themselves and sustain the outward flow of resources.

To the question of why extraction from the state becomes the dominant elite project in post-Communism, I will provide a Tillyan answer: it *works*. Those who triumph in this endeavor can delight in previously forbidden wealth. As the rapid ascent of Ilia Pavlov and the Orion group attests, they instantly acquire celebrity status much higher than that of simple businessmen and are accorded social recognition denied to increasingly impoverished ordinary citizens. In the aftermath of the implosion of state socialism, extraction works even better, and there are clear incentives to pursue it with heightened intensity, for at least two interrelated reasons. On the one hand, "democratization" and the campaign to introduce "the rule of law" are interpreted by predators as developments that render the imposition of swift and heavy sanctions increasingly likely. On the other hand, the vicissitudes of the democratic electoral process exacerbate the fears of entrenched elites that their strategic positions may be lost.

There is another, equally noteworthy implication of state-held resources being the primary target of extraction. Predatory elites in post-Communism lack what Thomas Ertman has called "the incentive for

---

31. On this symbiosis, see also Roumen Avramov and Kamen Genov, "The Rebirth of Capitalism in Bulgaria," *Bank Review* 4, no. 1 (1994): 1–27.
32. David Stark, "Not by Design," in *Strategic Choice and Path-Dependency in Post-Socialism*, ed. Jerzy Hausner, Bob Jessop, and Klaus Nielsen (Aldershot: Edward Elgar, 1995), 70.

infrastructural expansion," that is, the incentive to invest in the establishment of viable state institutions.[33] Those who extract from the state are only marginally concerned about flows of resources *into* the state domain and the maintenance of a coherent cohort of civil servants united by a common purpose. The chunks of wealth already available to predators are so huge and are distributed among so few key players that foregoing short-term opportunities in order to sustain extraction over the long run would be patently irrational.[34] Theoretically, predatory elites ought to benefit from the regular replenishing of the state locales they have occupied. And, of course, whatever assets trickle in to the state—the money of the occasional conscientious taxpayer or international financial assistance—will be promptly redistributed. But in practice predators are driven primarily by short-term considerations. If and when these elites are forced to abandon their strategic positions, there will be little or no "organizational residue" for future rulers to build on. The extraction from the state is invariably conducive to the atrophy and decay of the state's extractive agencies.

The historical peculiarity and institutional implications of the dominant predatory project in post-Communism may be better grasped when looked at though an analytical distinction articulated by Norbert Elias. There are two kinds of politically relevant competition, Elias avers: struggle for establishing a monopoly over means of governance, and struggle for control over an already existing monopoly. In certain situations, competing elites strive either to impose or to resist monopolies. Then, Elias points out, "from a certain point of development on, the struggle for monopolies no longer aims at their destruction; it is a struggle for control of their yields, for the plan according to which their burdens and benefits are to be divided up, in a word, for the keys to distribution."[35] The unique feature of post-Communism is that there is a string of keys to resource-rich "locales," and the best way to gain control over these locales is not to take possession of the entire chain (that may get you in a fight with lots of other contenders) but to demolish the chain and run away with the few keys you can get.[36] The waning capacity of the state to control its "own" resources is reflected in the shifting balance between political and nonpolitical forms of distribution. In a way resembling premodern

---

33. Ertman, *Birth of the Leviathan*, 315.
34. See also Steven Solnick, "Russia over the Edge," *East European Constitutional Review* 7, no. 4 (Fall 1998): 70–72.
35. Norbert Elias, *The Civilizing Process*, 2 vols. (Oxford: Blackwell, 1994), 353. The entire section 3 of chapter 2 ("On the Monopoly Mechanism") is quite pertinent to my discussion of the post-Communist political condition.
36. For a somewhat similar insight, see Stefan Hedlund, *Russia's "Market" Economy* (London: UCL Press, 1999), 329.

times, the success of networks of winners depends on the fracturing of the dominant "monopolist," that is, the state.

Furthermore, the social and economic structures amid which the dominant elite project unfolds are strikingly different from those described by Tilly. Under Communism—as well as immediately after 1989—all the means of production, natural resources, and financial assets were held by state agents, which meant that "economic structures" were entwined with administrative agencies. The social domain, on the other hand, was largely flattened: organized groups and intermediary organizations were nonexistent. Although an argument can be made that "subjects" under Communism enjoyed some room to negotiate relations in the workplace and indulged in small-scale strategies for resistance, there were no clearly articulated "interests" around which organized groups could begin to coalesce.[37] The capacity of civil society to monitor elite action beyond the extremely narrow confines of labor relations was nonexistent.

As a *social process*, then, extraction from the state is quite different from war making, and the major difference is easy to comprehend. For better or worse, post-Communist predators have absolutely no interest in the meager possessions held by the citizens inhabiting "civil society" (a circumstance that accounts for the surprisingly low levels of repression in Bulgaria's fledgling post-Communist democracy, as well as elsewhere in Eastern Europe). In post-Communism, rulers are not compelled to go out and acquire resources held by identifiable and potentially mobilizable social groups. That is why they have little incentive to become representative elites engaged in primarily formal modes of political competition. As the Bulgarian case demonstrates, a rescaling of elite predatory action occurs in post-Communism, from large-scale campaigns toward small-scale strategic transactions. Initial investments in massive, organized operations are not necessary—with the complicity of very few "insiders" operating exclusively from within state agencies, the success of the dominant elite project is ensured.

From that perspective, it becomes clear that the extraction from the state in early post-Communism gained momentum not by means of large-scale coercion but through a set of painless operations likely to encounter no sustained social resistance. Why did not anyone resist in a forceful manner the dominant predatory project? Because large segments of the population were *not* liable to feel immediate pain and suffer abuse at the hands of concrete "enemies." No individual citizen and no social group were *forced* to turn over their personal assets or property to someone else.

---

37. See also Jadwiga Staniszkis, *The Ontology of Socialism* (Oxford: Clarendon Press, 1992).

It was the eventual depreciation of such assets and the decay of the infrastructure whereby vital public services were provided that ultimately led to widespread social suffering and poverty in 1996–97. But the process was *gradual* and seemingly propelled by forces beyond the reach of common citizens. It was not associated with the instantaneous pain attendant on coercive interactions with *identifiable* social actors, such as the government or class rivals. In sum, during the crucial stages of the transformation of state structures larger constituencies were not involved, neither as victims nor as collaborators.

That the dominant elite project did not involve large-scale coercion is thus a historical specificity of post-Communist predation that goes a long way toward explaining the relative absence of resistance to the ransacking of the public domain. Tilly defines coercion as "all concerted applications, theoretical and actual, of action that commonly causes loss or damage to the persons or possessions of individuals and groups who are aware of both the action and the potential damage." He laments the "cumbersomeness" of this definition but argues that it makes it possible to draw a distinction between coercive elite projects and what he describes as "involuntary, inadvertent or secret damage."[38] His term *secret damage* dovetails quite nicely with the evidence from Bulgaria and is especially pertinent to the study of post-Communism. The extraction from the state takes place in arcane bureaucratic "spaces" from which the citizenry is by definition excluded. That is why—and this is a major difference in comparison with early modern Europe—the domain where extraction proceeds is not marked by the galvanization of mass participation and is not the immediate focal point of popular involvement. Insofar as it involved, so to speak, the extraction of the extracted, the dominant elite project in post-Communism does *not* have to be renegotiated by means of bargaining and compromise. Legal rules and regulations are not lacking; however, there is no mobilized social constituency capable of monitoring the management of state property and enforcing rules against predatory elites.

It bears emphasizing that when the post-Communist state was being stripped of its assets, it did not possess the institutional wherewithal to replenish its coffers. Writing about the rise of the "tax state" more than eighty years ago, Schumpeter predicted that "if socialism became a reality through the conquest of the economy by the power of the state, the state would annul itself by its very expansion."[39] Whether this is true or false in a general political sense is a matter of dispute; certainly,

---

38. Tilly, *Coercion*, 19.
39. Joseph Schumpeter, "The Crisis of the Tax State," in *The Economics and Sociology of Capitalism*, ed. Richard Swedberg (Princeton: Princeton University Press, 1991), 109.

however, the state under socialism "annulled" itself as a *tax* state. The collection of taxes as a function was completely swallowed up by the managerial function of the state as owner of the economy. As a political body, therefore, the post-Communist state relied for its financing—to use Max Weber's term—on "the existence of a productive establishment under [its] direct control."[40] The state had virtually no institutions designed to collect taxes from the citizenry and no institutions to reach out and "extract" resources from the private sector.[41] As the Bulgarian case shows, when this source of income dries up or is annihilated by the invasions of those who "convert political power into economic influence," the potency of state infrastructures is sapped. The argument is often made in the literature that it would be unreasonable to expect that institutions and practices that developed in the West in the course of decades and even centuries will be instantly replicated in the incipient democracies in Eastern Europe. This line of reasoning is usually followed in the analysis of party systems, the judiciary, and the institutional underpinnings of market exchange. It should be applied to the consolidation of the tax system as well. Given the lack of incentives for infrastructural expansion, the state, this most fundamental political organization, is stuck in an unenviable situation: as its brittleness becomes ever more pronounced, it also loses its main source of financing.

It should be also mentioned that the extraction from the state takes place in a propitious global context that logistically facilitates the looting of public domains. As the "happy" ending of the Orion saga makes obvious, the speed and opaqueness of computerized financial transactions is a sine qua non for the ultimate success of predatory elite behavior. In an international economy that affords ample opportunities for unencumbered "flexible accumulation" (to use a term coined by David Harvey), the prospect of impunity looms large in the calculus of those who loot public domains.[42] With ridiculous effortlessness, local predators may re-emerge as respectable, if somewhat obscure, "investors" in some of the nicer neighborhoods of the global capitalist village.

Thus the "reversed Tillyan perspective" furnishes a vantage point that allows us to analyze elite behavior not in the light of ahistorical assumptions about human nature (e.g., that rulers will inevitably steal whatever

---

40. Max Weber, *Economy and Society*, vol. 1 (Berkeley: University of California Press, 1978), 197.
41. See also Klaus Nielsen, Bob Jessop, and Jerzy Hausner, "Institutional Change in Post-Socialism," in *Strategic Choice and Path Dependence in Post-Socialism*, 3–46.
42. On "flexible accumulation," see David Harvey, *The Condition of Postmodernity* (Cambridge, Mass.: Blackwell, 1990).

they can put their hands on) or acontextual postulates about the nature of ruling (e.g., that its purpose is the maximization of power or revenue) but in a historically specific context.[43] It suggests that post-Communist predation is distinctly different from other forms of predatory behavior discussed in the literature on modern governance. Insofar as the extraction from the state targets the public domain rather than resources held by identifiable social groups, it is not predatory in the sense intimated by Douglass C. North, who focused exclusively on the activities of "a group or class [seeking] to extract income from the rest of the constituents in the interest of that group or class."[44] No such direct transfers have occurred in a post-Communist setting. To the extent that the extraction from the state does not entail the unrestrained physical and psychological victimization of weak civil societies, it is different from the mode of predatory behavior analyzed by Peter Evans. The main protagonists in the sad dramas explored by Evans are "rapacious incumbents who are autonomous from those above them and prey upon those below them."[45] As I have already noted, the attitude of predators toward "the masses" is one of indifference rather than violent aggressiveness. Finally, to the extent that the extraction from the state thrives on informal networking rather than formal policymaking, it is different from the state-led predation described by John Waterbury: "Through deficit financing and external borrowing the appetite of the state was sated at the expense of future generations."[46] As a rule, predatory actions in post-Communism are not grounded in a centralized budgetary process that runs amok and radically discounts the interests of future generations. These actions may be best characterized as privatistic forays that circumvent the political process altogether.

In Tilly's account, elites create a web of institutions in order to channel resources to the treasury and are forced to negotiate the terms of their predatory projects with mobilized social groups. The outcome is robust state structures. In post-Communism, elites emasculate existing state agencies in order to extract resources *from* the state; they do not have to reckon with societal counterparts or face enforcement of rules and conventions imposing constraints on their projects. The result is the decomposition of state structures.

---

43. On the theoretical assumption that rulers maximize revenue, see Margaret Levy, *Of Rule and Revenue* (Berkeley: University of California Press, 1988).

44. Douglas North, *Structure and Change in Economic History* (New York: W. W. Norton, 1981), 22.

45. Peter Evans, "Predatory, Developmental, and Other Apparatuses," *Sociological Forum* 4, no. 4 (December 1989): 561–87.

46. John Waterbury, *Exposed to Innumerable Delusions* (Cambridge: Cambridge University Press, 1993), 20.

The Paradox of Political Openings in the Contemporary World

That post-Communist societies are undergoing "multiple transitions" is by now commonplace in the literature. When the concrete dimensions of this "problem of simultaneity" are specified, however, the accent is habitually placed on the synergy of economic reforms and democratic consolidation.[47] The "reversed Tillyan perspective" enables us to see that a third, equally important process was unfolding in the 1990s: the reconfiguration of state structures. Research agendas designed to explore the puzzles of post-Communist politics will be considerably enriched if the problematic of state-building is considered alongside the well-known analytical issues related to marketization and democratization.[48]

Looked at through the prism of this triple-layered transition, the Bulgarian case suggests that the interplay of democratization, marketization, and state formation gives rise to a peculiar institutional conundrum that might be called "the paradox of democratic openings." The gist of this paradox is that there is a disjuncture between the *goals* post-Communist societies set out to pursue and the *means* available for the accomplishment of these goals. On the one hand, the collapse of state socialism was a major turning point that made it possible for society to expand its ideological horizons and engage in the pursuit of a wholly new set of variegated goals and values. On the other hand, the same phenomenon set off dramatic institutional changes that inflicted serious damage on the very tools that modern societies rely on in pursuing these goals: state bureaucracies, administrative agencies, and a corps of civil servants. The dramatic political changes that mark the end of authoritarian domination adversely affect existing infrastructures of governance.

Conceivably, the damage inflicted on the machinery of democratic rule may be traced back to ideological factors such as the antidemocratic worldviews of key segments of the civil service, or to political factors such as the intransigence of social forces loyal to the ancien régime. The evidence from Bulgaria shows, however, that in post-Communism the paradox of political openings—the situation in which heightened political expectations go together with the blunting of tools of governance—stems from

---

47. See, for example, Adam Przeworski, *Democracy and the Market* (Cambridge: Cambridge University Press, 1991).

48. Along the same lines, see Petr Kopecky and Cass Mudde, "What Has Eastern Europe Taught Us about the Democratization Literature?" *European Journal of Political Research* 37, no. 4 (June 2000): 517–39, and esp. Anna Grzymala-Busse and Pauline Jones-Luong, "Reconceptualizing the State," *Politics and Society* 30, no. 4 (December 2002): 529–54.

what a Weberian connoisseur might describe as "changes in the economic order." An economic order, according to Weber, is "the distribution of actual control over goods and services [and] the manner in which goods and services are indeed used by virtue of these powers of disposition which are based on *de facto* recognition."[49] The idea of "economic order" is juxtaposed to the ideal of "legal order," or de jure relations, which, according to Weber, "has nothing directly to do with the world of real economic conduct."[50] A student of historical episodes of state formation might easily imagine a socio-institutional environment in which a predatory state appropriates resources that legally ought to be beyond its reach. The opposite scenario, however, is also plausible: a state may operate with much less than it is entitled to because it is preyed upon by elite individuals or groups. It is this scenario that materialized in post-Communist Bulgaria. The most salient feature of the Communist legacy is that the domain of "goods and services"—to use Weber's expression—is *identical* with the "political" domain, that is, the domain of governance. The unfolding of the extraction from the state as a dominant elite project entails that the struggle for recognition between private competitors will be preceded, due to the historical circumstances, by a fight between agencies managing state property and their organizational rivals. The economic order of post-Communist political capitalism, then, is marked by the swift and massive reversal of de facto control over nominally state-owned assets.

The proper way to depict the key institutional reversal associated with the end of state socialism is not "elite turnover," "collapse of the socialist state," "regime change," or "transplantation of Western constitutional models." An analytically more fitting label would be "stratification of organizations." This rare mode of stratification is defined by Arthur Stinchcombe as "rapid structural change [that] introduces uncertainty and dissensus on the principles of ranking of organizations."[51] Under Communism, the main principle underpinning the hierarchy of organizations was clear and virtually uncontested. These societies were, to use a popular expression coined by T. H. Rigby, "mono-organizational": everyone was more or less coerced to follow the directives of the party-state, the vanguard of the people.[52] This was precisely the modus operandi that faded away in 1989. The end of Communist rule was marked by the proliferation of organizational units that complicated the previously flattened infrastructural landscape in post-Communist societies.

49. Weber, *Economy and Society*, 1:312.
50. Ibid.
51. Arthur Stinchcombe, "Social Structure and Organizations," in *Handbook of Organizations*, ed. James March (Chicago: Rand McNally, 1965), 169–80.
52. See T. H. Rigby, *Changing Soviet System* (Aldershot: Edward Elgar, 1990).

A penumbra of uncertainty hung over the principles for ranking of organizations. Although not all state agents switched their allegiance to newly formed organizations, many did. The organizational supremacy of the state was rapidly transformed from an unchallenged axiom into an uncertain proposition whose validity depended on the outcomes of daily contestations and logistical battles. The stratification of organizations and the attendant declassification of the state thus propelled the institutional dynamic underpinning the paradox of political openings.

One corollary of this paradox is that reformist strategies that assume functional state structures are just as utopian as the naive neoliberal assumption that market institutions emerge spontaneously once state regulations are relaxed. In fact, generating state capacity is the first task that reformers, irrespective of the content of their preferred policies, need to tackle. The fluctuations of stateness in post-Communist Bulgaria underscore that in the immediate aftermath of political openings state structures must be *created*, not simply "reformed."[53] The assumption that some sort of functioning administrative infrastructure actually exists and that what is needed is simply to improve its performance may be perilously misleading: it may lead not only to failure to recognize the magnitude of the task that lies ahead but to systematically inadequate choices of reform strategies or priorities in allocating scarce resources.

The historical-sociological perspective sheds much-needed light on the exact nature of "the hidden structures which frustrate some human aspirations while making others realizable, whether we appreciate it or not."[54] Although social predators do not target the institutions of liberal democracy, their predatory projects may undermine democracy by default. For example, low-intensity citizenship is a fact of life in post-Communism, not because of the reproduction of repressive social relations and entrenched class inequalities, but because the ongoing extraction from the state eats away the organizational basis of the state and thus renders impossible potentially salutary state action that might alleviate social suffering.[55] More generally, the stability of post-Communist democracies has been threatened not by the recrudescence of illiberal passions or the seductive appeal of authoritarian movements but by "rival games in town" that have reshaped the institutional and

---

53. For a similar insight, see Tony Verheijen, *Constitutional Pillars for New Democracies* (Leiden: DSWO Press, 1995), 41.

54. Dennis Smith, *The Rise of Historical Sociology* (Philadelphia: Temple University Press, 1991), 1.

55. On low-intensity citizenship, see Guillermo O'Donnell, *Counterpoints* (Notre Dame: University of Notre Dame Press, 1999).

organizational landscape of the fledgling polities without being subject to democratic control.

But the analytical benefits associated with the "reversed Tillyan perspective" go beyond the specification of what is it that frustrates enduring expectations about good governance in post-Communism. The state-centered line of analysis offered in this book has broader implications for the study of state structures—and hence the prospects of state-centered developmental projects—in the modern world. The kind of elite conduct observed under the peculiar conditions of post-Communism may be a harbinger of things to come as humankind moves into the twenty-first century. The post-Communist experience suggests that local predatory elites may turn themselves into a globally mobile, capital-flight caste whose ultimate objective is to consume extracted resources in some of the nicer neighborhoods of the global village. In other words, my analysis of the atrophy of state structures in post-Communism places back on the agenda an all-but-forgotten question: Why govern? By governing I mean creating the administrative wherewithal to respond to at least some demands of at least some domestic social constituencies at least some of the time.[56] The dominant mode of elite predatory action that transpired in post-Communism (which I term "extraction from the state") suggests that what might be called "the incentive to govern"—that is, the incentive to invest time, effort, and resources in the creation and maintenance of viable institutional infrastructures—may reemerge as an issue with heightened urgency in debates about politics in the twenty-first century. In that sense, looking at cases such as that of Bulgaria will provide an analytical lens for examining the paradoxes of political openings, stratification of organizations, and state debilitation brought about by changes in the Weberian economic order. This may increase our understanding of the complexities and conundrums that bedevil attempts to create functional democratic state structures in the modern world.

Summarizing his findings, Tilly argued that the political victories of ruling elites in early modern Europe "entailed administration."[57] My own analysis warrants the conclusion that in a post-Communist setting the success of predatory projects entails the opposite: the destruction of administration. I submit, therefore, that the emasculation of the state was unavoidable and would have transpired irrespective of the sequence of political events after 1989. In that sense, I would single

---

56. Compare Stephen Holmes, "What Russia Teaches Us Now," *American Prospect* 33, no. 8 (1997): 18–25.

57. Tilly, *Coercion*, 20.

out the decline of state capacity as the definitive attribute of the post-Communist condition. Concomitantly, I suggest that the resuscitation of democratic state structures is crucial for alleviating the social consequences of the paradox of political openings. Almost fifty years ago Alvin Gouldner noted that any effort to develop sound strategies for enhancing bureaucratic capacity was cast either as a dangerous exercise in futility or as a sinister prelude to the "ultimate loss of freedom," a reaction he described as "metaphysical pathos."[58] I do not want to go to the other extreme and radiate an equally misguided "metaphysic of hope" in the light of which the creation of efficient bureaucracies and logistically well-endowed administrative agencies will appear as the panacea to help post-Communist societies miraculously overcome all the evils that afflict them. But the lack of *political power* understood as a consensually created "medium of communication that allows binding decisions to be transmitted" is among the major problems that confront post-Communist states today, and this problem can be resolved only through a conscious, long-term commitment to institution-building projects backed by key social constituencies.[59]

At the end of this analysis of the transformation of state structures in post-Communist Bulgaria, it may be well worth remembering a genuinely prophetic statement made by John Stuart Mill 150 years ago: "Freedom cannot produce its best effects, and often breaks down altogether, unless means may be found of combining it with trained and skilled administration."[60] The message I have tried to convey is that the task of establishing the mechanisms and institutions of effective governance was the most daunting challenge facing the fledgling democracies in Eastern Europe—democracies where freedom is yet to produce its best effects. It would be a grave mistake to believe that while democratization and the establishment of functioning markets can only be brought about by means of popular mobilization, continued negotiations, commitment, and sustained organized action, the maintenance of state structures, this key challenge facing post-Communist polities, is merely a matter of legislation and institutional design. In fact, the problem of state–building in post-Communism is that, given the structural peculiarities of historical legacies, the selective destruction of institutional infrastructures is an almost natural development, and a major social effort is needed to reverse it. The success of this effort

---

58. Alvin Gouldner, "Metaphysical Pathos and the Theory of Bureaucracy," *American Political Science Review* 49, no. 2 (June 1955): 496–507.

59. For further elaboration on this concept of political power, see Nicklas Luhmann, *The Differentiation of Society* (New York: Columbia University Press, 1982), 147–65.

60. John Stuart Mill, "Considerations on Representative Government," in *Utilitarianism and Other Essays* (London: Everyman, 1993 [1861]), 267.

will be determined not only by political Don Quixotes seized with great visions but also by a multitude of bureaucratic Sancho Pansas for whom coping with the tensions and paradoxes of the post-Communist political condition is an everyday experience—and by self-reliant and active citizens for whom the realization that life is absurd is not an end but only a beginning.

Bibliography

Abbott, Andrew. *Time Matters: On Theory and Method*. Chicago: University of Chicago Press, 2001.
———. *Methods of Discovery: Heuristics for the Social Sciences*. New York: W. W. Norton, 2004.
Abrams, Philip. *Historical Sociology*. Somerset, England: Open Publishing, 1982.
Adams, Julia. "Culture in Rational-Choice Theories of State Formation." In *State/Culture: State Formation after the Cultural Turn*. Edited by George Steinmetz. Ithaca: Cornell University Press, 1999.
Amsden, Alice, Jacek Kohanowicz, and Lance Taylor. *The Market Meets Its Match: Restructuring the Economies of Eastern Europe*. Cambridge: Harvard University Press, 1994.
Ardant, Gabriel. "Financial Policy and Economic Infrastructure of Modern States and Nations." In *The Formation of National States in Western Europe*. Edited by Charles Tilly. Princeton: Princeton University Press, 1975.
Avramov, Roumen. "Macroeconomic Stabilization: Three Years Later." In *Economic Transition in Bulgaria*. Edited by Roumen Avramov and Ventzeslav Antonov, 7–37. Sofia: AECD, 1994.
———. "Tzenata na stabilizatzijata e ogranichen suverenitet" (The Price of Stabilization Is Limited Sovereignty). In *Ikonomicheska politika: nov pogled* (Economic Politics: A New Perspective). Sofia: Otvoreno Obshtestvo, 1996.
———, ed. *120 Years Bulgarian National Bank, 1879–1999*. Sofia: Bulgarian National Bank, 1999.
Avramov, Roumen, and Kamen Guenov. "The Rebirth of Capitalism in Bulgaria." *Bank Review* 4, no. 4 (April 1994).
Avramov, Roumen, and Jerome Sgard. "Bulgaria: From Enterprise Indiscipline to Financial Crisis." Document de travail No. 96. Paris: Centre d'études prospectives et d'informations internationales, 1996.
Azarya, Victor, and Naomi Chazan. "Disengagement from the State in Africa: Reflections on the Experience of Ghana." *Comparative Studies in Society and History* 29, no. 2 (April 1987): 106–31.

Badie, Bertrand. *The Imported State: The Westernization of Political Order.* Stanford: Stanford University Press, 2000.
Bagehot, Walter. *The English Constitution.* Ithaca: Cornell University Press, 1963.
Barkey, Karen. *Bandits and Bureaucrats: The Ottoman Route to State Centralization.* Ithaca: Cornell University Press, 1994.
Barkey, Karen, and Sunita Parikh. "Comparative Perspectives on the State." *American Review of Sociology* 17, no. 3 (1991): 523–49.
Bates, Robert H. "Letter from the President: Area Studies and the Discipline." *APSA-CP: Newsletter of the APSA Organized Section in Comparative Politics* 7, no. 1 (Winter 1996): 1. Available at http://www.nd.edu/~apsacp/pdf/APSA-CP_7_1.pdf.
Becker, Howard S. "Cases, Causes, Conjunctures, Stories, and Imagery." In *What Is a Case? Exploring the Foundations of Social Inquiry.* Edited by Charles C. Ragin and Howard S. Becker, 205–16. New York: Cambridge University Press, 1992.
Beer, Samuel. "Political Science and History." In *Essays in Theory and History: An Approach to the Social Sciences.* Edited by Melvin Richter, 41–74. Cambridge: Harvard University Press, 1970.
Benjamin, Walter. *Illuminations.* New York: Harcourt, Brace, 1968.
Berman, Sheri. *The Social Democratic Moment: Ideas and Politics in the Making of Interwar Europe.* Cambridge: Harvard University Press, 1998.
Bermeo, Nancy. "Democracy and the Lessons of Dictatorship." *Comparative Politics* 24, no. 3 (April 1993).
Bernhard, Michael. "Institutional Choices after Communism: A Critique of Theory-Building in an Empirical Wasteland." *East European Politics and Societies* 14, no. 2 (March 2000): 316–47.
Bernik, Ivan. "The Forgotten Legacy of Marginal Intellectuals." In *Transition to Capitalism? The Communist Legacy in Eastern Europe.* Edited by Janos Matyas Kovacs. New Brunswick, N.J.: Transaction, 1994.
Beyme, Klaus von. "Institutional Engineering and Transition to Democracy." In *Democratic Consolidation in Eastern Europe: Institutional Engineering.* Edited by Jan Zielonka. Oxford: Oxford University Press, 2001.
Bikov, Rumen, Margarit Mitzev, and Nacho Nachev. *Ikonomicheskata kriza v Bulgaria: prichini I posleditzi* (The Economic Crisis in Bulgaria: Causes and Consequences). Sofia: Sv. Georgi Pobedonosetz, 1992.
Blasi, Joseph R., Maya Kroumova, and Douglas Kruse. *Kremlin Capitalism: The Privatization of the Russian Economy.* Ithaca: Cornell University Press, 1997.
Boudon, Raymond. *The Unintended Consequences of Social Action.* New York: St. Martin's Press, 1982.
Bourdieu, Pierre. "Forms of Capital." In *Handbook of Theory and Research for the Sociology of Education.* Edited by John G. Richardson, 248–49. Westport, Conn.: Greenwood, 1986.
Boylan, Delia M. "Preemptive Strike: Central Bank Reform in Chile's Transition from Authoritarian Rule." *Comparative Politics* 30, no. 4 (July 1998): 443–62.
Bratton, Michael. "Peasant-State Relations in Post-Colonial Africa: Patterns of Engagement and Disengagement." In *State Power and Social Forces: Domination and Transformation in the Third World.* Edited by Joel S. Migdal, Atul Kohli, and Vivienne Shue. Cambridge: Cambridge University Press, 1994.
Bristow, John A. *The Bulgarian Economy in Transition.* Cheltenham, England: Edward Elgar, 1996.
Brovkin, Vladimir. "Fragmentation of Authority and Privatization of the State: From Gorbachev to Yeltsin." *Demokratizatzija* 6, no. 3 (Summer 1998).

Brubaker, Rogers. *Nationalism Reframed: Nationhood and the National Question in the New Europe.* Cambridge: Cambridge University Press, 1996.
Bryant, Christopher, and Edmund Mokrzycki, eds. *The New Great Transformation?* London: Routledge, 1994.
"Bulgarian Update." *East European Constitutional Review,* various issues (1991–97). www.law.nyu.edu/eecr.
Bulgarska Narodna Banka—Informatzionen Bjuletin (Bulgarian National Bank—Information Bulletin). November 1, 1991.
Bunce, Valerie. *Subversive Institutions: The Design and the Destruction of Socialism and the State.* Cambridge: Cambridge University Press, 1999.
Burawoy, Michael. "The State and Economic Involution: Russia through a China Lens." In *State-Society Synergy: Government and Social Capital in Development.* Edited by Peter Evans, 135–62.
Research Series No. 94. Berkeley: University of California, 1997.
———. "Transition without Transformation: Russia's Involuntary Road to Capitalism." *East European Politics and Societies* 15, no. 2 (Spring 2001): 269–90.
Burckhardt, Jacob. *The Age of Constantine the Great.* New York: Dorset Press, 1989.
Calhoun, Craig. *Critical Social Theory: Culture, History and the Challenge of Difference.* Oxford: Blackwell, 1995.
Carey, John M. "Parchment, Equilibria, and Institutions." *Comparative Political Studies* 33, nos. 6–7 (August–September 2000).
Carlin, Edward A. "Schumpeter's Constructed Type—the Entrepreneur." *Kyklos* 9 (1956): 27–41.
Carothers, Thomas. "The End of the Transition Paradigm." *Journal of Democracy* 13, no. 1 (January 2002): 1–17.
Carpenter, Daniel P. *The Forging of Bureaucratic Autonomy: Reputations, Networks, and Policy Innovation in Executive Agencies, 1862–1928.* Princeton: Princeton University Press, 2001.
Carruthers, Bruce G. *The City of Capital: Politics and Markets in the English Financial Revolution.* Princeton: Princeton University Press, 1996.
Chaudhry, Kiren Aziz. *The Price of Wealth: Economies and Institutions in the Middle East.* Ithaca: Cornell University Press, 1997.
Clark, Samuel. *State and Status: The Rise of the State and Aristocratic Power in Western Europe.* Cardiff: University of Wales Press, 1995.
Cohen, Stephen F. *Failed Crusade: America and the Tragedy of Postcommunist Russia.* New York: W. W. Norton, 2001.
Collins, Randall. *Conflict Sociology: Toward an Explanatory Science.* New York: Academic Press, 1975.
Comisso, Ellen. "State Structures, Political Processes, and Collective Choice in CMEA States." In *Power, Purpose, and Collective Choice: Economic Strategy in Socialist States.* Edited by Ellen Comisso and Laura D'Andrea Tyson, 19–62. Ithaca: Cornell University Press, 1986.
———. "Legacies of the Past or New Institutions?" *Comparative Political Studies* 28, no. 2 (1995).
Constant, Benjamin. "The Liberty of the Ancients Compared to That of the Moderns." In *Constant: Political Writings.* Cambridge: Cambridge University Press, 1988.
Coulloudon, Virginie. "Elite Groups in Russia." *Demokratizatsiya* 6, no. 3 (Summer 1998): 535–49.
Crawford, Beverly, ed. *Markets, States, and Democracy: The Political Economy of Post-Communist Transformation.* Boulder: Westview Press, 1995.

Creed, Gerald. *Domesticating Revolution: From Socialist Reform to Ambivalent Transition in a Bulgarian Village*. University Park: Pennsylvania State University Press, 1998.
Cukierman, Alex, Steven Webb, and Bilin Neyapti. "Measuring the Independence of Central Banks and the Effect of Policy Outcomes." *World Bank Economic Review* 6, no. 1 (Winter 1992): 353–69.
Dainov, Evgenii. *Politicheskijat debat i prehodut v Bulgaria* (Political Debate and Transition in Bulgaria). Sofia: Bulgarian Cultural Foundation, 2000.
Derluguian, Georgii. *Bourdieu's Secret Admirer in the Caucasus: A World-System Biography*. Chicago: University of Chicago Press, 2005.
Di Palma, Giuseppe. *To Craft Democracies: An Essay on Democratic Transitions*. Berkeley: University of California Press, 1990.
Downing, Brian. *The Military Revolution and Political Change*. Princeton: Princeton University Press, 1992.
Dunn, John. Preface to *Contemporary Crisis of the Nation State?* Edited by John Dunn, i–ii. Oxford: Blackwell, 1995.
Duverger, Maurice. "The Political System of the European Union." *European Journal of Political Research* 31, no. 1 (Spring 1997): 137–40.
Dworkin, Ronald. *Taking Rights Seriously*. Cambridge: Harvard University Press, 1977.
Easter, Gerald. "Preference for Presidentialism: Postcommunist Regime Change in Russia and the NIS." *World Politics* 49, no. 2 (January 1997): 184–211.
Eckstein, Harry. "Case Study and Theory in Political Science." In *Handbook of Political Science: Strategies of Inquiry*. Edited by Fred I. Greenstein and Nelson W. Polsby. Reading, Mass.: Addison-Wesley, 1975.
———. "Lessons for the 'Third Wave' from the First: An Essay on Democratization." In *Can Democracy Take Root in Postcommunist Russia?* Edited by Harry Eckstein et al. Lanham, Md.: Rowman and Littlefield, 1998.
Eley, Geoff. "The British Model and the German Road: Rethinking the Course of German History before 1914." In *The Peculiarities of German History*. Edited by Geoff Eley and David Blackbourn. Oxford: Oxford University Press, 1985.
Elias, Norbert. *The Civilizing Process*. Oxford: Basil Blackwell, 1978.
Elster, Jon. "Constitutionalism in Eastern Europe: Rebuilding the Boat in Open Seas." *Public Administration* 71 (1993).
———. "Constitutional Courts and Central Banks: Suicide Prevention or Suicide Pact?" *East European Constitutional Review* 3, nos. 3–4 (Summer–Fall 1994): 60–66.
———. "Miscalculations in the Design of the East European Presidencies." *East European Constitutional Review* (Winter 1994–Spring 1995): vol. 2, no. 4, and vol. 3, no. 1, 95–98.
———. "Transition, Constitution-Making and Separation in Czechoslovakia." *European Journal of Sociology* 36, no. 1 (1995): 105–34.
———. "Ways of Constitution-Making." In *Democracy's Victory and Crisis*. Edited by Axel Hadenius, 123–42. Cambridge: Cambridge University Press, 1997.
Elster, Jon, Claus Offe, and Ulrich K. Preuss. *Institutional Design in Post-Communist Societies: Rebuilding the Ship at Sea*. Cambridge: Cambridge University Press, 1998.
Ertman, Thomas. *Birth of the Leviathan: Building States and Regimes in Medieval and Early Modern Europe*. Cambridge: Cambridge University Press, 1997.
Evans, Peter. "Predatory, Developmental, and Other Apparatuses: A Comparative Political Economy Perspective on the Third World State." *Sociological Forum* 4, no. 4 (December 1989): 561–87.
———. "The Role of Theory in Comparative Politics." *World Politics* 48, no. 1 (October 1995): 2–10.

———. *Embedded Autonomy: States and Industrial Transformation*. Princeton: Princeton University Press, 1995.

———. "The Eclipse of the State? Reflections on Stateness in an Era of Globalization." *World Politics* 50, no. 4 (October 1997): 62–87.

———. "Government Action, Social Capital, and Development: Reviewing the Evidence of Synergy." In *State-Society Synergy: Government and Social Capital in Development*. Edited by Peter Evans. Research Series No. 94. Berkeley: University of California, International and Area Studies Digital Collection, 1997).

Evans, Peter, and Dietrich Rueschemeyer. "The State and Economic Transformation: Toward an Analysis of the Conditions Underlying Effective Intervention." In *Bringing the State Back In*. Edited by Peter Evans, Dietrich Rueschemeyer, and Theda Skocpol, 44–77. Cambridge: Cambridge University Press, 1985.

Fish, M. Steven. *Democracy from Scratch: Opposition and Regime in the New Russian Revolution*. Princeton: Princeton University Press, 1995.

———. "The Determinants of Economic Reform in the Post-Communist World." *East European Politics and Societies* 12, no. 1 (Winter 1998).

———. "The Dynamics of Democratic Erosion." In *Postcommunism and the Theory of Democracy*. Edited by Richard Anderson et al., 54–95. Princeton: Princeton University Press, 2001.

Fishman, Robert M. "Rethinking State and Regime: Southern Europe's Transition to Democracy." *World Politics* 42, no. 2 (April 1990): 422–40.

Frydman, Roman, Andrzej Rapaczynski, and John S. Earle, eds. *The Privatization Process in Central Europe*. Budapest: Central European University Press, 1993.

Frydman, Roman, Andrzej Rapaczynski, and Joel Turkewitz. "Transition to a Private Property Regime in the Czech Republic and Hungary." In *Economies in Transition: Comparing Asia and Eastern Europe*. Edited by Wing Thye Woo, Jeffrey D. Sacks, and Stephen Parker, 41–102. Cambridge: MIT Press, 1997.

Frye, Timothy. "A Politics of Institutional Choice: Post-Communist Presidencies." *Comparative Political Studies* 30, no. 5 (October 1997): 523–52.

———. *Brokers and Bureaucrats: Building Market Institutions in Russia*. Ann Arbor: University of Michigan Press, 2000.

Fukuyama, Francis. *The End of History*. New York: Free Press, 1992.

———. "The Primacy of Culture." In *The Global Resurgence of Democracy*. Edited by Larry Diamond and Mark Plattner. Baltimore: Johns Hopkins University Press, 1996.

———. *State-Building: Governance and World Order in the 21st Century*. Ithaca: Cornell University Press, 2004.

Gaddy, Clifford G., and Barry W. Ickes. *Russia's Virtual Economy*. Washington, D.C.: Brookings Institution, 2002.

Gambetta, Diego. "Concatenations of Mechanisms." In *Social Mechanisms: An Analytical Approach to Social Theory*. Edited by Peter Hedstrom and Richard Swedberg, 102–24. Cambridge: Cambridge University Press, 1998.

Ganev, Georgy. "Where Has Marxism Gone? Gauging the Impact of Alternative Ideas in Transition Bulgaria." *East European Politics and Societies* 19, no. 3 (Summer 2005): 443–62.

Ganev, Georgy, and Michael L. Wyzan. "Bulgaria: Macroeconomic and Political-Economic Implications of Stabilization under a Currency Board Arrangement." In *The Political Economy of Reform Failure*. Edited by Mats Lundahl and Michael L. Wyzan, 170–96. London: Routledge, 2005.

Ganev, Venelin I. "Prisoners' Rights, Public Services, and Institutional Collapse in Bulgaria." *East European Constitutional Review* 4, no. 4 (Fall 1995).

Ganev, Venelin I. "Emergency Powers in the New East-European Constitutions." *American Journal of Comparative Law* 45, no. 3 (Summer 1997): 585–612.
———. "Bulgaria's Symphony of Hope." *Journal of Democracy* 8, no. 4 (Fall 1997): 139–54.
———. "Semi-Presidentialism in Bulgaria." In *Semi-Presidential Regimes in Europe*. Edited by Robert Elgie, 134–58. Oxford: Oxford University Press, 1999.
———. "Notes on Networking in Postcommunist Societies." *East European Constitutional Review* 9, nos. 1–2 (Winter–Spring 2000): 101–7.
———. "The (Ir)Relevance of Postcommunist Constitutionalism." In *Democratic Consolidation in Eastern Europe*. Vol. 1. *Institutional Engineering*. Edited by Jan Zielonka, 186–211. Oxford: Oxford University Press, 2001.
———. "The Rise of Constitutional Adjudication in Bulgaria." In *Constitutional Justice, East and West*. Edited by Wojciech Sadurski, 163–89. The Hague: Kluwer Law International, 2002.
———. "The Politics of Ethnic Reconciliation in Bulgaria." In *National Reconciliation in Eastern Europe*. Edited by Henry F. Carey, 319–42. Boulder: Columbia University Press—East European Monographs, 2003.
———. "The 'Triumph of Neo-Liberalism' Reconsidered: Critical Remarks on Ideas-Centered Analyses of Political and Economic Change in Postcommunism." *East European Politics and Societies* 19, no. 3 (Summer 2005): 343–78.
———. "Ballots, Bribes, and State-Building in Postcommunist Bulgaria." *Journal of Democracy* 17, no. 1 (January 2006): 75–89.
Gellner, Ernest. *The Conditions of Liberty: Civil Society and Its Rivals*. London: Penguin Books, 1994.
Giddens, Anthony. *The Constitution of Society*. Berkeley: University of California Press, 1984.
Gill, Graeme. *The Collapse of a Single-Party System: The Disintegration of the Communist Party of the Soviet Union*. Cambridge: Cambridge University Press, 1994.
Goodman, John B. "The Politics of Central Bank Independence." *Comparative Politics* 23, no. 3 (April 1991).
Gotchev, Atanas, ed. *The Competitiveness of Bulgarian Export Industries*. Sofia: Albatross, 1997.
Gouldner, Alvin. "Metaphysical Pathos and the Theory of Bureaucracy." *American Political Science Review* 49, no. 2 (June 1955): 496–507.
Grabher, Gernot. "Adaptation at the Cost of Adaptability? Restructuring the Eastern German Regional Economy." In *Restructuring Networks in Post-Socialism*. Edited by David Stark and Gernot Grabher, 107–33. Oxford: Oxford University Press, 1997.
Granovetter, Mark S. "The Strength of Weak Ties." *American Journal of Sociology* 78, no. 6 (Spring 1973).
Gray, John. *Enlightenment's Wake*. London: Routledge, 1995.
Greskovits, Bela. *The Political Economy of Protest and Patience*. Budapest: Central European University Press, 1998.
Grzymala-Busse, Anna. "Political Competition and the Politicization of the State in East Central Europe." Paper presented at "The Postcommunist State" conference, Yale University, April 2001.
———. *Redeeming the Communist Past: The Regeneration of Communist Parties in East Central Europe*. Cambridge: Cambridge University Press, 2001.
Grzymala-Busse, Anna, and Pauline Jones Luong. "Reconceptualizing the State: Lessons from Postcommunism." *Politics and Society* 30, no. 4 (December 2002).
Guerrero, Eduardo. "Sociedad civil: Rival de la democracia? Polonia entre 1989 y 1995." *Politica y gobierno* 5, no. 2 (1998): 381–422.

Haggard, Stephen, and Robert K. Kaufman. *The Political Economy of Democratic Transitions*. Princeton: Princeton University Press, 1995.
Hall, John A., and G. John Ikenberry. *The State*. Minneapolis: University of Minnesota Press, 1989.
Hall, Peter A. *Governing the Economy: The Politics of State Intervention in Britain and France*. New York: Oxford University Press, 1986.
Hankiss, Elemer. *East European Alternatives*. Oxford: Clarendon Press, 1990.
Hanneman, Robert, and J. Rogers Hollingsworth. "Refocusing the Debate on the Role of the State in Capitalist Societies." In *State Theory and State History*. Edited by Rolf Torstendahl, 38–61. London: Sage, 1992.
Harvey, David. *The Condition of Postmodernity*. Cambridge, Mass.: Blackwell, 1990.
Hedlund, Stefan. *Russia's "Market" Economy: A Bad Case of Predatory Capitalism*. London: UCL Press, 1999.
Hellman, Joel. "Breaking the Bank: Bureaucrats and the Creation of Markets in a Transitional Economy." PhD diss., Columbia University, 1997.
———. "Constitutions and Economic Reform in the Post-Communist Transitions." In *The Rule of Law and Economic Reform in Russia*. Edited by Jeffrey Sachs and Katharina Pistor, 55–78. Boulder: Westview Press, 1997.
———. "Winners Take All: The Politics of Partial Reform in Postcommunist Transitions." *World Politics* 50, no. 1 (January 1998).
Hoeland, Armin. "Imposition without Adaptation? New Opportunities for Old Failure." In *European Legal Cultures*. Edited by Volkmar Gessner, Armin Hoeland, and Csaba Varga. Dartmouth, England: Aldershot, 1996.
Holmes, Stephen. "Back to the Drawing Board." *East European Constitutional Review* 3, no. 1 (Winter 1993): 24–28.
———. "Semipresidentialism and Its Problems." *East European Constitutional Review* (Winter 1994–Spring 1995): vol. 2, no. 4, and vol. 3, no. 1, 123–26.
———. "Constitutionalism." In *The Encyclopedia of Democracy*. Vol. 1. Edited by Seymour M. Lipset, 300–307. Washington, D.C.: Congressional Quarterly, 1995.
———. "Cultural Legacies or State Collapse? Probing the Postcommunist Dilemma." In *Postcommunism: Four Perspectives*. Edited by Michael Mandelbaum. New York: Council of Foreign Relations, 1996.
———. "What Russia Teaches Us Now." *American Prospect* 8, no. 33 (July 1, 1997), 30–35.
Holmes, Stephen, and Cass R. Sunstein. "The Politics of Constitutional Revision in Eastern Europe." In *Responding to Imperfection: The Theory and Practice of Constitutional Amendment*. Edited by Sanford Levinson. Princeton: Princeton University Press, 1995.
Horowitz, Donald L. "Comparing Democratic Systems." In *The Global Resurgence of Democracy*. Edited by Larry Diamond and Mark Plattner, 143–49. Baltimore: Johns Hopkins University Press, 1996.
Hough, Jerry. "Russia—On the Road to Thermidor." *Problems of Post-Communism* 41, nos. 2–3 (1994): 26–31.
Hristov, Lubomir. "A Role for an Independent Central Bank in Transition? The Case of Bulgaria." In *The Bulgarian Economy: Lessons from Reform during Early Transition*. Edited by Derek Jones and Jeffrey Miller. Aldershot: Ashgate, 1997.
Hunt, Lynn. "Charles Tilly's Collective Action." In *Vision and Method in Historical Sociology*. Edited by Theda Skocpol. Cambridge: Cambridge University Press, 1984.
Hutchcroft, Paul D. "Oligarchs and Cronies in the Philippine State: The Politics of Patrimonial Plunder." *World Politics* 43, no. 3 (Fall 1991): 414–50.
Ikenberry, G. John. "The Irony of State Strength: Comparative Responses to the Oil Shocks in the 1970s." *International Organization* 40, no. 1 (Winter 1986): 105–37.

International Journal of Comparative Law. Special issue on "Constitutional Borrowing," vol. 1, no. 2 (April 2003).
Immergut, Ellen M. "The Rules of the Game: The Logic of Health Policy-Making in France, Switzerland and Sweden." In *Structural Politics: Historical Institutionalism in Comparative Perspective*. Edited by Sven Steinmo, Kathleen Thelen, and Frank Longstreth, 57–89. Cambridge: Cambridge University Press, 1992.
Jackson, Marvin R. *Bulgaria's Attempt at "Radical Reform."* Cologne: Bundesinstitut for ostwissenschaftliche und internationale Studien, 1988.
Jepperson, Ronald J. "Institutions, Institutional Effects, and Institutionalism." In *The New Institutionalism in Organizational Analysis*. Edited by Walter W. Powell and Paul J. DiMaggio. Chicago: University of Chicago Press, 1991.
Johnson, Julia. *A Fistful of Rubbles: The Rise and Fall of the Soviet Banking System*. Ithaca: Cornell University Press, 2000.
Jones Luong, Pauline. "After the Break-Up: Institutional Design in Transitional States." *Comparative Political Studies* 33, no. 5 (June 2000): 563–92.
Jowitt, Ken. *The New World Disorder: The Leninist Extinction*. Berkeley: University of California Press, 1992.
Kahler, Miles. "Orthodoxy and Its Alternatives: Explaining Approaches to Stabilization and Adjustment." In *Economic Crisis and Policy Choice: The Politics of Adjustment in Developing Countries*. Edited by Joan M. Nelson. Princeton: Princeton University Press, 1990.
Kallas, Siim. "A Currency Board within a Central Bank: Reflections on the Estonian Hybrid." *East European Constitutional Review* 3, nos. 3–4 (Summer–Fall 1994): 53–56.
Kaviraj, Sudipta. "Crisis of the Nation-State in India." In *Contemporary Crisis of the Nation State?* Edited by John Dunn. Oxford: Blackwell, 1995.
Kirchheimer, Otto. *Politics, Law, and Social Change: Selected Essays of Otto Kirchheimer*. New York: Columbia University Press, 1969.
Kitschelt, Herbert, Zdenka Mansfelodva, Radoslaw Markowski, and Gabor Toka. *Post-Communist Party Systems*. Cambridge: Cambridge University Press, 1999.
Kohanowicz, Jacek. "Reforming Weak States and Deficient Bureaucracies." In *Intricate Links: Democratization and Market Reforms in Latin America and Eastern Europe*. Edited by Joan Nelson. New Brunswick, N.J.: Transaction, 1994.
Kolarova, Rumyana. "Bulgaria: A Self-Restricting Court." *East European Constitutional Review* 2, no. 2 (Spring 1993): 48–51.
Kolarova, Rumyana, and Dimiter Dimitrov. "The Roundtable Talks in Bulgaria." In *The Roundtable Talks and the Breakdown of Communism*. Edited by Jon Elster, 178–213. Chicago: University of Chicago Press, 1996.
Kopecky, Petr. "The Czech Republic: From the Burden of the Old Federal Constitution to the Constitutional Horse Trading among Political Parties." In *Institutional Engineering in Eastern Europe*. Edited by Jan Zielonka, 319–46. Oxford: Oxford University Press, 2001.
Kopecky, Petr, and Cas Mudde. "What Has Eastern Europe Taught Us about the Democratization Literature?" *European Journal of Political Research* 37, no. 4 (June 2000).
Kornai, Janos. *The Socialist Economy: The Political Economy of Communism*. Princeton: Princeton University Press, 1992.
———. "Paying the Bill for Goulash Communism: Hungarian Development and Macro-Stabilization in a Political Economy Perspective." *Social Research* 63, no. 4 (Winter 1996).
Kotkin, Stephen, and Andras Sajo, eds. *Political Corruption: A Skeptic's Guide*. Budapest: Central European University Press, 2002.

Kralevska, Nassja. *Bez zaglavie* (Untitled). Sofia: Rabotilnitza za knizhnina Vassil Stanilov, 2006.
Krassner, Stephen. *Defending the National Interest: Raw Materials Investments and U.S. Foreign Policy.* Princeton: Princeton University Press, 1978.
Krastev, Ivan. *Shifting Obsessions: Three Essays on the Politics of Anticorruption.* Budapest: Central European University Press, 2004.
Krygier, Martin. "Traps for Young Players in Times of Transition." *East European Constitutional Review* 8, no. 4 (Fall 1999).
Kryshtanovskaya, Olga, and Stephen White. "From Soviet *Nomenklatura* to Russian Elite." *Europe-Asia Studies* 48, no. 5 (1996).
Laitin, David D. "The Cultural Elements of Ethnically Mixed States: Nationality Re-Formation in Soviet Successor States." In *State/Culture: State Formation after the Cultural Turn.* Edited by George Steinmetz, 291–320. Ithaca: Cornell University Press, 1999.
Lardeyret, Guy. "The Problem with PR." In *The Global Resurgence of Democracy.* Edited by Larry Diamond and Mark Plattner, 175–80. Baltimore: Johns Hopkins University Press, 1996.
Leff, Carol Skalnik, and Gerardo Munck. "Modes of Transition and Democratization: South America and Eastern Europe in Comparative Perspective." *Comparative Politics* 29, no. 3 (April 1997): 343–62.
Levy, Margaret. *Of Rule and Revenue.* Berkeley: University of California Press, 1988.
Lichbach, Mark I., and Adam Seligman. *Market and Community: The Basis of Social Order, Revolution, and Relegitimation.* University Park: Pennsylvania State University Press, 2000.
Lijphart, Arend. "Comparative Politics and the Comparative Method." *American Political Science Review* 65, no. 1 (Winter 1971).
———. "Constitutional Choices for New Democracies." In *The Global Resurgence of Democracy.* Edited by Larry Diamond and Mark Plattner, 162–74. Baltimore: Johns Hopkins University Press, 1996.
Lilov, Alexander. *Dialogut na tsivilizatziite* (The Dialogue of Civilizations). Sofia: Zahari Stoyanov, 2004.
Linz, Juan J. "Some Thoughts on the Victory and Future of Democracy." In *Democracy's Victory and Crisis.* Edited by Axel Hadenius. Cambridge: Cambridge University Press, 1997.
———. "Introduction: Some Thoughts on Presidentialism in Postcommunist Europe." In *Postcommunist Presidents.* Edited by Ray Taras, 1–14. Cambridge: Cambridge University Press, 1997.
Linz, Juan J., and Alfred Stepan. *Problems of Democratic Transition and Consolidation.* Baltimore: Johns Hopkins University Press, 1996.
Linz, Juan J., Alfred Stepan, and Richard Gunther. "Democratic Transition and Consolidation in Southern Europe, with Reflections on Latin America and Eastern Europe." In *The Politics of Democratic Consolidation: Southern Europe in Comparative Perspective.* Edited by Richard Gunther, Hans-Jürgen Puhle, and P. Nikiforos Diamandouros. Baltimore: Johns Hopkins University Press, 1995.
Loewenstein, Karl. "Reflections on the Value of Constitutions in Our Revolutionary Age." In *Constitutions and Constitutional Trends since World War II.* Edited by Arnold J. Zurcher. New York: New York University Press, 1951.
Ludwikowski, Rett R. *Constitution-Making in the Region of Former Soviet Dominance.* Durham: Duke University Press, 1996.
Luhmann, Nicklas. *The Differentiation of Society.* New York: Columbia University Press, 1982.

Lukanov, Andrei. *Lukanov za krizata* (Lukanov on the Crisis). Sofia: Hristo Botev, 1992.

———. *Sotzialnata demorkatzija—alternativa za Bulgaria* (Social Democracy—An Alternative for Bulgaria). Pleven: Severno Eho, 1992.

Mann, Michael. "The Autonomous Power of the State: Its Origins, Mechanisms and Results." *Archives Europeennes de sociologie* 25, no. 2 (Fall 1984): 185–213.

Mann, Michael. *The Sources of Social Power*. Vol. 1. *A History of Power from the Beginning to A.D. 1760* Cambridge: Cambridge University Press, 1986.

———. *States, War and Capitalism*. Oxford: Blackwell, 1988.

McAuley, Mary. *Russia's Politics of Uncertainty*. Cambridge: Cambridge University Press, 1997.

McDermott, Gerald. *Embedded Politics: Industrial Networks and Institutional Change in Postcommunism*. Ann Arbor: University of Michigan Press, 2002.

McFaul, Michael. *Post-Communist Politics: Democratic Prospects in Russia and Eastern Europe*. Washington, D.C.: Center for Strategic and International Studies, 1993.

———. "The Allocation of Property Rights in Russia: The First Round." *Communist and Post-Communist Studies* 29, no. 3 (September 1996): 287–308.

McNeil, William. *The Pursuit of Power: Technology, Armed Force, and Society since A.D. 1000*. Chicago: University of Chicago Press, 1982.

Melone, Albert P. *Creating Parliamentary Democracy*. Columbus: Ohio State University Press, 1998.

Migdal, Joel. *Strong Societies and Weak States: State-Society Relations and State Capabilities in the Third World*. Princeton: Princeton University Press, 1988.

Mill, John Stuart. "Considerations on Representative Government." In *Utilitarianism and Other Essays*. London: Everyman, 1993 [1861].

Minchev, Ognian. *Stupki po putja* (Steps on the Road). Sofia: Universitetsk izdatelstvo Kliment Ohirdsksi, 1996.

Mitchell, Timothy. "The Limits of the State: Beyond Statist Approaches and Their Critics." *American Political Science Review* 85, no. 1 (March 1991): 77–96.

Mladenova, Zoya, and James Angressano. "Privatization in Bulgaria." *East European Quarterly* 30, no. 1 (January 1997): 495–516.

Montesquieu. *The Spirit of the Laws*. Cambridge: Cambridge University Press, 1989.

Moore, Barrington, Jr. *Social Origins of Dictatorship and Democracy*. Boston: Beacon Press, 1966.

Mosca, Gaetano. *The Ruling Class*. New York: McGraw-Hill, 1939.

Mumford, Lewis. *The Myth of the Machine: The Pentagon of Power*. New York: Harcourt, Brace, 1970.

Munck, Gerardo L. "Bringing Postcommunist Societies into Democratization Studies." *Slavic Review* 56, no. 4 (Fall 1997): 542–50.

Naishul, Vitalii. "Liberalism, Customary Rights, and Economic Reforms." *Communist Economies and Economic Transformation* 5, no. 1 (1993).

Nee, Victor. "A Theory of Market Transition: From Redistribution to Markets in State Socialism." *American Sociological Review* 54 (October 1989): 663–81.

Nelson, Joan, Jacek Kochanomicz, and Kalman Mizsei. "The Transition in Bulgaria, Hungary, and Poland: An Overview." In *A Precarious Balance: An Overview of Democracy and Economic Reform in Eastern Europe and Latin America*. Edited by Joan Nelson. San Francisco: Institute for Contemporary Studies, 1994.

Nenova, Mariela. "Finansovata politika v Bulgaria v uslovijata na prehoda kum pazarna ikonomika" Occasional Papers. Sofia: Bulgarian National Bank, June 1996.

Nielsen, Klaus, Bob Jessop, and Jerzy Hausner. "Institutional Change in Post-Socialism." In *Strategic Choice and Path Dependence in Post-Socialism: Institutional*

Dynamics in the Transformation Process. Edited by Jerzy Hausner, Bob Jessop, and Klaus Nielsen, 3–46. Aldershot: Edward Elgar, 1995.

Nikolov, Asen. *Vuzkrusvane na svobodata* (The Resurrection of Freedom). Sofia: Universitetsk izdatelstvo Kliment Ohirdsksi, 1998.

Nikolov, Jovo. "Organized Crime in Bulgaria." *East European Constitutional Review* 6, no. 4 (Fall 1997): 80–84.

Nikolva, Vjara, and Iren Ribarova, eds. *Protestut na 39te* (The Protest of the 39). Sofia: 2000.

North, Douglas. *Structure and Change in Economic History.* New York: W. W. Norton, 1981.

O'Donnell, Guillermo. *Counterpoints: Selected Essays on Authoritarianism and Democratization.* South Bend, Ind.: University of Notre Dame Press, 1999.

O'Donnell, Guillermo, and Philippe Schmitter. *Transitions from Authoritarian Rule: Tentative Conclusions about Uncertain Democracies.* Baltimore: Johns Hopkins University Press, 1986.

O'Neil, Patrick H. "Hungary: Political Transition and Executive Conflict; The Balance or Fragmentation of Power?" In *Postcommunist Presidents.* Edited by Ray Taras. Cambridge: Cambridge University Press, 1997.

Offe, Claus. *Varieties of Transition: The East European and East German Experience.* Cambridge: MIT Press, 1996.

Olson, Mancur. *The Rise and Decline of Nations.* New Haven: Yale University Press, 1982.

———. "A Theory of the Incentives Facing Political Organizations: Neo-Corporatism and the Hegemonic State." *International Political Science Review* 7, no. 2 (Summer 1986): 169–83.

———. "Why the Transition from Communism Is So Difficult." *Eastern Economic Journal* 21, no. 4 (Fall 1995).

Ost, David. *The Defeat of Solidarity: Anger and Politics in Postcommunist Europe.* Ithaca: Cornell University Press, 2005.

Pareto, Vilfredo. *Sociological Writings.* Totowa, N.J.: Rowman and Littlefield, 1966.

Peeva, Ralitza. "The Round Table Talks in Bulgaria." PhD diss., Department of Sociology, New School for Social Research, 2000.

Pei, Minxin. "Microfoundations of State-Socialism and Patterns of Economic Transformation." *Communist and Postcommunist Studies* 29, no. 2 (Spring 1996): 131–46.

Peukert, Detlev. *The Weimar Republic.* New York: Hill and Wang, 1993.

Pierson, Paul. *Politics in Time: History, Institutions, and Social Analysis.* Princeton: Princeton University Press, 2004.

Plutarch. *Lives.* Edited by Roman T. Bond. New York: Tudor Publishing, 1935.

Pocock, J. G. A. *The Machiavellian Moment: Florentine Political Thought and the Atlantic Republican Tradition.* Princeton: Princeton University Press, 1975.

Poggi, Gianfranco. *The State: Its Nature, Development, and Prospects.* Stanford: Stanford University Press, 1990.

———. *Forms of Power.* Cambridge: Polity, 2001.

Poznanski, Kazimierz Z. "Epilogue: Markets and States in the Transformation of Post-Communist Europe." In *Constructing Capitalism: The Re-Emergence of Civil Society and Liberal Economy in the Post-Communist World.* Edited by Kazimierz Z. Poznanski. Boulder: Westview Press, 1992.

———. "Building Capitalism with Communist Tools: Eastern Europe's Defective Transition." *East European Politics and Societies* 15, no. 2 (Spring 2001): 320–55.

———. "The Crisis of Transition as a State Crisis." In *Postcommunist Transformation and the Social Sciences.* Edited by Frank Bonker, Klaus Müller, and Andreas Pickel, 55–76. Lanham, Md.: Rowman and Littlefield, 2002.

Pridham, Geoffrey. "The International Context of Democratic Consolidation: Southern Europe in Comparative Perspective." In *The Politics of Democratic Consolidation: Southern Europe in Comparative Perspective.* Edited by Richard Gunther, Nikiforos Diamandouros, and Hans-Jürgen Puhle. Baltimore: Johns Hopkins University Press, 1995.

Prokop, Jane. "Industrial Conglomerates, Risk Spreading, and the Transition in Russia." *Communist Economies and Economic Transformation* 7, no. 1 (Fall 1995): 35–50.

Przeworski, Adam. *Democracy and the Market.* Cambridge: Cambridge University Press, 1991.

——. "The Neo-Liberal Fallacy." *Journal of Democracy* 3 (1993): 45–59.

——. *Sustainable Democracy.* Cambridge: Cambridge University Press, 1995.

Przeworski, Adam, Luis Carlos Bresser Pereira, and José Maria Maravall. *Economic Reform in New Democracies: A Social-Democratic Approach.* New York: Cambridge University Press, 1993.

Putnam, Robert. *Making Democracy Work: Civic Traditions in Modern Italy.* Princeton: Princeton University Press, 1992.

Raz, Joseph. "On the Authority and Interpretation of Constitutions: Some Preliminaries." In *Constitutionalism: Philosophical Foundations.* Edited by Larry Alexander, 152–93. Cambridge: Cambridge University Press, 1998.

Reddaway, Peter, and Dmitri Glinski. *The Tragedy of Russian Reforms: Market Bolshevism Against Democracy.* Washington, D.C.: United States Institute of Peace, 2001.

Reshenija I opredelenija na Konstitutzionnija Sud (Decisions and Rulings of the Constitutional Court). (Sofia: Akademia na naukite, 1993), various issues.

Rigby, T. H. *The Changing Soviet System: Mono-Organizational Socialism from Its Origins to Gorbachev's Restructuring.* Aldershot: Edward Elgar, 1990.

Rigby, T. H., and Ferenc Feher, eds. *Political Legitimation in Communist States.* New York: St. Martin's Press, 1982.

Rokkan, Stein. "Dimensions of State Formation and Nation Building: A Possible Paradigm for Research on Variations within Europe." In *The Formation of National States in Western Europe.* Edited by Charles Tilly, 562–600. Princeton: Princeton University Press, 1975.

——. *State Formation, Nation-Building and Mass Politics in Europe: The Theory of Stein Rokkan.* Oxford: Oxford University Press, 1999.

Rona-Tas, Akos. "The First Shall Be Last? Entrepreneurship and Communist Cadres in the Transition from Socialism." *American Journal of Sociology* 100, no. 1 (July 1994): 45–65.

——. *The Great Surprise of the Small Transformation: The Demise of Communism and the Rise of the Private Sector in Hungary.* Ann Arbor: University of Michigan Press, 1997.

Sabel, Charles E. "Learning by Monitoring: The Institutions of Economic Development." In *Handbook of Economic Sociology.* Edited by Richard Swedberg and Neil J. Smelser. Princeton: Princeton University Press, 1994.

Sajo, Andras. "Reading the Invisible Constitution: Judicial Review in Hungary." *Oxford Journal of Legal Studies* 15, no. 3 (Fall 1995): 253–67.

Sartori, Giovanni. *The Theory of Democracy Revisited.* Vol. 1. Chatham, N.J.: Chatham House, 1987.

Schamis, Hector E. *Re-Forming the State: The Politics of Privatization in Latin America and Europe.* Ann Arbor: University of Michigan Press, 2002.

Scheppele, Kim Lane. "Aspirational and Aversive Constitutionalism: The Case for Studying Cross-Constitutional Influence through Negative Models." *International Journal of Constitutional Law* 1, no. 2 (2003).

Scheuerman, William. *Liberal Democracy and the Acceleration of Time.* Baltimore: Johns Hopkins University Press, 2004.
Schumpeter, Joseph. *Capitalism, Socialism, and Democracy.* New York: Harper Colophon Books, 1975 [1942].
———. *The Theory of Economic Development.* New Brunswick, N.J.: Transaction, 1983.
———. *The Economics and Sociology of Capitalism.* Edited by Richard Swedberg. Princeton: Princeton University Press, 1991.
———. "Capitalism." In *Essays on Entrepreneurs, Innovations, Business Cycles, and the Evolution of Capitalism*, 201–2. New Brunswick, N.J.: Transaction, 1997.
Schwartz, Herman. *The Struggle for Constitutional Justice in Postcommunist Europe.* Chicago: University of Chicago Press, 1998.
Semler, Dwight. Introduction to "Focus: The Politics of Central Banking," a special issue of *East European Constitutional Review* 3, nos. 3–4 (Summer–Fall 1994): 48–52.
Sewell, William H., Jr. "A Theory of Structure: Duality, Agency, and Transformation." *American Journal of Sociology* 98, no. 1 (July 1992).
———. *Logics of History: Social History and Social Transformation.* Chicago: University of Chicago Press, 2005.
Sharlet, Robert. "Legal Transplants and Political Mutations: The Reception of Constitutional Law in Russia and the Newly Independent States." *East European Constitutional Review* 7, no. 4 (Fall 1998): 59–68.
Shlapentokh, Vladimir. "Early Feudalism—the Best Parallel for Contemporary Russia." *Europe-Asia Studies* 48, no. 3 (1996): 400–425.
Shugart, Matthew, and John M. Carey. *Presidents and Assemblies.* Cambridge: Cambridge University Press, 1992.
Sil, Rudra. "Problems Chasing Methods or Methods Chasing Problems? Research Communities, Constrained Pluralism and the Role of Eclecticism." In *Problems and Methods in the Study of Politics.* Edited by Ian Shapiro, Rogers M. Smith, and Tarek E. Masoud, 307–31. Cambridge: Cambridge University Press, 2004.
Skocpol, Theda. *States and Social Revolutions: A Comparative Analysis of France, Russia and China.* Cambridge: Cambridge University Press, 1979.
———. "Sociology's Historical Imagination." In *Vision and Method in Historical Sociology.* Edited by Theda Skocpol. Cambridge: Harvard University Press, 1984.
Smith, Dennis. *The Rise of Historical Sociology.* Philadelphia: Temple University Press, 1991.
Smith, Rogers M. "Science, Non-Science, and Politics." In *The Historic Turn in the Human Sciences.* Edited by Terence McDonald. Ann Arbor: University of Michigan Press, 1996.
Solnick, Steven. *Stealing the State.* Cambridge: Harvard University Press, 1998.
———. "Russia over the Edge." *East European Constitutional Review* 7, no. 4 (Fall 1998): 70–72.
Spassov, Milcho. *Imalo li e fashizum v Bulgaria* (Was There Fascism in Bulgaria?). Sofia: Otechestvo, 1998.
Spulber, Nicolas. *Redefining the State: Privatization and Welfare Reform in Industrial and Transitional Economies.* Cambridge: Cambridge University Press, 1997.
Stanchev, Krassen. *The Bulgarian National Bank and the Political Process.* Sofia: Institute for Market Economics, 1999. Available at http://ime-bg.org/bg/top_left.html.
———. "The Path of Bulgarian Economic Reform." *East European Constitutional Review* 10, no. 4 (Fall 2001): 56–61.
———, ed., *Anatomia na prehoda: stopanskata politika na Bulgaria 1989–2004* (Anatomy of the Transition: Economic Policy in Bulgaria, 1989–2004). Sofia: SIEMA, 2004.

Stanchev, Krassen, and Luisa Perrotti. *The Role of the Core Executive in the Privatization Process—Country Report: Bulgaria*. Sofia: Institute for Market Economics—OECD/Sigma World Bank Project, 1999.
Staniszkis, Jadwiga. *The Dynamics of the Breakthrough in Eastern Europe*. Berkeley: University of California Press, 1991.
———. *The Ontology of Socialism*. Oxford: Clarendon Press, 1992.
Stark, David. "Path Dependence and Privatization Strategies in East Central Europe." *East European Politics and Societies* 6, no. 1 (Winter 1992).
———. "Not by Design: The Myth of Designer Capitalism in Eastern Europe." In *Strategic Choice and Path-Dependency in Post-Socialism: Institutional Dynamics in the Transformation Process*. Edited by Jerzy Hausner, Bob Jessop, and Klaus Nielsen. Aldershot, England: Edward Elgar, 1995.
Stark, David, and Laszlo Bruszt. *Postsocialist Pathways*. Cambridge: Cambridge University Press, 1997.
Starodubrovskaya, Irina. "Financial-Industrial Groups: Illusions and Reality." *Communist Economies and Economic Transformation* 7, no. 1 (Fall 1995): 5–19.
Stavrakis, Peter. *State-Building in Postcommunist Russia*. Occasional Paper No. 254. Washington, D.C.: Kennan Institute for Advanced Russian Studies, August–October 1993).
Steinmetz, George. "Introduction: Culture and the State." In *State/Culture: State Formation after the Cultural Turn*. Edited by George Steinmetz. Ithaca: Cornell University Press, 1999.
Stinchcombe, Arthur. "Social Structure and Organizations." In *Handbook of Organizations*. Edited by James March, 169–80. Chicago: Rand McNally, 1965.
Stoica, Catalin Augustin. "From Good Communists to Even Better Capitalists?" *East European Politics and Societies* 18, no. 2 (May 2004).
Stone, Alec. *The Birth of Judicial Politics in France*. New York: Oxford University Press, 1992.
Stoner-Weiss, Kathryn. *Local Heroes: The Political Economy of Russian Regional Governance*. Princeton: Princeton University Press, 1997.
Strange, Susan. *States and Markets*. New York: Basil Blackwell, 1988.
Stranger, Alison. "Leninist Legacies and Legacies of State Socialism in Postcommunist Central Europe's Constitutional Development." In *Capitalism and Democracy in Central and Eastern Europe: Assessing the Legacy of Communist Rule*. Edited by Stephen E. Hanson and Grzegorz Ekiert. Cambridge: Cambridge University Press, 2003.
Sugarev, Edvin. *Bankovijat bankrut na Bulgaria* (Bulgaria's Bank Bankruptcy). Sofia: Fakel Press, 1996.
Szacki, Jerzy. *Liberalism after Communism*. Budapest: Central European University Press, 1994.
Szelényi, Iván, Gil Eyal, and Eleanor Townsley. *Making Capitalism without Capitalists: Class Formation and Elite Struggles in Post-Communist Central Europe*. London: Verso, 1998.
Tarrow, Sidney. "Mass Mobilization and Regime Change: Pacts, Reform, and Popular Power in Italy (1918–1922) and Spain (1975–1978)." In *The Politics of Democratic Consolidation: Southern Europe in Comparative Perspective*. Edited by Richard Gunther, P. Nikiforos Diamandouros, and Hans-Jurgen Pühle. Baltimore: Johns Hopkins University Press, 1995.
Thelen, Kathleen. "Historical Institutionalism in Comparative Politics." *Annual Review of Political Science* 2 (1999).
Tilly, Charles. "Reflections on the History of European State Making." In *The Formation of National States in Western Europe*. Edited by Charles Tilly. Princeton: Princeton University Press, 1975.

———. "War Making and State Making as Organized Crime." In *Bringing the State Back In*. Edited by Theda Skocpol, Peter Evans, and Dietrich Rueschemeyer, 169–91. Cambridge: Cambridge University Press, 1985.
———. *Coercion, Capital and European States, AD 990–1992*. Cambridge, Mass.: Blackwell, 1992.
———. *European Revolutions, 1492–1992*. Oxford: Blackwell, 1993.
Tocqueville, Alexis, de. *Recollections*. New Brunswick, N.J.: Transaction, 1992.
Tokes, Rudolph L. *Hungary's Negotiated Revolution*. Cambridge: Cambridge University Press, 1996.
Tsebelis, George. "Decision Making in Political Systems: Veto Players in Presidentialism, Parliamentarism, Multicameralism and Multipartyism." *British Journal of Political Science* 25, no. 1 (Fall 1995): 289–325.
Unger, Roberto Mangabeira. *Social Theory: Its Situation and Its Task*. Cambridge: Harvard University Press, 1990.
Vachudova, Milada Anna, and Timothy Snyder. "Are Transitions Transitory? Two Types of Political Change in Eastern Europe since 1989." *East European Politics and Societies* 11, no. 1 (Winter 1997): 1–35.
Valenzuela, J. Samuel. "Democratic Consolidation in Post-Transitional Setting: Notion, Process, and Facilitating Conditions." In *Issues in Democratic Consolidation: The New South American Democracies in Comparative Perspective*. Edited by Scott Mainwaring, Guillermo O'Donnell, and J. Samuel Valenzuela, 52–67. Notre Dame: University of Notre Dame Press, 1992.
Vaughn, Diane. "Theory Elaboration: The Heuristics of Case Analysis." In *What Is a Case? Exploring the Foundations of Social Inquiry*. Edited by Charles C. Ragin and Howard S. Becker, 173–202. New York: Cambridge University Press, 1992.
Verdery, Katherine. *What Was Socialism, and What Comes Next?* Princeton: Princeton University Press, 1996.
Verheijen, Tony. *Constitutional Pillars for New Democracies: The Cases of Bulgaria and Romania*. Leiden: DSWO Press, 1995.
Videnov, Zhan. *Otvud politicheskija teatur* (Beyond the Political Theater). Sofia: Hristo Botev, 1998.
Volkov, Vadim. "The Political Economy of Protection Rackets in the Past and in the Present." *Social Research* 67, no. 3 (Fall 2000): 1–35.
———. *Violent Entrepreneurs: The Use of Force in the Making of Russian Capitalism*. Ithaca: Cornell University Press, 2002.
Vorozheikina, Tatiana. "Clientelism and the Process of Political Democratization in Russia." In *Democracy, Clientelism, and Civil Society*. Edited by Luis Roniger and Ayse Gunes-Ayats. Boulder: Lynn Rienner, 1994.
Vulkanov, Velko. *Na kolene pred istinata* (Kneeling before Truth). Sofia: Bulvest 2000 [1996].
Wacquant, Loic. "Towards a Reflexive Sociology: A Workshop with Pierre Bourdieu." *Sociological Theory* 7, no. 1 (Spring 1989).
Wallerstein, Immanuel. *The Modern World System*. Vol. 1: *Capitalist Agriculture and the Origins of the European World Economy in the Sixteenth Century*. San Diego: Academic Press, 1974.
Wasilewski, Jacek. "Elite Circulation and Consolidation of Democracy in Poland." In *Postcommunist Elites and Democracy in Eastern Europe*. Edited by John Higley, Jan Pakulski, and Wlodzimierz Wesolowski. New York: St. Martin's Press, 1998.
Waterbury, John. *Exposed to Innumerable Delusions: Public Enterprise and State Power in Egypt, India, Mexico and Turkey*. Cambridge: Cambridge University Press, 1993.
Weber, Max. *Economy and Society*. Vol. 1. Berkeley: University of California Press, 1978.

Weber, Max. *The Russian Revolutions*. Ithaca: Cornell University Press, 1995.
Weingast, Barry. "The Economic Role of Political Institutions: Market-Preserving Federalism and Economic Development." *Journal of Law, Economics, and Organization* 11, no. 1 (Spring 1993): 1–23.
Wievorka, Michel. "Case Studies: History or Sociology?" In *What Is a Case? Exploring the Foundations of Social Inquiry*. Edited by Charles C. Ragin and Howard S. Becker, 159–71. New York: Cambridge University Press, 1992.
Wightman, Gordon, ed. *Party Formation in East-Central Europe*. Aldershot, England: Edward Elgar, 1995.
Whitehead, Laurence. *Democratization: Theory and Experience*. Oxford: Oxford University Press, 2002.
Whitley, Richard. "Transformation and Change in Europe: Critical Themes." In *Industrial Transformation in Europe: Process and Contexts*. Edited by Eckhardt Dittrich, Gert Schmidt, and Richard Whitley. London: Sage, 1995.
Williamson, Oliver. *The Economic Institutions of Capitalism: Firms, Markets, and Relational Contracting*. New York: Free Press, 1985.
Woo-Cumings, Meredith, ed. *The Developmental State*. Ithaca: Cornell University Press, 1999.
World Bank. *World Development Report 1997: The State in a Changing World*. Washington, D.C.: World Bank, with Oxford University Press, 1998.
Wyzan, Michael L. "Bulgarian Economic Policy and Performance." In *Bulgaria in Transition: Politics, Economics, Society, and Culture after Communism*. Edited by John D. Bell, 92–132. Boulder: Westview Press, 1998.
Yonkova, Assenka, Svetlana Alexandrova, and Latchezar Bogdanov. *Development of the Banking Sector in Bulgaria*. Sofia: Institute of Market Economics, 2000. Available at http://ime-bg.org/bg/top_left.html.
Zielonka, Jan. "New Institutions in the Old Eastern Bloc." In *The Global Resurgence of Democracy*. Edited by Larry Diamond and Marc F. Plattner. Baltimore: Johns Hopkins University Press, 1996.

Index

Abbott, Andrew, 24, 31–32
Adams, Julia, 178
Africa, 12, 17, 185
Agency for Economic Coordination and Development, 165
Agrobiznessbank, 87, 165
Agriculture, 51, 53, 54, 79–81, 83–85
"Angelus Novus" (Klee), 94
Antagonism stage, 112, 113
Aoristic power, 7–8
Aramco case, 76
Ardant, Gabriel, 179
Arms trade, 78, 101–2
Asia, 12, 17, 74
Assassinations, 108, 117, 119
Assets: and analytical perspectives, 189–90; and conversions of power, 74–75; polysemy of, 69–77; specificity of, 74–75
Asymmetrical effects, 94
Atanassov, Atanass, 110, 111
Audits, 70
Authoritarianism, 171, 195; and the separation of party and state, 34, 37, 59; and weak-state constitutionalism, 129, 145, 146–47
Avramov, Roumen, 87, 116–17

Badie, Bertrand, 185
Bagehot, Walter, 149

BAIB (Bulgarian Agricultural and Industrial Bank), 77–85
Balkans, politics and culture, 31, 144, 167
Balkanbank, 73
Banka Zemedelski Kredit, 87
Banking; and the BAIB (Bulgarian Agricultural and Industrial Bank), 77–85; and the BNB (Bulgarian National Bank), 86–87, 102, 152–58, 162–69, 171–74; and constitutional checks and balances, 151–74; and conversions of power, 65; and creditor-debtor relations, 85–91; and off-budget funds, 70–77; and the Orion case, 77–85, 186–87, 165, 168, 191; and post-Communist winning, 97, 102; and the separation of party and state, 53; and weak-state constitutionalism, 125, 139. *See also* Finance, international
Bank of England, 89, 163
Banks and Credits Law, 159
BANU (Bulgarian Agrarian National Union), 131
Barkey, Karen, 12, 116, 185
Bartex affair, 103n
Becker, Howard S., 26
Beckett, Samuel, 62
Beer, Samuel, 178
Benjamin, Walter, 94
Bermeo, Nancy, 172–73
Bernik, Ivan, 58

Berov, Ljuben, 100, 107, 137
Beyme, Klaus von, 126, 128
Biznes Banka, 87
Blagoev, Veselin, 102
Blueprints, ideological, 14, 19, 21, 31; and conversions of power, 71; and post-Communist winning, 115
BNB (Bulgarian National Bank), 86–87, 102, 152–58, 162–69, 171–74
Bosnia, 145
Boudon, Raymond, 64
Bourdieu, Pierre, 84, 93–94
Boylan, Delia M., 59
Brazil, 12, 17
Britain, 51, 57, 149. *See also* England
BSP (Bulgarian Socialist Party), 43–53, 73, 136, 139–43; and the BNB, 164, 166, 169, 171–72; and the Orion case, 78–81; and the Pirinski case, 160–61
Budget Law (1995), 108
Budgets, 59, 108, 163n, 164–65, 192
Bulgargaz, 104, 107, 108, 115
Bulgarian Business Bloc, 140
Bulgarian Communist Party, 32–52, 85–91, 159
Bulgarian National Bank (BNB), 86–87, 102, 152–58, 162–69, 171–74
Bulgarian Socialist Party. *See* BSP (Bulgarian Socialist Party)
Bulgarian Telephone Company, 79
Bulgartabak affair, 102, 103n
Bunce, Valerie, 5
Burckhardt, Jacob, 32
Bureaucracy, 186, 187, 190; and constitutional checks and balances, 166, 168; and conversions of power, 74–75, 92, 93; emasculation of, 10; and post-Communist winning, 115, 119; and the separation of party and state, 33, 34, 38, 56; and the state-centered perspective, 4, 9; and weak-state constitutionalism, 124–25, 148

Camus, Albert, 175
Canetti, Elias, 151, 174
Capital; and conversions of power, 63, 64, 66, 68–69, 89, 93–94; embezzlement of, 93, 84–85
Capitalism, 30, 184, 191; and conversions of power, 63, 64, 66–67, 78, 94; political, 50; and post-Communist winning, 121; and the separation of party and state, 45
Carey, John M., 147
Caritas case, 82–83

Carruthers, Bruce G., 88
Case studies; and analytical trade-offs, 23; defense of, 23; Eckstein on, 23; hypotheses-generating, 22–27; selection of, 27–32; and weak-state constitutionalism, 131
Castration, 61
Central Electoral Commission, 161
Central Committee of the Bulgarian Communist Party, 52, 159
Chaudhry, Kiren Aziz, 27–28, 178
Chemical industry, 106–10
Chirot, Daniel, 29
Citizenship, 161
Civil society, rise of, 12
Class, 120, 192; formation, 67; and the paradox of democratic openings, 195; political, use of the term, 41–43; struggle, 96
Cluj, 83
Coalitions, distributional, 120
Coercion, 182, 183–84, 186, 190
Cold war, 27
Collins, Randall, 116
Collusion stage, 112–13
COMECON (Council for Mutual Economic Assistance), 110
Commercial Code, 81
Committee for Party and State Control, 47
Committee on Energy, 104
Committee on Foreign Relations, 137
Committee on Mail and Long-Distance Communications, 79
Communist Party, 32–52, 85–91, 159
Compact discs, production of, 111
Comparative hypotheses, 34–35
Compartmentalization, 112
Computer technology, 52, 110–12
Constant, Benjamin, 173
Constantinescu, Emil, 42
Constitution (Bulgarian), 108, 130–50, 156, 157. *See also* Constitutionalism
Constitutional Court, 108, 133–37, 147, 151–62, 169–74
Constitutionalism; and banking, 151–74; and constitutional choices, 130–35; and constitutional practices, 135–44; pseudo-, 136; study of, overview of, 125–44; "thick," 135–36; "thin," 135; unbalanced, 149; weak-state, 123–50. *See also* Constitution (Bulgarian)
Consultative National Security Council, 141
Context, dynamic interpretation of, 148

Control, mechanisms of, 47–48, 60
Conversion costs, 63, 92–94
Conversion thesis, 63–69
Cooperatives, 79–80, 83
Coposu, Corneliu, 42
Corruption. *See* Crime
Council of Ministers, 52–54, 79, 107, 162
Creative destruction, notion of, 122
Credit millionaires, 87, 90
Creditor-debtor relations, 85–91. *See also* Debts; Loans
Crime, 32, 82; financial, 90; investigation of, 47; and mechanisms of control, 47–48; and post-Communist winning, 97; and weak-state constitutionalism, 146–47
Croatia, 16
Crowds and Power (Canetti), 151
Cukierman, Alex, 163
Currency Board, 32, 166–67
Czech Republic, 16, 24, 42

Dachev, Ljubomir, 73
Danov, Mikhail, 78, 79
Debts, 107–10, 165, 187. *See also* loans
Decentralization, 54–55, 65
Decision making, 59, 66, 92, 100, 113–15, 142–43
Decrees, 44, 49, 50, 54
Defection, separation as, 56–61
Deindustrialization, 111, 119
Deinstitutionalization, of information, 51–55, 60
Democracy, 2, 13, 30, 187, 193–98; and constitutional checks and balances, 151–52, 157, 159–60, 167, 170–71, 174; and conversions of power, 64, 88, 89, 91–92, 63; failure of, 28; and the hypotheses-generating case study, 24–25; and the separation of party and state, 34–61; and weak-state constitutionalism, 123, 126–31, 136, 139, 143, 145, 148. *See also* Elections
Deregulation, 19
Derluguian, Georgii, 27
Descriptive heuristics, 24. *See also* Heuristics
Diachronic analysis, 25
Dialectic, use of the term, 6
Dimitrova, Bistra, 164
Di Palma, Guiseppe, 134, 170
Dirty tricks, politics of, 119
Discretion, informalization of, 48–51, 60
Dobrev, Nikolay, 141–43

Donchev, Sasho, 110
"Dorian Gray Effect," 96–97, 120–22, 148, 171
DSK affair, 103n
Dunn, John, 175
DZU affair, 102–4, 110–12, 115, 118–19

Earle, Johns S., 65
Eckstein, Harry, 23, 25, 128
Eclecticism, and the hypotheses-generating case study method, 26
Economic Bank, 165
EEC (European Economic Community), 110
Egalitarianism, 129
Egypt, 57
Elatzite (company), 72
Elections, 25, 87, 112, 161: and analytical perspectives, 187; Fish on, 39–43; and the Orion case, 79; and the separation of party and state, 34–36, 38–44, 55, 59–60; and weak-state constitutionalism, 131–33, 137–38, 140–41. *See also* Democracy
Eley, Geoff, 31
Elias, Norbert, 10, 188
Eliot, T. S., 123
Elite, 2, 32, 63–66, 69, 90, 91; and analytical perspectives, 177, 179–87, 191–94, 196; behavior, assumptions about, 18–22; and constitutional checks and balances, 151, 153, 156, 169, 171–73; and the hypotheses-generating case study, 25; insouciance of, 32; non-Communist, 40, 41; and the paradox of democratic openings, 194, 196; and the policy-centered approach, 18–22; and post-Communist winning, 96, 100–101, 120; predatory, 178–81, 186–88, 190–96; and the separation of party and state, 40–43, 56, 58–62; and the state-centered perspective, 3, 7; and weak-state constitutionalism, 124, 130–31, 134–35, 144, 146–47, 149–50
Elster, Jon, 131–32, 157
Emergency powers, 136
England, 88, 89. *See also* Britain
Entrepreneurship, 9, 171; and conversions of power, 67, 68, 71–73, 76, 91, 92; and post-Communist winning, 97, 103, 112, 114; and the separation of party and state, 50
Ertman, Thomas, 176, 187–88

Ethnic groups, 12, 29, 31, 120
EU (European Union), 1, 63; Bulgarian's accession to full membership in, 138; loans from, 71
"Eumenes effect," 88
European Legal Cultures (Gessner, Hoeland, and Varga), 128
Evans, Peter, 17, 92, 192
Exchange rates, 167. *See also* Currency
Exports, 44. *See also* Trade
Extraction, problem of, 168–70, 183, 186–90, 192

Farming. *See* Agriculture
Filipov, Ljubomir, 102
Finance, international, 44–46, 53, 139. *See also* Banking; Currency
Fish, M. Steven, 23, 38–43, 59, 83, 159–60
Flexible accumulation, 82
Foreign Currency Commission, 45
France, 12, 105, 156
Freedom: House index, 160; Mill on, 197; of speech, 42, 139
Freud, Sigmund, 61
Frye, Timothy, 152
Fukuyama, Francis, 123, 128, 145
Funar, Georghe, 83
Functional perspectives, 5–6, 146

Gambetta, Diego, 146
Gambling, 102
Gas business, 104–6, 117
Gazprom, 104–6
Gelemezov, Spas, 102
Gellner, Ernest, 93
Germany, 79, 156
Getova, Edit, 73
Giddens, Anthony, 10
Gill, Graeme, 56n
Globalization, 12, 82, 111–12
GNP (gross national product), 139
Goodman, John B., 166
Gouldner, Alvin, 197
Governmental Commission on Foreign Currency Issues, 45
Governmental Commission on Scientific-Technological Cooperation, 45
Gradualism, 98
Gray, John, 15
Great National Assembly, 43, 131–33
Greece, 88, 78, 79, 154, 171
Greskovitz, Bela, 180
Grzymala-Busse, Anna, 11
Gunther, Richard, 11

Haggard, Stephen, 59
Hall, John A., 9–10
Hankiss, Elemer, 64
Harvey, David, 191
Hayek, Friedrich von, 15
Hellman, Joel, 67n, 97–99, 114, 118
Heuristics, 3, 24, 27, 152, 185
Himko-Kremikovtzi affair, 72, 101, 103–4, 106–10, 119
Hoeland, Armin, 128
Holmes, Stephen, 20
Hough, Jerry, 15
Hristova, Lilia, 110
Human rights. *See* rights
Hungary, 16, 23, 42, 66, 161
Hunger strikes, 132
Hursev, Emil, 163, 164
Hypotheses, and the case study method, 22–27, 66, 171; and post-Communist winning, 115; and the separation of party and state, 38–39, 52; and weak-state constitutionalism, 123, 128

Ideology, 14, 18, 19; and the paradox of democratic openings, 193; and the separation of party and state, 40, 45; and statism, 183, and weak-state constitutionalism, 135, 138–39
Ikenberry, John G., 9–10, 172
Iliescu, Ion, 83
IMF (International Monetary Fund), 16, 18–20
Immergut, Ellen M., 113
India, 12, 17
Information, deinstitutionalization of, 51–55, 60
Insiders/outsiders, notion of, 5, 56, 78, 87, 189
Institute for Social Governance, 52
Institute for State and Economic Management, 52
Institutional perspectives, 5–6
Institutionalism, 136, 184
Institutionalization, 119, 136
Insulation incentive, notion of, 59
Intelligentsia, 30
Intercom-Multigroup, 111
International aid, 71

Jankov, Krustyo, 102, 110
Japan, 184–85
Jepperson, Ronald L., 119
Johnson, Juliet, 65
Journalism, 30, 139. *See also* Media

Jowitt, Ken, 29
Justiciable law, 138

Kafka, Franz, 1, 5
Kahler, Martin, 20
Kalistratov, Dimiter, 108
Kaufman, Robert R., 59
Kaviraj, Sudipta, 51
Kintex, 78
Kirchheimer, Otto, 134, 137
Klee, Paul, 94
Kolarov, Ljubomir, 78, 79
Kolev, Ivan, 102
Kopecky, Petr, 13
Kostov, Ivan, 42, 106n
Krassner, Stephen, 76
Kredit Bank, 102
Kremikovtzi, 72, 101. *See also* Himko-Kremikovtzi affair
Krivoshiev, Nikolai, 78, 81
Krygier, Martin, 129
Kryshtanovskaya, Olga, 65

Labor. *See* Unions
Laissez-fair economics, 14, 19
Latin America, 12
Law enforcement, 47–48, 86
Law on Judicial Power, 160
Learning, political, 172
Legitimacy, upstream, 131–32
Lenin, V. I., 36
Licenses, 79, 86
Lichbach, Mark I., 93
Liechtenstein, 101
Lijphart, Arend, 24, 25
Linz, Juan J., 11, 37–39, 43, 59, 170
Loans, 71, 73, 85–91, 164. *See also* Debts
Lobbyists, 117, 121, 164
Loewenstein, Karl, 126
Loyalty, 36, 56, 164, 171
Lukanov, Andrei, 44–49, 52, 54–55, 104–5, 168
Luong, Pauline Jones, 11

Macedonia, 88
Malta, 101, 105
Mann, Michael, 7, 8, 56–57, 61
Marazov, Ivan, 140
Market(s), 63, 67–70, 76–77, 82, 86, 89–91; and analytical perspectives, 178, 191; and the policy-centered approach, 14, 16–18, 20; and post-Communist winning, 98, 101–2, 114–15, 117; and the separation of party and state, 39, 45, 50, 55; socialism, 45. *See also* Marketization
Marketization, 7, 115–116, 193. *See also* Markets
Marxism, 120
McAuley, Mary, 22
McDermott, Gerald, 24
McFaul, Michael, 65
MDK (copper mine), 72
Meciar, Vladimir, 16
Media, 30, 121, 139, 145, 160–61
Medzhidieva, Veska, 78, 79, 81
Mesopotamia, 57
Middle East, 12, 27–28, 51
Migdal, Joel, 17, 119
Military, 72–73, 182–84; Soviet, 101–2, 106; and weak-state constitutionalism, 133
Mill, John Stuart, 197
Ministry of Defense, 50
Ministry of Finance, 70, 90, 108, 166, 168
Ministry of Foreign Trade, 53
Ministry of Industry, 73, 115
Ministry of Internal Affairs, 50, 90, 102
Ministry of the Interior, 111, 117, 141
Ministry of Transportation, 50–51
Minstroi Holding, 102
Mitchell, Timothy, 76
Monarchy, 149
Monetarism, 16
Monitoring, 92, 168
Monopolies, 54–55, 86, 188–89; and post-Communist winning, 107, 114–15; and the separation of party and state, 36, 54
Montesquieu, Charles-Louis de Secondat, Baron de, 22, 170
Moore, Barrington, Jr., 181, 184–85
Mosca, Gaetano, 41
MRF (Movement for Rights and Freedom), 131, 140
Mudde, Cas, 13
Multiart, 101
Multigroup International Holding, 78, 95–96, 100–120, 164, 166, 181, 187
Mumford, Lewis, 181

Naishul, Vitalii, 66
Nation-states, formation of, 11–12
National Bank, 133
National Electric Company, 102
National Energy Committee, 102
National Sports Lottery (Toto), 102
Nationalization, 187
Nayapti, Bilin, 163

Nee, Victor, 66
Neoliberalism, 21, 25–26, 30–31, 115; and the separation of party and state, 46, 55; and the policy-centered approach, 14, 16, 18–22
New York Times, 145
Newspapers, 30, 145. *See also* Media
Nomenklatura, 35, 44, 57–58, 60, 187; and constitutional checks and balances, 168; and conversions of power, 63, 64, 65, 71, 87; and post-Communist winning, 103, 112
North, Douglass C., 192

O'Donnell, Guillermo, 16–17, 113
Off-budget funds, 70–77
Offe, Claus, 129
Oil industry, 49, 74, 102, 103, 104
Olson, Mancur, 89–90, 120, 121
One-party systems, 17, 57
"On Jean-Paul Sartre's La Nausée" (Camus), 175
Order No. 16, 54
Order on the Closing Down of Associations, 53
Orion case, 77–85, 165, 168, 186–87, 191
Orsov, Zlatomir, 78, 80, 81
Orthodox paradox, 20
Ost, David, 23
Ottoman empire, 185

"Parchment" institutions, 151, 153–54
Pareto, Vilfredo, 183
Parikh, Sunita, 12
Parliament, 156–57, 160, 166; and conversions of power, 70, 87; and post-Communist winning, 108; and the separation of party and state, 48, 49; and weak-state constitutionalism, 126–27, 132–33, 135, 137–38, 140–42
Parties, political, 23, 48–61; and the informalization of discretion, 48–51; and separation as defection, 56–61; and the state, separation of, 33–61, 62
Party-State Commission on Scientific and Technical Development, 110
Patrimonial political culture, 96, 158
Pavlov, Ilia, 101–2, 104–6, 109, 112n, 117, 187
Pei, Minxin, 114
Pensions Law, 159
People's Union, 140
Petrol, 103
Peukert, Detlev, 38

Pharmacy (company), 72
Pierson, Paul, 125
Pinochet, Augusto, 59
Pirinski, Georgi, 160–61
Pluralism; 62, 158; and the separation of party and state, 34, 36–37, 58; and weak-state constitutionalism, 144
Plutarch, 88, 154, 172
Pocock, J. G. A., 89
Podkrepa trade union, 102
Poggi, Gianfranco, 3, 7
Poland, 2n, 15, 39, 42, 50
Polanyi, Karl, 14
Policy-centered approach, 13–22
Political parties. *See* Parties, political
Political repression, 47, 147, 189
Polysemy of resources, 75–76
Ponzi scheme, 82–83
Popov, Angel, 107
Popov, Vassil, 102
Populism, 145
Power: "ballast to resist other," in Montesquieu, 170; Canetti on, 151; and constitutional checks and balances, 151–74, 160, 173–74; conversions of, 8–9, 62–94, 187; despotic, 58; networks of, Mann on, 7, 8; and the polysemy of assets, 69–77; and post-Communist winning, 96, 99–100, 112–18; and the separation of party and state, 34–36, 39, 41–42, 44, 57–59, 61; and the state-centered perspective, 7–8; veto, 9, 25, 44; and weak-state constitutionalism, 136, 142–43, 148, 150
Poznanski, Kazimierz Z., 33n
Predatory elites, 178–81, 186–88, 190–96. *See also* Elites
Premyanov, Krassimir, 49, 164, 168
Presidential regimes, 126–30, 133, 135–41, 158, 161
Prezeworski, Adam, 15
Pridham, Geoffrey, 170
Prikhvatizatzija, use of the term, 65
"Primacy of Culture, The" (Fukuyama), 128
Privatization, 19, 50, 171–72, 187; and conversions of power, 64–67, 69, 71, 83, 91; and post-Communist winning, 109–10, 114–15; and the separation of party and state, 48, 50–51
Private property. *See* Property
Privatization Agency, 102, 171
Problems of Democratic Transition and Consolidation (Linz and Stepan), 37–38

Index   **221**

"Problems of Our Laws, The" (Kafka), 1
Prokuratura, 47
Property, 89, 97, 173; and conversions of power, 65–67, 76, 89, 90, 91; right to sell and lease, 50
Purva Chatsna Banka, 87

"Quick resuscitation" scenario, 63

Raidovski, Krassimir, 79
Railway systems, 74–75
Rapaczynski, Frydman, 65
Rawls, John, 158
Raz, Joseph, 135, 138–39
Realism, 115
Rechtsstaat, 137
Redistribution, of wealth, 96, 112–22
Reforms, 18–20, 64, 83, 195; and post-Communist winning, 98–99, 119; and the separation of party and state, 39, 40, 44, 46–47, 55; and weak-state constitutionalism, 124, 130
Religion, freedom of, 139
Rent; dismantling, 114; extraction, 113; -seeking schemes, 117–18, 109, 146, 187
Restructuring, 71
Rigby, T. H., 194
Rights, 134, 136, 139, 144
Rokkan, Stein, 181
Romania, 35, 40, 42, 82–83
Rona-Ras, Akos, 23
Rule of law, 187
Russia, 20–23, 51, 65, 104–6; and the DZU affair, 111; railway system in, 75

Sabel, Charles E., 92
Sartori, Giovanni, 113
Sartre, Jean-Paul, 175
Saudi Arabia, 28
Schamis, Hector E., 7, 114
Scheppele, Kim Lane, 157
Scheuerman, William, 21
Schmitter, Philippe, 143
Schumpeter, Joseph, 67–68, 92, 97, 122, 146; notion of creative destruction in, 122; on the rise of the "tax state," 190
Secret service, 78, 79, 102
Seligman, Adam, 93
Sewell, William H., Jr., 69, 75
Shakespeare, William, 172
Shareholders, 80–81
Shevarshidze, Nikita, 104, 105
Shivarov, Svetoslav, 80
Shlapentokh, Vladimir, 82

Shock therapy, 16, 31, 45
Shopov, Grigor, 101
Shugart, Matthew, 147
Sil, Rudra, 26
Simultaneity, problem of, 193
Singapore, 74
Skocpol, Theda, 62–63, 184
Slovakia, 16, 58
Smith, Rogers M., 182–83
Social capital, of the state, 9, 84
Socialism, 2, 13, 177–78, 186–87, 194; and constitutional checks and balances, 155; and conversions of power, 67, 71; market, 45; and the policy-centered approach, 13–15, 17; and post-Communist winning, 97, 114, 117; Schumpeter on, 190–91; and the separation of party and state, 38–39, 40, 45, 50
Social security, 134
SOEs (state-owned enterprises), 71–73, 80, 104, 162; and credit-debtor relations, 87; and the DZU affair, 111, 112; and Himko, 107
Sofia District Court, 104
Sofiyanski, Stefan, 106n
Sokolov, Dimiter, 102
Solnick, Steven, 57, 74–75
South Africa, 81
South Korea, 17
Sovereign creditors/debtors, 88–89. *See also* Debt
Soviet Union, 12, 28, 101–2, 106
Sovmorflot (Soviet Black Sea military fleet), 101–2
Spain, 156, 171
Spassov, Roumen, 78, 81
Spulber, Nicolas, 65
Staniszkis, Jadwiga, 50, 64
Stara Zagora, 110, 111
Stark, David, 18
State-building: and analytical perspectives, 177–98; and constitutional checks and balances, 167, 152–74; and conversions of power, 63, 89; and the formation of nation-states, 11; and post-Communist winning, 100; Tilly on, 12; two dimensions of, 9, 140–50; and weak-state constitutionalism, 123–50
State-centered perspective: and conversions of power, 91–94; described, 3–13; and the separation of party and state, 34, 35, 46, 59, 61
State Gazette, 133

State Savings Bank, 79, 86–87, 109, 164
State Security, 78, 101, 102
State transformation, use of the phrase, 2
State weakness. *See* Weak states
Statism, 82, 116, 183
Steel industry, 72, 107
Steinmetz, George, 21
Stepan, Alfred, 11, 37–39, 43, 59, 170
Stinchcombe, Arthur, 194
Stock market, 88
Stoica, 83
Stomana steelworks, 72
Stone, Alec, 158
Stoner-Weiss, Kathryn, 124
Stoppard, Tom, 95, 121
Stoyanov, Petar, 42, 140, 141
Strange, Susan, 50
Stranger, Alison, 130
Subsidies, 18
Supreme Administrative Court, 133, 137, 157
Supreme Court, 81, 161
Supreme Court of Cassation, 133, 137, 157
Supreme Party Council, 78
Switzerland, 110–11
Szelényi, Iván, 66

Tabula rasa premise, 17
Tarrow, Sidney, 21
Taxation, 90, 160, 185, 186, 190–91
Thelen, Kathleen, 153
Tilly, Charles, 4, 12, 172, 177, 180–96; on the collapse of the Soviet empire, 12; on political relations and the maintenance of modern states, 4
Tismăneanu, Vladimir, 29
Tobacco industry, 102
Tocqueville, Alexis de, 146
Topenergy affair, 103–6
Trade: arms trade, 78, 101–2; and post-Communist winning, 101–3; and the separation of party and state, 44, 53, 54; and weak-state constitutionalism, 139
Transition costs, 63
Transportation, 50, 51, 53
Tsvetkov, Trifon, 102
Tudjman, Franjo, 16

UACB (Union of the Agricultural Cooperatives in Bulgaria), 79–81
UDF (Union of Democratic Forces), 42, 112n, 131–32, 140
Ukraine, 16

UN (United Nations), 51
Unemployment benefits, 134
Unions, 23, 54, 79–80, 84, 102
Utopianism, 14, 115–16

Vaughn, Diane, 26–27
Verdery, Katherine, 29, 82, 83
Veto mechanisms, 112–18, 133, 137
Videnov, Zhan, 49, 100, 107–8, 139–41, 165; and the Orion case, 79; resignation of, 81; and SOEs, 73; Topenergy affair and, 104
Volkov, Vadim, 6, 48
Vorozheikina, Tatyana, 64
Vouchers, 80
Vratza, 107, 109
Vuchev, Kliment, 71–76, 92
Vulchev, Todor, 163, 164
Vulkanov, Velko, 161

Waiting for Godot (Beckett), 62
War making, historical analysis of, 182–85
Warterbury, John, 192
Waste Land, The (Eliot), 123
Weak states, 3, 9–11, 31, 123–50, 175, 177; and constitutional checks and balances, 154–55, 172; and conversions of power, 62–63; and the hypotheses-generating case study, 22, 23, 25, 27; and the policy-centered approach, 13, 22; and the separation of party and state, 46
Webb, Steven, 163
Weber, Max, 136, 191, 194
Weimar Republic, 38
Weingast, Barry R., 97
White, Stephen, 65
Whitehead, Lawrence, 157
Wilde, Oscar, 120
Winning, post-Communist, 95–122
Withdrawal of the state, metaphor of, 17–18, 20
World Bank, 1, 105
World War II, 126
Wyzan, Michael L., 145

Yemen, 28
Yugoslavian embargo, 51

Zadgranichni druzhestva (Companies Abroad), 53
Zhelev, Zhelyu, 42, 133, 137–38, 140, 141
Zhivkov, Todor, 30, 44–45, 55

www.ingramcontent.com/pod-product-compliance
Lightning Source LLC
Chambersburg PA
CBHW030136240426
43672CB00005B/145